Is It Utopia Yet?

An Insider's View of Twin Oaks Community in its Twenty-Sixth Year

by Kat Kinkade

Cartoons by Jonathan Roth

Chapter-head Illustrations by Hildegard Ott

Twin Oaks Publishing

Contents

A Foreward by the Author i

Introducing the Community
  An Overview of the Basics for Those Who Don't Know Us 1

In The Beginning 9

Government 101 17

Equal Is As Equal Does:
  Twin Oaks' Famous Labor Credit System 29

Money Equality: A Close Look at a Communal Economy 42

City People Earn a Living in the Country 52

Collective Consumption 63

Housing and Other Buildings: The Early Years 78

Why I Left Twin Oaks, and Other Personal Things 84

A Lot Happens in Nine Years 91

Branch Experiments and the Small Living Groups 96

The Return To Twin Oaks 104

Problems and Progress of Recent Years 111

Grow A Tomato, Eat A Tomato 115

The Builders 123

The Serenity to Accept the Things I Cannot Change 138

Suffer the Little Children 143

Cows and Concrete 155

Turnover 165

Sex, Love, and Jealousy 175

Living in a Diverse Community 192

On Being Different 200

A Little Crime, a Little Punishment 212

Movements and Causes 223

Power and Leadership 232

Some Leaders Who Made a Difference 242

Art, Music, and Theater 268

Adventures with Internal Revenue 279

Whose Book is it, Anyway?—The Chapters I Didn't Write 285

Demographics and Some Remarks About Aging 292

Twin Oaks Plants an Acorn 300

And in Conclusion... 307

Index 310

A Foreward
by the Author

When I was 17, I thought I was a communist. What I meant by that was that I believed every human on earth had a right to an equal share of the world's goods and advantages, and any arrangement short of that was a cheat. I never gave much thought to "Capital C Communism," didn't follow world events, didn't join any organizations. All my inspiration had come from the writers of Utopian fiction, in particular Edward Bellamy's *Looking Backward*. I couldn't see anything wrong with Bellamy's vision for America.

My own life became busy with marriage, jobs, childbirth, college, divorce. It wasn't until I was 34 that I first conceived of utopian communism as anything more than an ideal. That was the year I read B.F. Skinner's *Walden Two*.

Walden Two, like *Looking Backward,* is fiction, but it is set in the here and now, in ordinary rural America, and it concentrates on a single community. The seductive element of *Walden Two* is that it reads like a practical guide to a community that could actually exist.

I was disappointed to learn that no one by that date, fully fifteen years after the book's publication, had created a community based on the fictional model. Nevertheless, I thought it could be done, so I set about getting in touch with other people who shared my enthusiasm.

When we founded Twin Oaks in 1967, my attention had to be focused mostly on practical matters: the Community's organizational framework, labor system, property agreements; the sheer difficulty of holding the group together long enough for it to ensure its own survival. Nevertheless, behind all the practical challenges the ideal remained the same as it had ever been. That ideal was essentially "communist," as I understood it, and its name was Equality.

A rigorous dedication to equality does away with the obvious problems of a free enterprise laissez-faire economy. There are no big winners and losers, no rich or poor, and so forth. The egalitarian systems that Twin Oaks invented with such idealistic passion in the Sixties have stood up fairly well, not only for economic stability, but also for all the social and emotional benefits of cooperation and the pursuit of common goals.

Just the same, at age 62 I no longer think of myself as a communist. I still pursue Utopia, but I no longer hold to a single economic theory as a sure way of getting there. Equality goes just so far. Having achieved it (more or less), Twin Oaks is in a good position to evaluate the problems it solved and those it has failed to solve. We are even beginning to acknowledge that it has created a few problems.

This book is partly a report on how an egalitarian community is doing in its 25th anniversary year, and partly a record of my personal relationship with the community I helped to found, as it has moved beyond the original vision and become a creature of its time. I am the only one of the original founders to continue to live at Twin Oaks.

This is my second book about Twin Oaks Community. The first one, which tells of the Community's founding and early years, was published in 1973 under the title *A Walden Two Experiment.* Between my two books there is another, called *Living the Dream,* by Ingrid Komar, concentrating on the years 1979-1982. The latter can be ordered from us at this address:

Twin Oaks Community
Route 4, Box 169
Louisa, VA 23093

Though I would like to sell those books, I have tried to write this one in such a way that it can be understood independent of background reading. I have quoted briefly from the earlier books, sometimes for ironic contrast. We did not do everything we thought we were going to do the way we thought we were going to do it!

Among other radical departures, I should mention that Twin Oaks no longer claims any connection other than historical with *Walden Two* or Skinner. Many parts of our organization and culture were in fact derived from *Walden Two*, based on some of Skinner's good intuitions. However, his central idea, behaviorism worked out on a community scale, was abandoned long ago.

Now about those cartoons: This was a bonus. Jonathan Roth joined Twin Oaks just about the time I started writing this book, and he hadn't been here a month before he began satirizing the Community with his cartoons. I liked them so much I asked for permission to include a selection along with my manuscript. If his view of the Community doesn't exactly match mine, don't be surprised. We are both telling the truth as we see it, and neither of us claims to be completely objective.

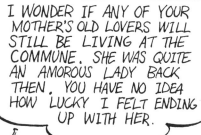

Introducing the Community
An Overview of the Basics
for Those Who Don't Know Us

What is an Intentional Community

For those who never heard of Twin Oaks before, I should explain that it is an "intentional community." That means it's a community with its own clear borders and membership. Some people call it a "utopian" community. The essential element in any intentional community, ours included, is that people who want to live in it have to join, be accepted by those who already live there, and go by its rules and norms, which may in some ways differ from those in society at large.

We list over 375 intentional communities in North America in our *Directory of Intentional Communities.* Among these, only a few are of our type—income-sharing, experimental, economically self-sufficient, without a charismatic leader. In this modest company Twin Oaks is considered "famous." Some foolish newsperson once called us the "Colossus of the commune movement."

We used to get a lot of press coverage because of our historical connection to B.F. Skinner's *Walden Two.* When Skinner wrote a best seller, TIME magazine, among others, dipped back into his literary history in search of a human-interest angle and found us. They sent out a reporter and a photographer, and about twenty of us appeared in the magazine, posed on top of the oldest, rattiest wooden shed the photographer could find, dressed in our briefest summer cutoffs and smiling amiably at the camera. (The mother of one of our members called him up when she saw it and tearfully told him that this was definitely not the way she had hoped to see his picture in TIME.)

Just the same, you don't need to be embarrassed if you never heard of us. Several million people haven't.

Some Twin Oaks Statistics

Let me introduce Twin Oaks, using some facts and numbers for starters. As of spring 1993 we are a group of eighty-five adult members and 15 children, and those numbers are subject to change at any time in either direction. The adults range in age from nineteen to sixty-eight, the children currently between infancy and sixteen, not counting the baby we're expecting later this year. Our population keeps changing as some people join each year and others go on to other things. At least forty current members have lived here for five years or more, and nine of us for over ten years.

Each adult member (whether single or married) has a private room in one of seven large residences. We share bathrooms (about one bath for every eight people) and living rooms, some of which double as libraries.

Most of the time Twin Oaks houses, in addition to its members and children, a handful of visitors who are considering joining us in the future, and a few personal guests of individual members.

We earn our living by a variety of cottage industries, chiefly the manufacture of rope hammocks. We have a modest income, considered "poverty" by national standards and "luxury" by some other intentional communities.

The Community owns eleven cars and small trucks, which are on the road most of the time and are usually maintained by our own mechanics. We also have two tractors and a couple of big trucks.

Twin Oaks Physical Description

Here's what you'd see if you drove up the front driveway tomorrow. The road would take you past a well-tended two-acre vegetable garden and then to the edge of a grassy courtyard surrounded by four buildings, most of them sided in unpainted rough oak.

Perhaps the strongest visual impression is that Twin Oaks is very green. We have made small clearings in our forested land and built our houses in them. Several acres that were once cultivated or used for pasture have been returned to woods. Even the courtyard is dotted with trees and ornamentals.

A second strong impression is that this is definitely not suburbia. The careful, manicured look of the institution that needs to impress visitors is entirely absent. Twin Oaks' loveliness is of the home-made, home-consumed variety. Here the forsythia sends out flowered shoots in random and uncontrolled directions, and the daffodils, past their peak flowering, are allowed to sit in place until they are ready to bloom again. The oak siding on the buildings warps here and there, and wasps build their nests under the eaves until we get around to dealing with them.

Rope hammocks are everywhere in evidence, including a few that are still on the jigs being woven for future sales. Twin Oaks is a lavish user of its own products, and the courtyard is much used as an extension of the hammock shop. Many hundreds of hammocks have been created by barefoot communitarians in this outdoor environment. If you come on a nice day, you can probably lie in one hammock and watch somebody weave another one at the same time.

There'd be a few people about, dressed very casually. They might be working in the yard or overseeing children or just walking between buildings.

The buildings around the edge of the courtyard include an office (once the original farmhouse), the hammock shop (source of most of the Community's income), and three residences. These buildings were once the whole Community, but later you'll find there are several more residences and other workshops within a few minutes' walk.

Most members take their meals in the central dining hall called Zhankoye. It is not near the courtyard but is tucked among the trees about a five-minute woodland walk away. (Most of the buildings are named after other communities, either historical or fictional. Zhankoye was a pre-Zionist Jewish settlement in Russia.) Zhankoye is not the only kitchen at Twin Oaks. Most of the residences also have kitchens, which are used for snacks and small meals.

A Commune and a Home

Twin Oaks is a commune, not in the sense that was stereotyped by the press in the Sixties, (sex, drugs, and cockroaches) but in the nineteenth century sense of a place where the inhabitants share many things communally—including, and especially, income. It is highly organized but very flexible. Its labor system is unique, its money economy fairly conventional but entirely controlled by the Community's members. By the way, we tend to avoid the word "commune," because of its misleading connotations, and generally use the word "community" instead, but for an income-sharing group like ours, both terms apply.

I hope it's a Saturday afternoon that you turn up our driveway, because that's the day we welcome strangers. We give them a tour of the place and answer their questions. The other six days we discourage drop-ins, because Twin Oaks is not merely an institution; it is our home.

Like any home, it's the place we eat and sleep and wash the dishes and take care of the kids. Unlike most homes, it is also where we earn our living, run our government, learn new skills, sing and play music, dance and put on plays, fall in and out of love. It is not merely the center of our lives; in many ways it defines our lives. We may be parents and managers and builders and gardeners and mechanics, but we are also consciously Twin Oakers.

Where the Members Come From

Do you wonder where we all came from? From many different states and a few foreign countries. From suburban families and city apartments and farms and colleges and other communities. We were drawn here by one or more aspects of what this communal life offers.

Do you imagine that we are all of a type, more or less alike? A week in our company will change that impression. For better or for worse, we have different backgrounds, different ideas, different goals. What, then, holds us together? To tell the truth, we don't know. We've read that we're supposed to have a strong common religion or a powerful, inspirational leader in order to prevent our disintegration as a community. We have neither. The generalizations derived from studies of nineteenth century communities do not seem to explain our viability.

4

Some Reasons for Twin Oaks' Survival

I once tried to figure out what the factors are that account for Twin Oaks' success to date. As I compared us with other successful and unsuccessful groups, I hazarded that there are probably at least twenty big questions that influence viability, and each community has to get good answers to about twelve of them in order to survive and prosper. Here are some of the ones that Twin Oaks has found satisfactory ways of dealing with:

... We get the work done, and we have enough work equality so that members don't feel badly ripped off by each other. There are a lot of different ways to do this. Our way is a labor credit system, which I'll describe in detail later.

... We keep enough money coming in. There has to be enough to cover the basics and a few amenities. There has to be some pocket money. Good food, adequate shelter, medical care, and the like are taken for granted here.

... We maintain a communal economy and hold a rein on personal consumption. The big advantage of the communal over the merely cooperative is that in a communal system what money there is can be plowed back into the Community, rather than dribbled away by individuals. In a cooperative, members have personal CD players and bicycles. A communal group is much more likely to have things like sewage treatment and sidewalks. When people leave, they take the bicycles with them, but the sidewalks stay put.

... We keep the door open. Our visitor program has provided us with a stream of new members to take the places of those who decide to do something else. Failure to seek and accept new members is a major reason some groups have failed.

... We leave people's minds alone. We really do not insist on intellectual or spiritual conformity. This has its costs, but it nets us a rich harvest of members who could not be happy in a community with a narrower focus. One might say that we appeal to a "market" that had been untapped before we came along.

... We have systems. Though we leave room for individual action as much as we can, we're too big to be very casual about work, money, auto use, and so forth.

... We have freedom. Within our systems there is an enormous flexibility that makes it possible for our members to do almost any decent and wholesome thing they want to do, within the limits of our resources.

... We're big enough to survive upheavals and turnover. I figure thirty people with their land and housing held in common is about minimum for security. We reached that population in our third year.

I see I've named only eight. Others could be "We have an environment congenial to love and mating; we provide for our children; we live in a healthy environment; we have opportunities for many different kinds of learning and growth, including widely-spread leadership; we never stagnate but are constantly changing and growing; we are a people of essential good will; we inspire hope."

I don't know how many of the above are really necessary for a successful community. At some point in this thinking I begin to blur the distinction between basic essentials and a loving description of Twin Oaks. At any rate, we are here, we are twenty-five years old and vigorous.

Too many generalizations make a dull book. I want to leave this overview behind and zoom in on the detail.

Courtyard in Winter, view from the air

Hammock weaving in the courtyard

8

Chapter 2

In The Beginning

When I read a story, I like to read it in order—what happened first, followed by what happened after that. If other people are like me in this way, they'll want me to start somewhere near the beginning. Much has been written about early Twin Oaks, but I'll summarize those early years briefly.

The People and Activities

There were eight of us founding communitarians, and of those eight, only five were seriously committed to the Community. We had 123 acres of farm and forest land, which we had little idea what to do with, a house that was far too small for our needs, and several barns, one of which most of us slept in. After we pooled all our money, the bank balance stood at a little over $2,000.

We also had a sort of blueprint for community in the form of the book *Walden Two*. Our plan was to create the community described in that book. Of course we couldn't literally do this, partly from lack of money, but we came as close as we could.

The basic feeling among the core members was that we were creating a new world. Other than the vague directions we derived from Skinner's novel, there were few assumptions. We felt free to change the clock or the calendar, take new names, raise children

9

by unproven theories, and redefine economic and political justice. We proceded to do all of these.

The reason we didn't collapse within six months was that we also had some common sense, and our vision included economic stability and tolerance of diversity. We built a house, went to work to earn money, took in new members to replace people who left.

Some of us were happy. Central to my own happiness was my conviction that there was no task on earth more important, or certainly more interesting, than the building of an egalitarian community. I merged my own interests and the Community's so thoroughly that there was almost no difference between the two. I wrote a little newsletter during this period that we called *The Leaves of Twin Oaks*. We put it out every month, and it was full of cheerful and homely tales of our small activities, our theories, even our pets. I was conscious that we Twin Oakers were characters in a book about starting a community, and that avid readers might well be inspired to join us, or at least renew their subscriptions. I wanted it to be a happy story, so I suppressed all the problems and conflicts. This came naturally to me at the time, because I was fundamentally happy myself.

There were so few of us and so much to do that each of us naturally did dozens of different tasks. I, for example, cooked and cleaned, made sausage from our fresh-killed hogs, suckered tobacco plants, canned tomatoes, tin-snipped ductwork for our first building. I went to Feedbacks and Encounter sessions; I was involved in planning and administration. I gave visitor tours and press interviews.

Since I was among those who stayed on while others came and went, I became a symbol of security and permanence to the little Community. Perhaps for this reason I was allowed to use my judgment in a vast array of business, including areas where that judgment really wasn't very good. For example, I remember that my personal enthusiasm for braided rugs translated itself into a belief that the Community needed a huge braided rug in its living room. From there it was an easy step to allowing full work credit for people to sit on the floor stitching the braid together, even though common sense should have told me there was no way to preserve the rug from dirty boots and ubiquitous mud, and no way to clean it. (These days I make small braided rugs quietly in my own room on my own time. In a way this symbolizes the changes in my relationship to this Community.)

I even remember that I used to insist that everyone recycle the tops of soda bottles by using them as gravel on one of our muddy driveways. People protested that bottle tops were ugly, but I was unmoved. Since I was interested in recycling, I figured everybody should be.

Dwight, an early member who was critical of me, once told me that I went around giving instructions, acting as if Twin Oaks were my duchy. While I don't remember this, I can see why it might have been true. It was natural for me to deal with everybody's questions, because I was more likely than anyone else to know the answers, all the way from "What is the purpose of community?" to "Where do we keep the baking soda?"

Early Troubles

In the meantime, a lot of perfectly awful things were happening. My husband got fed up and decided to leave the Community. He asked me to choose between him and Twin Oaks, and I chose Twin Oaks without hesitation. My teenaged daughter assumed full independence at the age of 16 and took off thumbing her way to California in pursuit of a boyfriend. The average new member stayed about 3 months. An "underground" developed among the youngest members, who stayed up late in the smoking room, listening to the popular music of the time and criticizing the "Establishment," meaning me and others who were deeply invested in the Community.

We squandered time and energy in projects doomed to failure, like making rammed-earth bricks, trying to market products we hadn't perfected, and especially pouring labor into the full-time communal care of one small child who was destined to leave a year later. We ran our cars without maintenance, were helpless in the face of frozen water pipes, planted crops on a flood plain (which duly flooded), let two cows die of starvation, built a house on an asphalt foundation, wasted months of time fashioning window frames from scratch.

Nevertheless we prospered and grew. Early residences were not very well built, but they housed members. Members often didn't stay long, but they accomplished things while they stayed.

Word spread. Within a year several newspaper articles had featured us. People wrote to us, visited, joined.

Response to Criticism and Skepticism

There were perhaps times when I felt some uncertainty. One day in 1970 a young man came to visit us, having read some laudatory article in a newspaper. He spent several hours looking around at Twin Oaks' physical plant, growing more morose with each hour. Finally he cornered me where I was typing on my first book and interrupted me to say, "What I can't figure out is what you people are so proud of. I never saw such a run-down dump in my life. I can't see what you've proven except hippies can run a farm."

In point of fact we hadn't proven even that, but I didn't like having our obvious problems pointed out so rudely. I turned to him and said, "Get out." He expostulated, "Now, wait a minute…" but I could no longer stand his presence. "Don't come into my home and tell me it's a dump," I said. "Who invited you anyway? I live here. Go away. Go on, get out!" I believe he went, but he had ruined my day. I sat and looked at the room I was in. The rudely-sheetrocked walls were unpainted and dingy. The window openings had no glass in them yet and for two years had been covered by a double layer of dirty polyethylene. Raw boards on concrete blocks held piles of books and magazines, among which spiders and wasps carried on their tiny lives. A torn carpet lay wrinkled on the asphalt floor. The Community's typewriter rested on a desk that had been rescued from the dump.

What had we proven? As far as I knew at that time, we had proven that equality can work as an economic system. Intelligently applied, the principle of equality does help get the work done and does give satisfaction to a group that must share both the work and the results of it. People can and usually will do their best, even without personal economic incentives, if they are doing it for their own community.

Our accomplishments, in that fourth year, went further than that. We had proved that people can work peaceably under a chosen government without giving the decision-makers any benefits beyond what everybody got. We had demonstrated again that it is not the material plane that generates happiness or unhappiness, but the relationships between people. We had already permanently changed the lives of dozens of people who had come through Twin Oaks and been members for a while.

A year later we got glass in the windows and paint on the walls, and that was a good thing, too.

Feelings about the Pioneer Years

There is no one here at Twin Oaks today to share with me those memories of the first five years, but we all share the inheritance of the work those early members did and the institutions they created. This edifice of Community was erected on that asphalt floor. Current members hear my stories of the early days and frequently comment, "I wouldn't have joined a place like that; I couldn't have stood it." Their tone seems to say, "I'm glad you did, but Ugh! How could you?"

Occasionally we'll get a member who feels differently. I remember one who told me frankly, "I was born too late. Everything important is done already. I envy you the pioneer days." I laughed at him and told him to go out and start another community. There is no shortage of pioneer experience in the world for those who crave it.

It was not a love of pioneering that motivated me in 1967. It was a vision of community. Those conditions that are considered hardships now were irrelevant when they were happening. The only thing that mattered was the glorious goal: Walden Two or bust!

I didn't get Walden Two, and this book explains why not and what happened instead. Walden Two idealism is nothing now but a quaint and somewhat embarrassing part of our history. What we created instead is a sturdy, modestly prosperous, self-governing community with no one ideological name tag beyond "egalitarian."

Though Walden Two was thrown out, the work we accomplished in the first five years was not. Our passion was equality, and everything we did was a working out of that central idea. Our work was not wasted. The cows may have died and the roofs leaked, but the governmental and labor systems survived. For good and for evil, these are the legacy of the first few years. Let me tell you about them.

14

Chapter 3

Government 101

Twin Oaks uses what we call the Planner-Manager form of government. We got it straight out of *Walden Two*, and it has worked remarkably well over the years.

"Planner" refers to a board of three members who serve eighteen-month staggered terms and during that time make long-range policy, control and dispense resources, and do whatever else comes up to take care of the overall well-being of the Community. "Managers" are the people in charge of various specific areas of work or authority.

Managers

On the surface our system looks like a hierarchy, workers reporting to Managers and Managers to Planners. In practice the system is largely non-hierarchical. Nobody "reports" to anybody. Managers are almost autonomous, fellow-workers looking to them only for direction. The Food Manager decides what foods we will have available; the Auto Manager decides when to replace an aging vehicle. The Garden Manager determines which vegetables we grow. All of these decisions are usually made after seeking input from others, but they are still managerial-level decisions.

The theory behind the design of our managerial system is that it is desirable to spread authority as broadly as possible. We tend to attract people who distrust hierarchies and want to cooperate with, rather than report to, other Community members.

Furthermore, we're all "workers," and at least three quarters of us are managers in addition. We tend not to work full time in any one job, so members who are managers of one area are workers in somebody else's area. All of us take as much responsibility as we feel we can handle, and nobody bosses anybody else around.

We have over time created about seventy-five managerships. We have around eighty-five members. This does not mean we all have one managerial job apiece. By no means all of our members are prepared to take on such responsibility. Some members are very new, and not ready. Others are preparing to leave, and are dropping the jobs they had. Some people do not like responsibility and will not accept a managership. There are even a few who on principle do not believe anyone should have authority and therefore cannot very well assume any. Including the committee-run managerships, like the Membership Team and the Health Team, the real numbers are more like one hundred administrative jobs divided among sixty people.

Not all managerships are equal. There is a great deal of difference between, for example, the GMT (General Managerial Team in charge of the rope products businesses), and the Bees Manager. It's the difference between not running out of honey and not running out of money.

Then there's House, which makes sure we don't run out of soap, and Auto Maintenance, which keeps the cars running out (and in).

Obviously there is enough managerial work for everyone who wants some, and some people pick up as many as six managerial tasks at a time.

You get a managership by signing up for one when there's a vacancy. A group of related managers (called the Council) interviews candidates and chooses one. Councils are as likely to choose a new member as an old one. They use their judgment.

Managerial Turnover

Responsible people tend to overload themselves. Eventually they will have to let something go, because they're just not doing it justice, and at that point the job is posted once more for volunteers. Thus the managerial cycle turns.

Managerial jobs (with a couple of exceptions) have no set term limits, and visitors sometimes ask if this does not lead to entrenched power. This has not become a serious problem yet. Managers tend to quit a job when it ceases to interest them, and the average job by this means gets a new Manager every two or three years.

Taking on a new managership is one of the more stimulating things a member can do. New managers usually have ideas and energy for their areas, and managerial turnover is frequently healthy for the Community. Members sometimes change jobs when they become bored or frustrated or feel the need for a new challenge.

Planners

Then there is the plannership. To be a Planner means to take responsibility for the Community. Most of the time this isn't as frightening as it sounds, because the Community has so much momentum that it mostly just goes along from month to month without much guidance. In any case it is seldom in danger. Also, the plannership is a team, three or four people working together.

New Planners get their jobs by first being selected by the other Planners from among volunteers. They then go through what we call "veto process," in the course of which as few as twenty percent of the Community members have the power to reject them by secret ballot. In other words, anyone who takes office as a Planner necessarily has either the support or the acquiescence of a minimum of eighty percent of the Community members.

The Planner term is eighteen months. Planners are not allowed to serve two terms in a row, but can be reappointed after they have been out of office for at least six months. No one so far has ever taken the job back quite so quickly.

Why don't we have a direct election? Partly because we usually don't have two candidates. It is hard enough to find one person who is both willing and able to fill this job. When there are two applicants, the one not chosen is usually content to wait until the next slot opens in a few months. In addition, voting between two candidates might generate competitive feelings we prefer to avoid.

The voting we do have (i.e., the veto box) is a quiet affair. There is absolutely no campaigning. The box, sealed, but with a slot for votes and comments, sits in the dining room appropriately marked, and a notice is posted announcing the candidate and the voting deadline. A week later the Planners open the box and tell the candidate yes or no. That week can be anxiety-filled for a candidate uncertain of the Community's mood, but there is usually a happy ending. In the rare cases where there is an effective 20% veto, the Planners tell the candidate what reasons people gave for their veto votes, but do not normally disclose the names of the negative voters.

The Planner Job

Planners meet two or three times a week for three hours at a time. At these meetings they discuss whatever proposals are on their agenda, argue their merits, organize means of getting opinions from the Community members, read and discuss such feedback after they get it, and eventually reach and post decisions. The Planners discuss and decide small resource allocations that come up between the yearly economic plans. For one month of every year they spend most of their time working on next year's economic plan. All meetings are legally open to any member who wants to come, but people seldom do. Planners also talk to any member who wants to approach them directly about anything.

Of course there are public meetings held about all significant issues, and it is the Planners' duty to schedule them, attend them, and pay attention to the input they get from them.

In addition, for the duration of their eighteen-month term, Planners are pretty much on call for conversations with individuals about Community concerns. They also keep their eyes and ears open for issues that may be surfacing even though no one has put them in the form of a proposal. Many proposals, in fact, are Planner-generated in response to felt Community needs. For example, after years of seasonal dispute about the legality and advisability of requiring women to wear shirts in hot weather, the Planners finally made a general, Community-wide nudity policy, in which certain areas of the Community are set aside as "clothing-optional." Other than those areas, women are supposed to keep their shirts on.

Planners also make the final decisions (after input from members) on the site choices for new buildings. This is a difficult and tedious business, because there are always objections to any given site (too close, too far away, too wooded, too sunny, etc.). They also give the go-ahead (or not) to new businesses, major business or borrowing decisions, the design of new buildings, and a hundred other matters of general, rather than managerial, concern.

Checks on Power

At all levels of Community government, there are legal checks on power. Any time any Community member disapproves of a decision, whether Planner level or Managerial, that decision can be appealed. Managerial decisions are appealed to a group of related managers called a Council, Council decisions to the Planners, and Planner decisions to the members as a voting body. A simple majority of the members can have its way about anything except bylaws changes, which take a higher percentage.

Appeals are uncommon, because the average Manager or Planner group avoids making decisions that are likely to be overruled. Living in a group of less than a hundred people, we don't often misread public sentiment. Once in a while we do, of course. Those are always interesting times.

Public Opinion

It is the legal checks and appeals system that qualifies us technically as a democracy, but actually, our democratic practices are far deeper than these. Planners and managers do not sit around thinking "How can I use my position to get something I think is important, without getting overruled?" (At least not often.) They think "I need to find out if the Community is ready for this step that I think is important." Then they set about finding out.

We have several communication devices, but the most important by far is called the O&I Board. "O&I" stands for "Opinion and Idea." This bulletin board has been in use since 1970. Currently it has 24 clipboards available for people to post their opinion papers on, and these are always full. Members read the O&I the way many people outside of Community read the daily newspaper, though in our case the "newspaper" is mostly one big editorial page, with many editors. It is our custom to attach blank pages to the backs of our papers, so that others can comment on our ideas. The comments may be supportive—"Good paper. I especially liked your idea about..."; or they may take issue with the paper—"I don't think this would work, because..." No one has ever declared a limit on the length of a comment, and sometimes they go on for pages. The norm is shorter than that, and many people limit their comments to a sentence or two, or to ditto marks under someone else's comment.

Some O&I papers are proposals which will eventually go to the Planners or relevant managers for decision. Planners customarily watch the O&I Board, and if they can see a path of useful action, they will add the current issues to their agenda.

Alternate Ideas About Governance—Consensus and Democracy

The other major governmental systems in use in secular community circles are (1) consensus, which requires the consent of every member before a decision can be made; and (2) direct voting democracy, under which each member votes on every issue. Both have their adherents. Neither of these seems to me practical for Twin Oaks at this time. As time goes by and we learn to use the system we have, it seems less and less likely that we will do a major governmental system change.

Consensus and direct voting democracy both require, as far as I know, attendance at meetings in order to participate in government. Everything I have read about consensus starts out with the assumption that people are gathered in one room with the intent of reaching a decision. But Twin Oakers will not gather in one room more than perhaps once a year. Most of them will come to meetings only to discuss things that are vital to them personally, and in such cases they expect the meetings to be scheduled to their reasonable convenience—that is, not when they are taking a vacation and not when they have to cook or take care of children or milk cows. When you consider that Twin Oakers take an average of eight weeks vacation per year, entirely at their personal convenience or even sudden whim, and that somebody is fixing a meal or milking a cow or caring for children almost all the time, it's hard to imagine how we would find a slot for a regular meeting time, and even harder to imagine getting more than 25 people, if that, to attend.

The Planner-Manager system, however, does not depend solely on meetings. It uses them, but the input it gets from the membership as a whole is grabbed by whatever means fits in with people's schedules. The O&I Board, with its written and signed comments, is a principal tool. Those who don't like the O&I may be reached by personal conversation or a survey. By one means or another, the Planners and managers attempt to get a sense of the Community that is simply not available in meetings. I don't claim complete success in this. I merely think we get more complete input than any system that depends primarily on meetings. Like consensus procedures (but unlike direct democracy), our system enables us to make compromises that include minority interests. Unlike consensus, it doesn't always leave everyone feeling satisfied. But it takes much, much less time than consensus, and that time is precious to us.

Like direct democracy (but unlike consensus), the Planner-Manager system lets us make decisions in a hurry if we have to.

Unlike direct democracy it does not leave every member feeling that he or she has an equal vote, win or lose. But we get a lot closer to widely accepted decisions, and that, too, is precious.

The above defense of the planner system, as opposed to consensus, has drawn strong objections from some people within the communities movement who have read this manuscript. The essence of their rebuttal is that consensus procedures, properly practiced, do not have to take a long time. They say that the use of consensus process requires education, but once people understand how to use it, it need be no more cumbersome than the planner system and will result in better feelings in addition. In response I will merely say that if I ever saw this demonstrated in a large community with numerous pressing, controversial issues that affect the members' personal lives, I would be convinced. So far I'm not.

The Bylaws

More powerful than Planners, managers, or even a majority overruling vote is the written document, the Twin Oaks bylaws. These outline the general direction of the Community and add a substantial amount of detail in certain areas, such as membership and personal property. No Board of Planners can overrule them, and nobody can ignore them, either. If they are to be changed, the changes must go through formal and tedious process and require a high percentage of Planner and member signatures in order to go into effect. This is seldom done, and the bylaws thus serve a function of protecting the original goals of the Community from rapid change.

History and Evolution of our System and Remarks on Power

Twin Oaks did not reach its current level of governmental sophistication without going through several years of experimenting. We started out by lifting from *Walden Two* the system Skinner had envisioned for a thousand people and doing our best to apply it to our intitial group of eight. Here is what I said about it in my first book, written in 1971:

> A Walden Two community is not a hierarchy. Nobody is on top of anybody. The job of decision-making requires decision-making skills, just as the job of salesperson requires selling skills. The plannership is not a position to be awarded to the Manager who rates promotion, any more than a managership is a promotion for a regular member with good behavior. Managerships are positions of responsibility and trust...Planners are just managers of miscellaneous

decisions that don't come under other managerships. The job requires agility of mind, reasonableness of judgment, commitment to the goals of the Community, and sharp self-awareness.... It does not give orders. It has no power to legislate anything that the group as a whole does not want, no means of enforcement except persuasion. It does not deserve, expect, or want prestige. Planners are in every sense regular members of the Community, subject to their own regulations....

Rereading now what I wrote twenty years ago, I note that the fundamental Community ideology concerning power is stated accurately enough. Nevertheless there is something basic missing from that description. It fails to mention the fact that we have power struggles in spite of our ideology. It dismisses these struggles as simple political incorrectness and doesn't look at the reasons for them.

The plain fact is that a whole lot of people, regardless of their leadership talent or lack of it, have ideas about how their community should work, and they want to see those ideas implemented. In short, though we tried hard to deny it, power is a goody, and many people want some.

What we thought then, and said, was that power shouldn't be a goody. It shouldn't be an end in itself. One shouldn't want to rule others. We believed it, and we denied such impulses when they appeared in our own behavior. We (I mean we who covertly competed for power within the Community) wanted only enough influence to guide the Community in the way it should go. As long as the group was on the right track, it didn't matter who filled administrative jobs. Critics immediately asked the obvious question: Whose right track? My answer was straightforward: Those who agreed with the original vision.

We had never idealized or offered political equality. Any reading of *Walden Two* makes it clear why not. We did not want *equal* government; we wanted *good* government. I knew there were increasing numbers of people joining Twin Oaks who did not share the vision of excellence in government, preferring a broad franchise. I thought they were good members, but I didn't think they belonged in leadership positions, because they didn't have the "right" beliefs. When they began to seek a full share in leadership, I felt not only threatened but betrayed.

Before the first five years had passed, the people I considered usurpers had outnumbered the old-timers, and of course needed to legitimize their position as full equals. In 1974 conflict on this issue became intense, and Twin Oaks hired outside facilitators to help it deal with its internal power struggles. The outsiders, predictably, viewed all members as having an innate right to political equality. One of the exercises they directed the group to do was to form itself into a line, everybody standing close to the other members they usually agreed with, and far away from those with opposing views. The line, when it eventually got itself formed, stretched from one side of the courtyard to the other, and on out into the middle of Central Field. From that basis the facilitators successfully guided the Community into accepting ideological diversity as a basic and working from there. At that point the Community stopped advertising itself as Walden Two related, and started including in its recruitment material the basic statement that no one ideology was predominant.

"I will never forgive them," said Gerri, a leader of the old guard and a believer in Walden Two. "They enfranchised everybody. They destroyed our goals."

Recalling beliefs and emotions I shared with Gerri at one time, I sympathize with that statement. Just the same, I have forgiven those facilitators long ago, because I have learned something in the meantime. Legitimizing multiple philosophies at Twin Oaks was inevitable. We couldn't keep out people with different philosophies and goals. We needed people for sheer survival, and there weren't enough Walden Two enthusiasts to go around. We didn't have, had never had, the power to accept people's presence and their labor and deny them political influence.

People, even very nice people who don't believe in power, do as well for themselves as they can. Majorities make law for themselves. Since the early founders of Twin Oaks couldn't command a majority, couldn't even manage the place without the energy of the newcomers, the original philosophy was doomed and was duly overrun. It wasn't an outrage. It was just an ordinary event and should have been predicted.

How the Changes Affected Me

Since I hadn't predicted it, I had a very hard time in the years of transition between the original vision of the Planner system and the modified hodge-podge that it was destined to become. Not only had I believed that a community should be guided by the wisest heads available, but it was clear to me that I was one of them. I saw in myself the qualities I thought of as essential— "agility of mind, reasonableness of judgment, commitment to the goals of the Community, and sharp self-awareness," and as far as I could see, I had them in more generous measure than most members. I also had a strong desire to be in charge, and though I

25

recognized the dangers inherent in this, I thought that my awareness of this drive, together with my good intentions and the safeguards in the bylaws, was sufficient to keep it under control.

I could see that some other people envied my position in the Community. They wanted that sense of control and centrality, and the prestige that went with it. I didn't blame them. In fact, I felt sorry for them, because I saw them as having ambitions beyond their abilities, an inherently frustrating situation.

I did not see my own flaws, and maybe this wasn't entirely my fault. Certainly there was nobody around to give me any guidance. Such peers as I had shared my belief in the importance of high quality decision-making and didn't quarrel with my self-estimate. When people criticized me, I tried to listen. Unfortunately, what they had to say to me was usually, "You have too much power." As far as I was concerned, this was not a legitimate criticism, and I ignored it. If they had said "You bruise too many egos," I'd have understood better.

The big thing I didn't understand was that, no matter how sound my decisions seemed to me, the people who disagreed and the people who envied me would eventually find a way to take my place, for better or for worse. It happened first and most painfully in 1970, when we were short of experienced and capable leaders, and I was nominated to serve another Planner term, less than a year after my previous term had expired. The members overwhelmingly vetoed my appointment, not because they thought I made bad decisions, nor because they had another candidate in mind, but simply because I had "too much power," and they were tired of it.

The big shock was discovering how much I minded it when it happened. For me, it wasn't just theory that Planners didn't deserve or want prestige; it was basic morality. I had always despised people who wanted high office for ego reasons. Now I found myself deeply depressed because I had been effectively deposed. My "sharp self-awareness" went through the painful process of becoming even sharper.

I had a choice: I could either despise myself or I could change my theory. I chose the latter. Realizing that it wasn't realistic to expect other decision-makers to remain entirely above personal ego if I couldn't do it myself, I adjusted my thinking to take egos into account.

The new leaders needed time to try out their methods, and I needed time to recover my emotional balance, so at that point I stepped back from government and turned my attention to writing a book.

THIS IS OUR COMMUNICATION CENTER, THE **O AND I BOARD**. ON THESE VERY CLIPBOARDS THE IDEAS ABOUT HOW OUR COMMUNITY SHOULD BE ARE INDICATED, EVALUATED, DEMONSTRATED, REPLICATED, COMPLICATED, DEBATED, CONSECRATED, INCORPORATED, ASSIMILATED, DESECRATED, ANTIQUATED, ELIMINATED, RUMINATED AND DEFECATED BY A NUMBER OF OUR MEMBERS.

WAITING LIST: ① GODOT ②

TOILET SEATS: UP OR DOWN? THE DEBATE CONTINUES

101 FUN WAYS TO CONFUSE VISITORS

RAISE HELL TO LOWER QUOTA

HMMM... SO WHY'S IT CALLED THE **O AND I BOARD**?

CAUSE EVERYTIME I SEE IT I SAY **OI**!

JONATHAN

27

28

Chapter 4

Equal Is As Equal Does:
Twin Oaks' Famous Labor Credit System

I say, "famous" in the context of the communities movement. All over the country, when Twin Oaks' name comes up, people are likely to say, "Oh yes, that's where they have labor credits." This is true, and after twenty-five years, I still think labor credits are, in spite of various drawbacks, more a solution than a problem.

Basically labor credits are Twin Oaks' internal economic currency. One credit equals one hour of work. Other than the obvious exceptions for the sick and the aging, every member is required to work an equal number of hours for the Community each week. We call this "doing quota." Quota is set by the Planners according to the needs of the Community. This year it's forty-six hours a week.

To people accustomed to a forty-hour work week, this may sound high at first, but it turns out to be a leisurely pace when one considers how much it covers. The following things are here considered creditable work: house cleaning, shopping, childcare, laundry, cooking, mowing the lawn, doing household repairs, volunteer work for charitable organizations, going to the doctor, voting in local elections, writing letters to Congress, going to relatives' funerals, and repainting our own rooms, in addition to virtually unlimited sick time. Every year we add some new projects to that list. Dozens of administrative and planning meetings are creditable, too.

Counting our work in hourly units gives us a great deal of flexibility. Members may and usually do choose to vary their days and weeks by doing several different jobs. Some people specialize in their own favorite work areas, but others deliberately alternate active physical work with clerical tasks or meditative production routines. To as great an extent as possible, members choose their own work.

People may well want to do more work in the course of a week than the minimum requirement. We allow this work to be counted as "over quota" labor credits and to be accumulated for future leisure time. By this means most members earn a substantial amount of vacation time.

It takes two people about two days to do the labor assigning each week, juggling the personal requests with the Community's varying needs for different kinds of labor. This sounds like a job for a computer, but so far we haven't succeeded in reducing labor assigning to the level of machine judgment. Out of this investment in clerical labor we get (1) individual labor schedules; (2) general schedules posted where everyone can find out who is scheduled for what; (3) bookkeeping in which members' surplus credits or deficits are recorded and data on all work areas is summarized and tallied. (The computer does what it is good at after the human has completed the part requiring judgment.) All jobs are covered with assigned workers; all members have a fair share of the work.

Of course there are simpler ways of distributing work, but none that grants a comparable degree of flexibility and personal choice. This is the main reason the basic system has survived for twenty-five years, in spite of numerous acknowledged flaws.

The Variable Credit Experiment

The idea of the labor credit was originally inspired by Skinner's *Walden Two,* but the way we use the system now is different in one fundamental way from the system suggested in the book. Skinner, having read Edward Bellamy's *Looking Backward,* was impressed with the idea that different kinds of work should be rewarded differently. That is, the more onerous a task, the more credit it should earn. The fictional members of Walden Two got 1.4 credits per hour for working in the sewers, and only .2 for puttering in the flower gardens.

Part of the charm of this idea, which we dubbed the "variable credit," is that it reverses the traditional remunerative formula (that reward for work is determined by supply and demand, and therefore skilled work, however pleasant, pays better than unskilled, however wearing or demeaning.) We agreed with Bellamy and Skinner that the traditional scheme is unfair and unnecessary, and we embraced the variable credit with a fervor almost ideological.

Ultimately we rejected the variable credit, both in theory and practice, but in the five years during which we honored and experimented with it, we assumed the principle was basic and important, and we therefore gave it a very serious try. Our first problem was to find a fair and objective method to determine which jobs were in fact less desirable than others, so they could be given a higher credit value.

It didn't work just to ask people what they thought. The lure of higher credit tended to set people into competition with each other, sometimes squabbling with each other in their rival claims to personal suffering and sacrifice. ("Milkers deserve more credit because they have to get up at five in the morning on cold winter mornings." "Cooks have to slave over a hot stove on broiling August afternoons.")

A system in which each person rated all the jobs according to *personal* preference (the value of the credit varying accordingly) held a certain logic, and we used it for over a year. This sometimes resulted in having two people on a shift, doing identical work, but one getting more credit than the other. Intuitively this felt bad to people, no matter how logically it had been arrived at. We kept trying to foolproof the system, but there were always people who figured out how to manipulate it for their own benefit, which created bad feelings in those who either couldn't or wouldn't engage in such manipulations.

We experimented with at least four variations on the variable credit system, and meanwhile vocal discontent with it grew louder and more convincing. What Skinner didn't have any way of knowing is that a group of 40 members or more will have a broad enough range of taste and preference so that it becomes pointless to define "more (or less) desirable work." Skinner didn't imagine (nor did I until experience showed me) that some people would rather dig a ditch than balance a checkbook. There is almost no type of work that does not attract someone. When we do run across jobs that nobody wants to do, manipulating the credit does not help.

The variable credit idea failed to make sense as soon as we were faced with any very large or endless task. Though it is pleasant to make hammocks in our sociable, relaxed workshop, making 12,000 of them every year gets tiresome, and toward the end of a high-production season, members complain. The same thing happens when we process hundreds of jars of tomatoes and peppers. No matter what the work, it will attract workers unless and until there is too much of it. Then it suddenly becomes "undesirable."

A corollary is that work seems very desirable when there is not enough of it to go around. I remember a time when the Community had not done any construction for a couple of years and then decided to build a new residence. Under the bidding system, members were competing to be construction workers. Some said they would build for .8 of a credit per hour; then others offered bids of .7 and .6. In desperation someone said that if he was appointed to the crew, he would do it for no credit. Then someone else claimed to be willing to do it for negative credits—paying for the privilege from his labor balance. We eventually made up the crew by drawing lots and assigning an arbitrary .8 per hour for the work. Within two weeks of the start of the building, the workers realized what they had done to themselves by competitive bidding. They could not meet quota. In order to get forty-six credits, they would have to work a steady fifty-eight hours a week throughout the construction season. Besides, after the first few days, construction work did not turn out to be as much fun as it had seemed.

During the same period, people forced the value of managerial work down to .9 per hour, on the theory that planning and managing are more fun than other jobs. Some managers responded by quitting their jobs. The people who replaced them soon discovered they didn't want the responsibilities after all, especially not at reduced "pay." We pronounced the variable credit system a failure in 1974, and since then almost all work earns one credit per hour.

Getting the Dishes Washed

Even so, we have to take turns washing the dishes. Though a few people rather like washing dishes, and many people do not mind it, there are not enough such people to cover all the dishwashing that a community needs. For years we attempted to assign that task only to those who minded it least, but they tired of it.

The move to a mandatory kitchen shift did not take place without a struggle. Two members adamantly refused to go along with it. They claimed that they not only hated kitchen work, but they hated it more than other people did. This was proved, it was said, by the fact that they were willing to make a public issue of it. Why would they deliberately subject themselves to resentful criticism if not because staying out of the kitchen was very important to them? Joshua stood on principle. He had joined the Community, he said, under the conditions that work was distributed according to preference. He saw the switch to a mandatory rotation as a violation of principle, and he, for one, would not consent to it. He would not wash dishes, and that was that. If we put it on his labor credit sheet, he would ignore it.

After a good bit of indignant grumbling, the Community decided to put the new rotation into effect over the objections of the two holdouts. Everybody else would wash dishes. Those two men would not be assigned. Eventually one of them offered to clean bathrooms as a substitute, an offer very welcome to the Community, since we had almost as much trouble getting bathrooms cleaned as we did getting volunteers for dishwashing. Joshua held out to the end, but when he left after many years as a member, there were those who still remembered his rebellion and who said "Well, at least now there are no exceptions."

No Unemployment in Community

People sometimes point out as an advantage of communal living that we have no unemployment. The concept of unemployment doesn't have any meaning in our environment. We do the work that we need or want to do, and we spread it out more or less evenly. If we run out of valuable things to do, the labor quota goes down for everybody, and we all get more vacation. If sales and income go down, we all take the "cut in pay" in the form of the Community's buying fewer or cheaper amenities or postponing them for a more prosperous year.

Dealing with the Non-Worker

In 1972 I claimed that if a Twin Oaks member consistently worked less than quota, we would eventually ask him or her to leave the Community. I believed it when I wrote it, but the idea has been severely tested in the intervening years. Twin Oaks is just comfortable enough that it can support a few dependents. When an adult member slides into dependency, we don't always rise up in indignation against him or her, not right away at least.

Let's take a hypothetical member named Fulano*—not a real person but a composite of several case histories. Fulano does less than quota for several weeks and accumulates a deficit. We call this "being in the labor hole." Various people talk to him about it, but he is not impressed by bureaucratic types. His friends never mention the subject to him, and defend him to others, saying "I'm sure he does his share but forgets to write it down," or "Labor credits aren't the only way to value a person's contribution," or "He's been going through some personal stuff and needs time off."

Since all of these are possible or even likely, and since the bureaucratic types don't want to make enemies, and since the Community seems to be surviving in spite of it, the matter gets postponed. It used to be that several months could go by before somebody would get angry enough to force the matter to group attention. By this time the deficit might have reached perhaps 400 credits—about nine weeks. It would be obvious that Fulano was never going to get out of the hole, and a lot of people would envy him his nine weeks of unearned vacation time.

On one such occasion a particular "Fulano" openly defied the group to kick him out. He went public with his refusal to work, and the group astonished itself by voting to take him at his word and throw him out. But it was an unusual case. The fabric of community is not tough enough to bear expelling a member every year or two. There was a period when a few people were getting away with doing little or nothing.

We patched this hole in 1987 with something called the "labor hole policy." Its essential provision is that any member remaining in the hole for seven months out of the last twelve automatically reverts to provisional membership. There are benefits to that. The member starts over with a clean slate, no deficit. But in exchange, his or her continued membership eventually may become subject to a poll of the current members, and that poll is taken by secret ballot. If I had been playing fast and loose with the labor credit system (which amounts to living off other people's labor), I would fear a secret ballot, and I think most people do.

What? Punishment in a Walden Two community? No, not punishment. Contingency management. The Community offers several different ways to remain in good standing. There are vacations, occasional leaves of absence, time extensions, second

---

*In Mexico, "Fulano, Sultano, and Mengano" are the rough equivalent of "Tom, Dick, and Harry." I lived in Mexico for a while and have found the trio useful when I don't want to use real names. There is no intentional connection between the name "Fulano" and the English word "fool," and the term in not pejorative in either language.

chances, counseling, and a wide choice of work, all before encountering the teeth of the labor hole policy. There is even a chance one might go unscathed through the dreaded poll. But eventually, one way or another, we all have to do our share of the work or leave, because it is not healthy for a large part of the Community to be angry and feel ripped off.

Advantages of the Labor Credit System

As I write all this, something is nagging at me, saying that I'm not getting at the main point. The point is not that we have some difficulties and have figured ways around them. The point is, the labor credit system works. Several people from other communities have come here to observe it, and that is because we have solved numerous problems that some other groups have bogged down over. An institution doesn't last twenty-five years in a group like ours if it isn't working. Here's what it does for us:

It is our security that everybody is doing a fair share. It is a way of earning free time and taking that leisure whenever we want it. It allows us to work in a variety of areas that interest us, without giving up one for the other. It gives immense flexibility in scheduling. There is plenty of room within the labor credit system to personalize it to suit one's work preferences.

It helps minimize resentment and guilt. We do not look askance at a person who is lying in a hammock at ten O'clock in the morning. We just figure he or she is using up vacation credits, or has already worked a full share or soon will.

We get up and go to bed when we please, work the hours that suit us, take on responsibility when we feel ready for it, work with other members whom we get along with, and participate in the Community decision-making that controls how we define creditable work. I don't think our system can be matched, anywhere in the world, for that combination of freedom and responsibility.

Problems with the Labor Credit System

In no way do I deny that there are problems with it. I'll name a few of them:

The labor credit system does nothing to control those few people who lie on their labor sheets. If there are members who seriously mean to take advantage of our loose controls, nothing stops them until their abuse is so obvious that people begin to complain. We've had a few such cases. What usually happens is that the person becomes demoralized enough to leave the Community after a while. This is not a triumph for the system, but neither does it seriously threaten the Community.

Some people can't handle the freedom. The expectations of the Community are very broad and lenient. People who are accustomed to a firm schedule, with supervision, suddenly find themselves adrift with more freedom than they can manage. Without any habits of self-discipline, they find themselves postponing work until late in the week, at which time they can't possibly make quota. A few weeks of this and they're in trouble. These people need a much more tightly organized system than Twin Oaks provides.

The system's most serious flaw is one it shares with the wage system. There are sometimes people who set about earning labor credits as if they were dollars, and their whole attitude toward their work is colored by the thought of the credit. This distracts them from the intrinsic worth and enjoyment of the work they are doing. They begin to feel that labor credits are the way the Community expresses its approval or indifference, and therefore if an activity isn't labor creditable, that means the Community does not value it—or them.

The labor credit is so central in some people's thinking that they want labor credits for everything they do—going to meetings, participating in local good works, doing art and music, talking to their children—everything, we sometimes say, except brushing their teeth, and that will probably be next. This is one reason that Twin Oaks' labor system is controversial in the communal movement. People are put off by what they call the "labor credit mentality."

I think they are quite right. People who get caught in that trap are not getting as much out of our system as the people who simply devote themselves to their work and use the credit as a way to keep track of it. I wish we could think of a way to solve this problem. In the meantime I think we are getting more out of the system than it is costing us. The benefits seem to be worth the tradeoffs.

I am not very disturbed by the criticisms of the labor credit system. I expect all systems to have flaws. For me personally, this is part of the interest. Problem solving is what we do here.

38

41

Money Equality:

A Close Look at a Communal Economy

Definition of "Communal Economy"

When I say that Twin Oaks has a fully communal economic system, I mean that we generate income almost entirely from on-premises activities, and all of that money goes into a communal bank account. We are not employees, and we get no wages. Instead, the Community takes care of all our needs.

By "all our needs" I mean food, clothing, housing, medical and dental care, toiletries, furniture, automobiles and trucks and their maintenance, recreation, and a dozen other things. I do not mean "all our wants," which is different. The Community buys food, but not candy. It keeps vehicles on the road, but not luxury cars, and usually not new. It subsidizes parties, but within a modest budget. It does not buy cigarettes or private booze. It does not pay for much vacation travel.

The Community reserves the right to determine what is and is not a "need," and this will vary according to our income. In spite of these exceptions, I consider that we have complete social security within the Community.

Sick leave is unrestricted. If you get sick, you don't have to work. If a doctor sends you to a hospital, you don't worry about the bill. Either we qualify for financial aid because of our low per-capita income, or we will pay the bill, and in either case it's taken care of by the office people.

Members don't have personal checking accounts, electric bills, or installment payments. Their contact with money is simply to check some out from the office for either personal spending (charged to their monthly allowance) or their managerial area, if they are in charge of something. For these purposes they may write checks on the Community's account. One of our check signers will sign them, and the accounting will be done later.

The pocket-money allowance this year is $50 per person per month (cumulative), kept in the Community's bank account until called for, and spent entirely at the member's discretion. This is where the gifts, cigarettes, phone calls, candy bar, etc. will come from. The allowance has no connection whatever with productivity. The person who was sick all month gets the same allowance as the people who managed a business. Children get an allowance, too, about half the amount given adults.

The legitimacy of any business or domestic expense is decided by the Manager of that area within the budget. The Library Manager decides (after seeking input from the group) which magazines to subscribe to; the Clothing Manager determines whether a member really needs new boots; the Utilities Manager buys the parts needed to fix the leaking shower head.

There are no privately owned vehicles. Any member who wants to drive somewhere checks out an available car at the office. The cost of this travel is charged to the managerial area or personal allowance of the member who signed it out, as appropriate.

The Practical Problems—Different Needs

This general arrangement is pretty standard for a fully communal society. It is very similar to what is done in the Israeli kibbutzim. In its social security aspects it is also much like the large religious societies. It is classical utopian communism.

Does it work? Is this rigid egalitarian economy really stable and satisfactory? It's a good question, and the answer is, "Well, mostly."

There are problems and exceptions. Humans are always wanting something that isn't easy to get, and general budgets sometimes don't serve them. Some examples:

Alice wants to take voice lessons. She thinks she wants a career in music. She made an official request at economic planning time, but it was turned down. Now she is considering leaving the Community and getting a job in order to finance this dream.

Tony feels a need to visit his parents in Italy at least once a year. They are getting old, and family ties are strong. The allowance is not nearly adequate for this. He feels bad about leaving the Community, and his skills are valuable to us.

Charlene simply can't stay in one place all the time. She is prepared to make a lifetime commitment to Twin Oaks, but she has to spend about 2 to 3 months every year traveling, or she'll go nuts, she says.

Donald wants to go camping in the mountains, which is easy enough to do on a Twin Oaks allowance, but he wants first class hiking and camping gear. Especially he wants a good down jacket and boots more expensive than the Clothing Manager will buy. He's only talking about a few hundred dollars, but he doesn't have it.

Here's the question: Are these "needs?" It depends on what you're comparing them to. It is absurd to call them "needs" if you're making comparisons to the lifestyle of the average inhabitant of this planet, or even with that of one's own grandparents. Ordinary people two generations ago didn't travel, didn't aspire to the entertainment profession, and didn't expect expensive equipment for a hobby. They kept their expectations down to the level of their income.

Twin Oaks's income is about $5,000 a year per person. Why is it some of our members do not automatically adjust their financial "needs" realistically to the Community's per-capita income? My guess is that it is because they are accustomed to thinking in terms of the income of their parents and peers outside the Community. For them, music lessons, plane tickets, and camping equipment seem like perfectly ordinary expenses.

Furthermore, they plead, they are not asking the Community to pay for these things. They understand that we cannot afford to finance the yearnings of all our members equally, and they also understand that we cannot in good conscience do it selectively. All they are asking is to be allowed to earn the money themselves in their own free time.

Attempts at Solutions—Vacation Earnings and Gift Money

Thus was born the policy we now call "V.E." (for Vacation Earnings). Members may, while on vacation away from the Community (vacation they have earned by working more than their quota), earn money for purposes like those I have mentioned above, without turning this money over to the Community.

In a separate piece of early legislation we agreed to allow members to accept gifts, including cash, from parents and other outsiders. Normally this money is expected to be used on vacation, not spent on envy-causing consumption here.

These rules were well meant when we wrote them, and they do solve some people's individual financial problems. In spite of this, they have proved a headache. The catch is that not everybody can easily get a job and make a little money in the vacation time available, and not everybody has sources outside the Community from which to expect gift money. We are also unequal in the amount of energy we have available to earn the extra vacation credits in the first place. Thus, in our egalitarian Community, some are richer than others.

How much richer? On the average, a few hundred dollars a year. Compared to our total income (in goods and services) it is only a few percentage points of difference, but it rankles. Every time one of us claims proudly that Twin Oaks has a truly equal economic system, someone will sneer and say, "Not really." Every time the Planners deny someone a special privilege on the grounds that we cannot extend the same privilege to everyone, the disappointed person will grumble about selective equality.

We have several times tried to do away with V.E. in order to stop the angry (and perhaps justified) cynicism of those who cannot profit from it, but we've never even come close to a decision to abandon it. Probably half the Community's members do a little V.E. work from time to time and value the privilege. As to the half that doesn't, a lot of them consider the matter petty. An increasing percentage of members does not consider absolute economic equality very important. They have come to community for entirely different reasons. The bitter complaints come from a handful of people, but they are not necessarily a quiet handful, and can create unrest.

Weeds and Knots

We took a bold step the year we introduced "Weeds and Knots." This is a committee that distributes small amounts of money upon request to individuals who apply for it. ("Weeds and Knots" is a kind of spoonerism for "Needs and Wants.") People who envy those who easily earn V.E. are free to apply to Weeds and Knots for travel money or any other expense. (I got some once for a correspondence course I wanted to take.) These grants are usually small—less than $100 at a time—because the committee tries to make its budget cover as many requests as possible, and it has only about $2000 a year all together. The hope for this committee is that it will give mostly to people who don't have other resources but do have unsatisfied financial wants.

OPP

What many people want us to do is to provide a way to earn personal money within the Community, without having to go away. If we could do this, it would do a lot toward satisfying our desire to treat all members equally. Unfortunately, our tax lawyer tells us that we absolutely cannot pay our members any wages if we are to retain our valuable tax status, which I will explain later.

There is nothing, however, to prohibit our having an incentive program that benefits the Community, rather than individuals. We started such a program a few years ago, and it has been quite effective. People will work without labor credits for goals of their own choosing, even though they do not end up owning the purchased items. For example, people have used the program to earn CDs for the hammock shop music library, books for the Women's Library, and donations to causes they care about.

We call the program "OPP," which stands for "Overquota Products for Projects." An extension of this idea has been to make it available for community travel, such as a group going to visit another community or to a conference on vital topics. As long as the trip benefits the Community in an observable way, it qualifies. This is not the same as being able to earn money directly for personal travel, but it does satisfy some people and eases the strain caused by the desire to travel and the shortage of money.

Progress or Backsliding?

Gift money, V.E., and OPP would all have disgusted me in the early years. I assumed then that absolute financial equality should be a basic requirement. The very idea of any member wanting to hold out on the group by having a private bank account or a private source of income, or some economic privilege that other people lacked made me curl my lip in contempt. My attitude to every request for special privilege was always the same: "Why you?" In other words, what is there about you that makes you deserve to have more than other people? You say you work harder? It was blind luck and genes that gave you the body and the capacity to work harder. You say you want to set something aside for your children? What makes your children more deserving than anybody else's children? And so forth. I was known as a hard-nosed egalitarian, and this is one of the reasons people called me "very idealistic." It wasn't always a compliment.

It took me about seven years and a fair amount of self-examination, as well as observation of the people I lived with, to discover some unsettling things about my equality theory. For one thing, I came to see that my ideological purity, though a hardship on other people, wasn't any hardship on me. I had no financial assets when we started. I had no money in the bank, no reliable car, no generous relatives, no time and energy for earning money in my spare time. Because I was so engrossed in the Community itself, I got rich satisfaction from my life without feeling any need for spending money. In short, I had nothing to gain from making our financial rules more flexible. Most of the people who agreed with my hard line principles were in similar situations.

Also, in truth, I coveted for the Community every dollar anybody could find, and every hour they could contribute. When I used the "Why you?" argument, there was another motive behind it—the desire to build the Community faster and make it more secure. I didn't want those resources diverted.

The people who wanted the financial agreements to be looser generally had some money or skill or opportunity they wanted to use for their own benefit. They weren't wholeheartedly engrossed in the Community, so they weren't getting the emotional payoffs that I got all the time.

I remember when I was in the tenth grade I had a gray-haired history teacher named Mrs. Cooper, who told us, with amusement and glee, "Your politics will be determined by your pocketbook." I protested indignantly. I swore that I would be an exception. I was certain that when I grew up I would remain a radical, no matter how rich I got. Now I'm the one with gray hair, and I agree with Mrs. Cooper. But the process isn't quite as simple as she made it sound. It is not that I abandoned my principles as soon as I had something to lose. It is that having something to lose put me in touch with the complexities of the problem.

I can now answer the question "Why you?" The answer is basically this: Because most people value small liberties more than they value small equalities, and therefore society works better if the rules aren't too rigid. Equality is a means, not an end.

People will and do work for the common good. If they did not, Twin Oaks would be impossible. But they work harder for more direct personal benefit, and it would be dishonest to deny it. When the Community desperately needs to have a great deal of work done in a hurry (making a lot of hammocks for a rush order, for example), it relies about ninety percent on good will, personal conscience, the labor system, and community feeling. But if we're going to get the other ten percent, we need to add an incentive program of some kind, some method by which added effort gets added reward.

Gradually I noticed that almost everybody behaves in this way. Then I faced the fact that I was no better than the rest of them. The question "Why you?" is still unanswerable in terms of absolute justice. But I have lowered my sights. We're not going to create absolute justice. The best we can manage is a a reasonable amount of equity. We have a great deal more justice within Twin Oaks than I see in my country as a whole, and I am willing to let it be fuzzy around the edges.

So some members have outside bank accounts*, and others have prosperous parents who buy them plane tickets. Some can earn a lot of over-quota credits and use their vacations to make $10 -20/hr doing freelance computer programming or construction, and others can just barely make quota and will have to apply to Weeds and Knots when they really want something. I accept it all.

Actually, I once gave another try at increasing justice. I proposed to the Planners that we determine which members were getting a lot of gift money from their parents, and then create a fund to make up the difference to the members who did not have this source of income. We took a survey to determine who was who. Not a single member we asked admitted to getting any gift money. This was absurd, because we knew for a fact that almost half the Community's members received birthday checks and plane tickets and so forth. But those people claimed that the money they received was not really theirs. The parents were merely paying for trips home, a mixed blessing for the member. They (the members) had no more freely spendable cash than those who were too poor to make such visits. If the Community proposed giving away money selectively to our own poor, suddenly everybody was poor.

These days people don't call me "idealistic" any more. They call me "cynical." But that isn't true, either. I have learned that personal gain is, not a stronger motivation than the good of the Community, but a more reliable one. I accept that now. I no longer think it is evil or disgusting. I think it's ordinary.

Twin Oaks as a group has not caught up with my conclusions (or not backslid to them, depending on your point of view). When

---

* Such accounts remain frozen for the duration of a person's membership.

I returned to this Community after spending nine years in other places (a story I'll tell in a later chapter), I looked carefully at my own willingness to live by a code I had myself created but no longer fully believed in. I decided that Twin Oaks had a right to expect me to live by its rules, however naive I now thought its principles. So that's what I do. I no longer preach absolute equality. I live, along with other communitarians, a rough equality that doesn't create gross differences or engender severe envy. To the extent that we still find economic equality important, I keep within the limits of our law and common practice.

Some Effects of a Communal Economy

I ask myself how we have been affected, overall, by our relatively strict financial rules. Here's what I come up with:

...We wipe out any gross economic differences among members. This is basic to our original goals, and we tend to take it for granted, so much so that this fundamental equality gets buried in the avalanche of communal self-criticism. Because we are not absolutely 100 percent equal about everything, we sometimes forget that we are indeed mostly equal about most things.

...Communal earning and spending allow us to prioritize, as a group, expenditures that are basic to health and well-being, and to make sure they are covered before going on to less vital purchases. As individuals we might be willing to forego dental care, for example, and use the money for travel or hobbies. As a Community we never do that. Luxury spending is something we can sometimes do and sometimes not. The money for the dentist is always there.

...We have a meaningful tax advantage by being fully income-sharing.

...We do not get rich members. They are simply unwilling to give up the income from their investments. Interestingly, when we were very poor, we did occasionally attract people who had large sums of money. But now that we do not literally need this money, incoming people appear to resent giving it up. In the early years we got outright donations from members, and put up buildings with them. These days we virtually never get any money from members except what the bylaws require.

By the standards of the outside world, our rules are still strict. Members of Twin Oaks cannot run a business from our property or earn any money anywhere within Louisa County unless they turn the earnings over to the Community. We don't have private homes or cars. Interest on bank accounts and the like remains

Community property. Social security payments and child support come to the Community. We retain the general principle that one cannot become personally richer while being a Community member.

In spite of the little exceptions, I consider Twin Oaks truly communal, in the same general sense that an Israeli kibbutz is communal. Like the kibbutzim, we have holes in our system, but, also like them, the overall economic system is so much bigger and more important than the exceptions that it would be out of proportion and unfair to dwell on them.

These days I believe that secular communal economies must, to be successful, be full of holes. I think that if they are too tight, too "equal," they will fail, because people would not be able to stand the constraints. Give people a little chance to serve themselves on the side, and they will give heartily out of their core efforts for the group. We do, anyway.

Chapter 6

City People Earn A Living
In The Country

Quoting from A Walden Two Experiment: 1972

We were very naive about money when we started. In many ways I am sure we are still. But in the back of all our minds was one bit of knowledge that saved us from worrying about it too much. That was that, if we had to, we could and would get ordinary jobs in the city.

We hoped for a while that it might not be necessary. The tobacco crop* we worked so hard on would bring in some money. We had a friend who was sending us $200 a month to get started on. There was a house in Washington that two of us owned equity in. And we had some ideas for small industries that we hoped would put us on our feet.

As a matter of fact, the tobacco crop brought in about $300 total, the friend eventually stopped sending the checks, the house could not be sold for even its equity, and our industrial ideas didn't do too well.

The fact is that in 1968 we did have to go out and get jobs, and we still have to. We will continue to do it as long as necessary to keep the

---

*In today's political climate it is shocking to hear that Twin Oaks ever considered raising tobacco for a living. In 1967 we didn't give it much thought. We had bought a farm that had a tobacco allotment. That meant guaranteed income for us, more vital by far at that time than arguments against tobacco.

Community going. This is the main reason Twin Oaks has continued where dozens of communes with similar beginnings have failed. Our naivete about everything financial was counteracted by our willingness to work for wages.

Getting Serious About Hammocks

Outside work came to an end in 1973, shortly after the above was published. In 1974 there was a financial crisis, which was caused simply by ignorance of financial planning. Twin Oaks spent more than it earned by a large margin, deceived by the substantial bank balance at the end of our hammock sales season. When the money ran out quite suddenly, Twin Oakers volunteered to go get jobs, which they hadn't had to do for several months. One of the outside workers was Ken. He got a job mowing lawns for some institution. One day while he was riding around on the mower, he said to himself, "I'd rather make hammocks at home. I wonder if the Community would allow me to spend all my time making hammocks instead of working at this pointless job, if I promised to take the business seriously and spend some real effort selling." He made the proposal, and the Community decided to let him try. The most effective salesperson turned out to be a member named Steven, but Ken, true to his word, put his whole attention on the hammock shop. Together with two friends he changed the shop from a mostly deserted space to a lively and interesting place to be. The three of them kept up a running conversation, told jokes, and learned to weave hammocks at speeds not previously attained. This atmosphere attracted many other workers. Meanwhile, Steven went on the road and talked gift shops and an occasional department store into trying our product.

The other outside workers came home for the last time in 1975 when Twin Oaks got the first big order from Pier One Imports. Though there have been a few scares in the years since then, our "What if Pier One drops us?" fears have not yet been realized, and this customer has been the backbone of our income for the last 18 years.

Questions About the Dependence on Pier One

There are people who think that if Twin Oaks had not lucked into the Pier One account, the Community would have folded, like so many others. I don't think so. I think we'd have found other ways to keep going.

I acknowledge that we have become somewhat soft as a result of our secure income and the amenities we have provided for ourselves over the years, and I would expect financial disaster to be an unpleasant shock. Would the people who long for more of the "simple life" continue to admire simplicity if it included not being able to take a child to a doctor for a sore throat? It's hard to know what to predict, but my offhand guess is that our population would, under adverse conditions, diminish slightly, but we wouldn't go under.

Twin Oaks is simply not fragile. We haven't experienced hard times for several years, but I believe the quality of people we have and attract, and their attachment to this Community, are enough to guarantee our survival.

A couple of years ago the Planners asked, on one of their surveys, what the members thought of the Pier One Strategy. The most frequent answer was "I never heard of it. What is it?" The Pier One Strategy is the opposite of what it sounds like. It consists of a series of steps we want to take to reduce our frightening dependence on Pier One for income. In theory what we want to do is find some more medium-sized accounts that could be relied upon to buy hammocks from us regularly, so that the Pier One account would eventually be a smaller percentage of our income. This solution is more easily conceived than accomplished. We've been after those medium-sized accounts for years, and every once in a while we get one, but our competitors are after them, too.

Another part of the Strategy is encouraging the development of middle-sized businesses that will bring in a reasonable dollar-per-hour and have nothing to do with hammocks. The first of these grew out of the hammock business, the manufacture of a hanging chair with an oak frame.

The Hanging Chair

When Twin Oaks brought out the hanging chair in the 1970s, the Community decided to get a patent on the design. A search through the patent files showed us nothing similar. There were "hammock chairs" consisting of a brief hammock for one person, but nobody had patented anything with a back, not to mention the attractive rope work that keeps our swinging chair in place. In taking out a patent we thought we were being extra cautious, but the caution didn't help much. Some heir of the patent-holder on a backless hanging "chair" saw our product and, smelling money, sued us for patent infringement. I have always thought we would have won the case if it had ever gone to court, but Twin Oaks elected to settle the case for several thousand dollars.

Craft Fairs

The hanging chair gives us entry into handcrafted furniture shows and craft fairs, which, in their turn, are also a minor Twin Oaks business bringing in a good income per hour.

These days the members who sell at craft fairs are allowed a cheap hotel room if we have no friend in the area who can offer hospitality, but there was a time when they were expected to camp. Most fairs are held in cities, with no camp ground conveniently available. Our sales people frequently slept in or near the van. On one occasion when the van was full of merchandise and it rained, they had to crawl with their sleeping bags underneath the van for shelter. In the morning they freshened up with wrinkled clothing from their backpacks and a brief wash in the public restroom.

These conditions did nothing to reduce the willingness of members to do this work. Craft fairs are one of the more popular ways to earn labor credits. People like to travel, enjoy the stimulation of the work, and see the advantage of being forced by the circumstances to work twelve-hour days, allowing them to pile up labor credits for future vacations.

Another pleasure of doing fairs is trading for the merchandise sold by other crafts people. It is a custom at these fairs for the sales people to examine products in other booths and bargain for exchanges. Thus one of us might come home with pottery or stained glass, perhaps for Christmas gifts to our parents, giving in exchange a hammock, which we then earn by making extra hammocks for the Community without credit after we return home. Twin Oakers are not usually sharp bargainers. We have one member who traded an Oakweave chair (a standing chair with a woven rope seat) worth $150 for a piece of metalicized ribbon in the shape of a bow tie. Her friends remonstrated with her for bad bargaining, but she could only say "The guy who sold them was so cute."

Indexing

In 1982 we added the indexing of books to our list of enterprises. This little business is good for us, because it calls for an entirely different kind of labor and uses some of the brain-power and education the Community has in good supply.

Our entry into indexing was the gift of an admirer named Bill. This man had been indexing books to supplement his professional academic income for many years. He became interested in intentional community and saw a way to help. He was willing to provide us an entry into the business by persuading one of his own customers to give us a try. Our first indexing project was a large technical work on heat exchangers. For weeks the new indexing crew went around muttering phrases like "Eddies, turbulent."

When Bill first came to visit Twin Oaks and to talk about his idea, he was referred to Taylor, who was New Industries Manager. Generally speaking, the job of a New Industries Manager is to provide a small budget and guidance for any member who has an idea for a new income area. If the fledgling business shows promise on a small scale, it will be given the resources to expand.

Taylor was very good at this job. She had the experience to know that most of these efforts would cost us a few hundred dollars and some labor credits and probably come to nothing in the end, but she never tried to discourage anyone with an idea. She recognized that Twin Oaks really does have a need for viable businesses, and she kept her mind open.

Bill never asked us for a cent for his aid in teaching us indexing and then finding initial customers for us. He visited Twin Oaks while we were doing our first index and stood ready to give help. He dearly loved to talk, and naturally he liked to be listened to. I remember when I was trying to help out on the heat exchanger index, I would occasionally ask him a question, such as whether two expressions were sufficiently similar to be indexed under a single entry. That was Bill's opportunity. He knew all about the principles of heat exchange. For the next twenty minutes I sat with glazed eyes listening to a science lecture and thinking, "Does this man have any idea of the value of time? Does he know I'm taking labor credits for sitting here nodding and smiling and saying, 'I see,' (which I didn't) ?" At the end I timidly repeated my original question—should it be one entry or two? "Oh," said Bill, "don't worry about it. It will be taken care of in the final editing."

Indexing is exacting work. All the entries need to be correct. If the index says that Wang Li Cheong is mentioned on page 437, one had better be able to find the reference there. It was perhaps the demanding nature of the job, along with the suspicion that ninety percent of one's work will never in fact be used, that inspired one of our early Indexing Managers to play a small joke. We were working for the U.S. State Department at the time, indexing the volumes of documents that were freshly being declassified. The current volume was on Korea, and the indexer was reminded of the TV show M*A*S*H*. He had an inspiration. Wouldn't it be fun to insert a fictional character in the index? Probably nobody would ever notice it, and it could be our private joke. So he entered the name "Potter, Colonel S." into the index, and we all giggled.

Alas, somebody did notice. The State Department didn't giggle at all. They called Bill in Washington and waxed indignant about his recommendation. Bill then called our indexer and transferred the Government's wrath to him, in an hour-long lecture about professionalism and good faith recommendations and the like. It was not, said the State Department, funny. On the contrary, said Bill, it was childish and highly embarrassing.

Our indexer squirmed and groveled, ate crow, donned sackcloth and ashes, and promised never, never, never, never to do it again. In addition, he internalized the scolding, and these days probably nowhere in the nation is there a more scrupulous indexer than he. He was so embarrassed about his misplaced levity that as long as he was a member, he wouldn't allow this story to be published. Now he's gone, years have passed, and his reputation as an indexer is solid, so I'm taking the liberty. I disagree with the State Department. I think it's hilarious.

Even then we were good indexers, and we didn't lose the State Department job. Apologies were accepted, and we did twenty more volumes of declassified documents. Over a ten-year period we have also indexed over three hundred other books on topics ranging from computers to literary criticism.

Tofu

Most popular of the income-earning efforts is our new tofu-making plant. We buy organically grown soybeans and make tofu and related products, which we then sell to health food stores, Chinese restaurants, and distributors in nearby cities. This business is in its first year as I write this, and it is too soon to know how well it will serve our needs for income. Although the work of making tofu is not particularly easy, some of our members like to do it because they believe in it. Hammocks and fancy chairs are luxury products made with non-renewable resources, and indexing is merely a convenience for students and scholars. Tofu, however, is a basic foodstuff, low on the food chain, highly nutritious, and so forth.

The tofu business brings out ideological fervor that is much lacking in the hammocks business. It attracts people who believe in tofu, who think of it as part of a solution to the world's biggest problems. This consideration keeps people volunteering to make tofu, in spite of the fact that the work itself is hard, hot, and heavy. I hope that spirit can be sustained.

Vertical Integration

Another potential for improving our income is "vertical integration." This means making for ourselves the materials for our products, materials that we otherwise would have had to buy. We have done this in two areas of our hammock business: rope-making and stretcher-making. (Stretchers are the two wooden sticks that keep the hammock open.) Both of these operations were instantly profitable, of course, because they had an automatic internal market, and no effort had to go into selling. Selling remains one of our poorest skills. This year we are experimenting with vertical integration of the tofu business as well, by growing some of our own soybeans.

Special Problems Operating in the Business World

There are things about Twin Oaks social customs that work against our success in business. Chief among them is the fact that people change their areas of work at will, and seldom remain in the same job for more than a couple of years. Also, members may (and do) take vacation whenever they choose. Managers who are themselves faithful to their commitments find this easy-going attitude of their co-workers exasperating in the extreme.

One might ask how, under these circumstances, we can stay in business at all, in competition with firms that conduct themselves in a less lackadaisical fashion. Part of the answer is that Twin Oaks virtually never actually makes what the Outside World calls a profit. All we make is an hourly income on the level of a wage. When we say that the hammock business earns us $7.50 an hour, we mean that the total net income from the business, divided by all the hours that go into the business, comes out to that figure. That includes administrative and sales hours as well as production. We have no executive officers getting a larger salary than other people (or indeed any salary at all). There are no sales bonuses. We don't even have many supervisors. We also have no shareholders or investors with a stake in our businesses. We finance ourselves entirely from previous earnings.

The Payoff

What all of us get (production workers, clerical workers, administrative workers, and support people in areas like cooking, laundry, and child care) is a comfortable, secure life, a lot of freedom, opportunities to do untraditional work and learn new skills, and a chance to work at our varying ideals. Nobody gets any cash. Nobody "gets ahead." There's no place special to get ahead to.

In 1991 Twin Oaks paid taxes on an income of $5,200 per member. In 1992 it went down to $3,500. By outside standards both numbers sound like poverty. By American communal standards it sounds like prosperity. There are several reasons it amounts to a better living than the numbers would indicate. One, of course, is our ability to purchase food and other things in bulk. Another is our willingness to put in labor instead of money where it makes sense to do so and thus get some necessities (such as potatoes) and some luxuries (such as solid oak wood trim) by harvesting them from our own property

A third source of invisible income takes the form of internal services. We take for granted such personal services as baby-sitting (we call it "primary time"), personal shopping, sick care, individual tutoring, building construction and maintenance, and of course cooking and (to the degree that we do it) house-cleaning. The parents of our school children can frequently find some other Community member to volunteer to drive a child to a play practice or a soccer game. We have one member who teaches piano for labor credits, one who leads classes in aerobics, and another who teaches dance and gymnastics. None of this involves any transfer of cash and is therefore not part of our "income." But it is part of our good life.

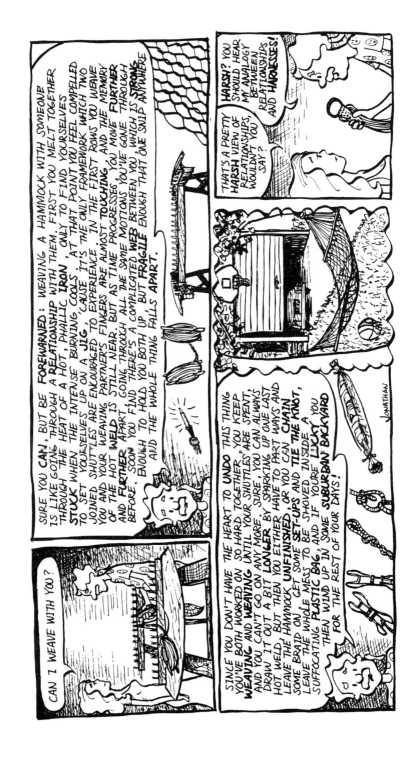

CAN I WEAVE WITH YOU?

SURE YOU **CAN**, BUT BE **FOREWARNED**: WEAVING A HAMMOCK WITH SOMEONE IS LIKE GOING THROUGH A **RELATIONSHIP** WITH THEM. FIRST YOU MELT TOGETHER THROUGH THE HEAT OF A HOT, PHALLIC **IRON**, ONLY TO FIND YOURSELVES **STUCK** WHEN THE INTENSE BURNING COOLS. AT THAT POINT YOU FEEL COMPELLED TO SET YOURSELVES UP ON A **JIG**, 'CAUSE IT'S THE ONLY FRAMEWORK WHICH TWO JOINED SHUTTLES ARE ENCOURAGED TO EXPERIENCE. IN THE FIRST ROWS YOU WEAVE YOU AND YOUR WEAVING PARTNER'S FINGERS ARE ALMOST **TOUCHING**, AND THE MEMORY OF THE HOT **WELD** IS STILL NEAR. BUT AS TIME PROGRESSES, YOU MOVE **FURTHER** AND **FURTHER** APART. GOING THROUGH ALL THE SAME MOTIONS YOU'VE GONE THROUGH BEFORE. SOON YOU FIND THERE'S A COMPLICATED **WEB** BETWEEN YOU, WHICH IS **STRONG** ENOUGH TO HOLD YOU BOTH UP, BUT **FRAGILE** ENOUGH THAT ONE SNIP ANYWHERE AND THE WHOLE THING FALLS APART.

SINCE YOU DON'T HAVE THE HEART TO **UNDO** THIS THING YOU'VE BOTH WORKED ON SO HARD TOGETHER, YOU KEEP **WEAVING** AND **WEAVING** UNTIL YOUR SHUTTLES ARE SPENT, AND YOU CAN'T GO ON ANY MORE. SURE, YOU CAN ALWAYS DRAW IT OUT A BIT **LONGER** BY SPARKING UP ONE LAST HOT WELD, BUT THEN YOU EITHER HAVE TO PART WAYS AND LEAVE THE HAMMOCK **UNFINISHED**, OR YOU CAN **CHAIN** SOME BRAID ON, GET SOME **SET-UPS** AND TIE THE **KNOT**, LEAVE THE WHOLE MESS TO BE SHOVED INSIDE A SUFFOCATING PLASTIC BAG, AND IF YOU'RE **LUCKY** YOU THEN WIND UP IN SOME **SUBURBAN BACKYARD** FOR THE REST OF YOUR DAYS!

THAT'S A PRETTY **HARSH** VIEW OF RELATIONSHIPS, WOULDN'T YOU SAY?

HARSH? YOU SHOULD HEAR MY ANALOGY BETWEEN RELATIONSHIPS AND **HARNESSES!**

JONATHAN

60

62

Chapter 7

Collective Consumption

No one will be surprised when I say that spending money presents fewer problems than earning it. However, Community-style spending has its own challenges. Principally, we have to decide as a group what to spend our money on. This is a process we basically do once a year, in December, frequently with an update in mid-July.

The Tradeoff Game

The Community over time has invented a device called "The Tradeoff Game" to help us decide democratically how to use our money and labor. The Game isn't as much fun as the name would imply. Really, what each "player" does is fill out a long, complicated survey. Each member gets a copy of all the relevant figures that would affect economic decisions for the forthcoming year. As clearly and concisely as possible, the survey sets out how much money and labor each area used for the last two years and how much the Managers are asking for this year. The task of each player is then to evaluate these requests and express individual opinions in numeric form.

For instance, on my Game I see that the Rollie, the Building Maintenance Manager, is asking for a substantial increase in both money and labor over last year's budgets. I note that he overspent both the previous year. I think about what has been accomplished since he took the managership, and I feel pleased at his commitment and the progress I have seen. I think about the future of the area. There is still a backlog of maintenance that needs to be attended to. I am inclined to vote Rollie a big increase, because I think the Community will get its money's and labor's worth. So I express my approval and encouragement by writing on the Game form the same number that Rollie requested. Then I go on to the next area and do the same kind of thinking.

This is all pleasant enough, but there's a catch, and therein lies the essence of the Game: The bottom line is fixed. There is just so much money and labor to go around. If I treat every Manager as generously as I do Rollie, I won't have enough. My Game has to balance to that bottom line. Everybody who does a Tradeoff Game works with a pencil and eraser, and a conscientious player will probably devote at least 4 hours to the task.

When all the Games are analyzed and (usually) averaged, the Planners have a very good guide for making up the next year's economic plan.

OTRAS

We generally expect to have somewhat more money than we absolutely need for our ongoing expenses. We can also usually predict a labor supply larger than those ongoing areas require. Even so, individual Game players have to be careful how they allocate resources, because we want to have some left over for the area we call "OTRAs."

OTRA is both an acronym and a pun. It stands for "One Time Resource Allocation." It is also Spanish for "Other," meaning, in this case, other than the regular ongoing activities of the Community. People playing the Tradeoff Game determine by their votes what extra projects the Community will devote resources to in the coming year. In a typical year, the Community will vote about half the extra money into items or projects with an extended lifetime, like a tractor or a woodshed, and the other half into immediately consumed items, such as allowance raises or charitable donations.

In recent years, the ongoing areas of the Community have cost us about $180,000 per year, or about $2400 per member. This is in addition to baseline expenses like insurance and utilities, costing an additional $170,000 or $2300 each. Our recent income has permitted us to spend about $30,000 a year on OTRAs. This money goes for a wide variety of things.

Here is a partial but representative list of the items we have voted to purchase or support during the last two years:

Honey extractor	$ 369	Coffee & juice	3000
Fruit trees	141	Hay barn	1555
Raise turkeys	160	Children's books	205
Home school	1222	Lumber shed	435
Rewire a residence	412	Wood lathe	215
Replace water main	1200	Fire exit	1535
Various donations	6000	Cat food	325

Evaluation of the Game

There are people who consider filling out the Tradeoff Game to be a lot of trouble, but historically the Game is a solution to an old problem. Before it was invented, Planners had to make economic decisions on their own (on a very small income at that point in history), and their chosen plan frequently got a lot of criticism from disappointed members, who would make such remarks as "The Planners don't care about agriculture" or "They never give us anything I want." The Planners, who were trying hard to please, as well as to protect the Community's interests, were frustrated by the grumbling, because the discontented never seemed to realize that the total amount of money was limited. In vain Planners would ask "What did you want us not to buy?" With the invention of the Tradeoff Game, every Community member must personally answer this question.

The Game and I

The first year that I did a Tradeoff Game was just after my nine-year absence (which I'll explain later). In a sense I was a "new" member and tended to associate with other new members. A small group of us decided to fill our Games out together, thinking we could maximize our influence acting in combination. We had a good time. I remember a young man named Todd looking up from his Game and saying "This is the way the United States ought to do its budgets." We spent a few minutes fantasizing about that. Given the opportunity, we decided, we would definitely cut the defense budget and give more to schools and health care. I don't believe we dealt with the national debt.

Getting back to the task at hand, our little group decided to cut back on the garden and milk-processing labor budgets, because we thought we had way too many tomatoes, and the homemade cheeses of that time were truly awful. There were eight of us working together, and when our Games were turned in, the Planners were appalled to see those eight votes threatening the well-established garden and milk-processing budgets. "It's Kat influencing all those new people!" they fumed. There was not supposed to be any difference made between the input from old members and new ones, so they worried. They could not ignore the eight votes, but if they gave them much credence, they would upset a great many people. As a solution, one of the Planners leaked the information to her personal friends (gardeners all), who retaliated by changing their Games to raise the garden and milk processing budgets beyond the original requests. The Planners could then average the input and maintain the status quo. I look back on this incident and laugh. I'm glad the Planners outsmarted us, because we really were new to the Game, and we really didn't understand the Community well enough to be throwing our numeric weight around.

The Tradeoff Game is at this point a fundamental institution at Twin Oaks, and as such is a fair target for gentle satire. Our choir sings a song about it, the words fitted to a Gilbert and Sullivan tune from "Patience." It goes like this:

The Tradeoff Game Song

Oh, Come, Let us harness our minds to the task
Of the Plan for the coming year.
The figures are in from the year just past.
The computer has made them clear.

First off we must pay for the regular things
That we hardly can do without
Like food and the like for our well-beings
Too boring to sing about.

But when it is done there may still be a sum
We have earned and is ours to use.
There's a wishbook of goodies to browse among
We have only to pick and choose.

Let's have a new house for the needs of the old,
And a pool in our own backyard.
We need recreation, so I've been told,
Or we might work much too hard.

We could buy a van or a pickup or two,
Though we seem to have some to spare
But whenever we need them most, it's true,
There's only the dump truck there.

It's time that we started to travel at ease,
With allowance to pay the bill.
One hundred a month will surely please,
Or at least I think it will.

We live on a planet where some are bereft
Of the means to get them through.
Let's give to the needy who lean to the Left.
It's the least that we can do.

And while we're about it, let's think of the Earth,
And earnestly guarantee
To buy things Organic for all we're worth,
And save lots of Energy

Chorus:
The new year will be like the old year has been
For there's much that remains the same
But some will acquire what their hearts desire
In the yearly Tradeoff Game

If this song doesn't amuse you, it's probably because you don't live here. It has a lot of in-jokes and is a big hit at performances.

Beyond the Game—Income, Spending, and Ideology

What the Tradeoff Game does not address is the basic question of how much money we are willing to earn in total, and how hard we ought to be working to maintain or increase our current spending level. On this, as on many subjects, we are not in complete agreement. A substantial subgroup of the Community would like to see us cut back on both earning and spending. They argue

67

that we have much that we could well do without. This is obviously true. Our sister community, Sandhill Farm, spends less than a quarter of what we do per person.

As a community Twin Oaks has yet to come to grips with what it would mean to take this seriously. No matter what kind of expenses we might choose to cut back on, somebody would feel deprived. We are much more diverse than Sandhill, and possibly more diverse than some of our members want us to be. It is our diversity that keeps us putting out money for first one special interest and then another. For example, we maintain a full dairy program even though some of us do not consume dairy products; we contribute to charitable and political causes that only some of us believe in; we fund dances and parties that many people don't attend; we support children when some of our members would prefer an all-adult community; and so on.

Meanwhile we maintain the basics for everybody. That means that we are going to pay for utilities, insurance, medical expenses, and a wide variety of food choices, even though individual members could easily go without some of those things. One could say that this is a fundamental problem with group purchasing. It is of course offset by many savings that only groups can accomplish.

Standard of Living vs. Expansion

We used to have a recurring controversy which got dubbed "Standard of Living versus Expansion." I will quote from *A Walden Two Experiment,* 1972:

> Expansion versus the Quality of Life is probably the most enduring argument we have. The beginning of this argument was in 1969, when Simon wanted meat on the table, and Dwight wanted us to tighten our belts for the revolution. As I look back on it, it seems odd that the subject didn't come up until 1969. We have never ceased talking about it since. Dwight, Brian, and I shared the vision of large community. *Walden Two* suggested a thousand as a reasonable population number to shoot for (and after you get to the thousand, you divide the group; half of you go to a new location and start another community; the other half stay where they are and accept new members to fill the vacated spaces, and so on, *ad infinitum*). Implicit in the expansion idea is the assumption that we have a task to perform for the world's population, and that we will not be living up to our responsibilities unless and until a good part of that population can make community living (*Walden Two* style) one of its choices. Simon was the first to give us any argument. He held that nobody had any moral obligation to anybody but himself. He lived up to his philosophy

> pretty well . . . His blatant selfishness kept us from taking his point of view seriously, so we didn't meet "quality of life" as an issue until it came up again in later years, this time presented by people who quite seriously meant that they preferred a smaller community, that we should use our money and labor to improve our surroundings, rather than building for more members, and that, though we might have a responsibility toward people who have not yet had a chance to join, we have a greater responsibility to ourselves to make our own lives more rewarding. I am not really capable of presenting the quality of life argument very well, since I am a heavy partisan for the other side. No matter how it is argued, I can always hear the ring of "me first" in it, and I cannot help asking, "Why you?"

I feel both irony and nostalgia as I reread that chapter. Actually, the Quality of Life versus Expansion argument changed its form many years ago. It turns out that prosperity and a larger population, far from being opposed to each other, are in fact partners. A little experience with financial statistics shows us why. Each worker produces a surplus, either in cash or in goods or services of some kind. The accumulated surpluses allow us to buy or build useful things. Obviously, the more people contribute to this surplus, the more easily we can handle large or basic amenities. It is easy enough to piddle away $500, but $5,000 makes you stop and think.

Each "generation" of communitarians contributes to the pool of physical wealth that we own in terms of land, housing, soil improvement, dairy herd, and so forth. In the early years the apparent "costs" of providing housing for people we hadn't met yet disguised the fact that we were, in so doing, accumulating a kind of wealth. A few people have suggested that we stop building for the future and simply live off what has been accumulated in the past, without adding anything in our turn. To date they have not persuaded the group.

This does not mean that we no longer argue about population growth. We do, but we no longer argue about it as if it were in opposition to material prosperity. Instead people argue that increased population produces psychological crowding, more institutionalization, and the like.

Also, we no longer use the terms "standard of living" and "quality of life" as if they mean the same thing. Of course I have always known better. It is ironically amusing to me to be lectured on the subject by new members who are at pains to point out that material goods aren't as important as emotional, social, psychological, or spiritual experiences.

It doesn't really matter who is giving the lecture. It is wonderful that we all know this for sure. We spend money, and we enjoy what we spend it on, but none of us, not even the worst spendthrift among us, believes that the accumulation of goods is a key to happiness. If we ever believed it, we left the notion behind when we first drove up the driveway and unloaded our suitcases.

71

I NOTICE I'M NOT THE ONLY ONE STARING AT THE WOMEN AS THEY GO BY. AFTER SO MANY YEARS ON THE FARM, YOU MUST FIND CITY GIRLS QUITE ATTRACTIVE, HUH?

ATTRACTIVE?! **HARDLY!** THEY LOOK LIKE VICTIMS OF **RADIATION POISONING!** ALL THEIR BODY HAIR HAS FALLEN OUT.

THIS HAS BEEN SOME AFTERNOON! I DIDN'T REALIZE THAT BRINGING YOU TO TOWN FOR THE FIRST TIME IN 13 YEARS WAS GOING TO BE SUCH AN ADVENTURE!

ICE CREAM

I THINK I'M GETTING THE HANG OF IT, THOUGH. I WAS ABLE TO GET THIS NEW WINTER COAT WITHOUT ANY HELP FROM YOU.

IT'S A NICE COAT, TOO. HOW MUCH DID YOU HAVE TO PAY FOR IT?

BACK TO S.A

HELP W

PAY?

STOP!

JONATHAN

Chapter 8

Housing and Other Buildings
The Early Years

We started Twin Oaks in June, 1967, and we needed decent shelter before winter. All we had were a small farmhouse and two barns to house the original eight members. Though both house and barns served as sleeping quarters for several months, putting up better housing was a high priority. We went through a number of experiments before we got a serious start on a building. First there was rammed earth (far more work per brick than we could contemplate); then geodesic domes (too leaky, too hard to insulate, and too round for rectangular furniture). Refurbishing a barn seemed a sensible thing to do, but we discarded the plan when we did cost estimates. It turned out to be nearly as expensive as a new building and more trouble.

We had one member with the confidence to engage us in new construction. We followed his lead (also used his money) and put up the big square shop/residence that we now call "Harmony."

Harmony was followed by Oneida, a badly built structure that we cursed and altered for years but which housed twenty-eight people and thus gave us the population foundation the Community needed.

Henry's Influence

Then when the Community was about four years old, an architect named Henry joined Twin Oaks. He stayed several years and contributed heavily to the design and construction of at least six of our present buildings.

I have been told that toward the end of Henry's Twin Oaks career he became a controversial and troublesome figure, but I wasn't around for that part of our history, and I'm glad I missed it, because my memories of Henry glow with untainted admiration.

When he first came, Henry was a miracle. He had been living in Richmond, working for an architectural firm, and he came to visit Twin Oaks a couple of times. He got interested in the Community and started drawing possible designs for our next residence. He got so interested, in fact, that he couldn't resist quitting his job and joining us as a member. Twin Oaks urgently needed buildings, specifically a place to raise our children. After that we would need a sewage treatment plant, more workshops, and, as the Community grew, additional residences.

What made Henry so wonderful was that he had the power to engage the entire Community in his design process. He would draw up some preliminary ideas and show them to anyone who would look at them. Since at the time we had very few places to socialize, we naturally congregated near the main food source, the original farmhouse (called Llano). There on a dining table he would shove aside the catsup and newspapers and lay out the latest plan. I remember being afraid to criticize the drawings, because they looked so pretty. Henry would say, "Now maybe we could put a hallway here instead, and the rooms could go like this . . ." and I would gasp with dismay as he carelessly drew with a marker across the lovely drawings. He kept saying, "Don't worry about these drawings. They're just lines on a piece of paper. Say what you think. We can make lines go anywhere."

Of course all along he had some idea where the plan might be heading, but he paid careful attention to any suggestions we made, either including them in the next version or explaining why they wouldn't work. We would criticize as best we could, and he would take the drawings away and draw some fresh ones—not a month later (the more recent norm) but the very next day. He would lay out the new one and say, "Now look at these changes. What do you think?"

I always thought they were terrific. I didn't have enough information to do any intelligent criticism. I did not know, for example, that Henry was both innovative and relatively inexperienced. He was reading a lot in his field and wanted to try out new ideas. With the Community's enthusiasm, a little money, and our willingness to follow his leadership, he had a valuable opportunity to use experimental building techniques and designs. In later years some of those techniques proved faulty, and I have been around to hear recent building maintenance people curse him for his non-standard methods, particularly when he kept within our meager budgets by using minimal structural timbers.

Henry

Henry not only designed but took a major role in the construction of all those buildings. He got up early and worked long hours, and he would take the time to instruct amateur and even casual workers. In later years he complained about these working conditions, as any construction manager would; but at the time they were happening, I never even knew that he felt any hardship.

In the last year before I left Twin Oaks for the East Wind venture (1972), I was going through some uncertainties about my role at Twin Oaks and feeling the sadness of my first loss of influence and a consequent sense of uselessness. I had reached a place where I could not think of anything I wanted to do at Twin Oaks. The days stretched ahead drearily and gray, and I had difficulty making myself get up in the morning. There was only one thing that really interested me, and that was community growth. I was, as I shall recount, extremely frustrated with Twin Oaks' unwillingness to increase its population at that time. In a desperate effort to revive my morale and become a useful citizen again, I approached Henry about using me on his construction crew. Putting up a new building had symbolic meaning to me. I thought it might cheer me up.

At the time we were in the initial stages of building Degania, the children's building, a partially-underground structure made principally of concrete. The work consisted of mixing concrete in a small mixer, dumping it into wheelbarrows, wheeling each load over a ramp and pouring it into a plywood form, and then holding onto a giant vibrator while it agitated the concrete mixture to encourage any trapped air-bubbles to come to the surface. The next day the forms had to be removed from the drying concrete wall, cleaned up, oiled, and placed ready for the next section to be poured. It sounds very tedious as I think of it now. Why didn't we build a whole lot of forms and pour the concrete all at once, from a truck? Why did we choose to mix our own? I believe it was because we couldn't afford to buy so much plywood which would be waste material at the finish of the construction. Henry was working within our money constraints. Also, since Degania is placed among standing trees and dug deeply into the ground, it would have been extremely difficult to find an access for a concrete truck to pour from. At the time I didn't even ask these questions. I supposed that the way Henry did things must be the way they were done in the Outside World.

Back to my part in the construction of Degania: Henry, who already had enough incompetent help to frustrate a saint, took pity on me and accepted me onto his crew. He chose tasks that a person of my strength could do. I mixed concrete. Someone else handled the wheelbarrows, and I held onto the vibrator. I removed forms, cleaned and re-oiled them. I clipped rebar* into proper lengths and joined pieces of it together with wire, using heavy work gloves and a pair of pliers. It was winter time, and I remember struggling with the rebar in the cold. Sometimes I was on the site all by myself, and I'm now guessing that on those occasions someone, probably Henry, came along behind me and redid some of my work. But I didn't guess it at the time. I felt fully employed and useful. Whenever Henry was around, he encouraged the crew and made me feel part of it. Never once did he imply that I was a nuisance.

Now in actual fact, I am worth more using a typewriter or a calculator for one hour than I ever was or could be working on a construction site for four hours. But at that time I needed to do construction, and Henry somehow understood and helped me out. Is it any wonder that to this day I can listen to no criticism of Henry?

Other Builders

With Henry's encouragement, other people began to believe that they, too, could design buildings. It was Steven who designed Morningstar residence, and Tupelo residence is the work of three different amateur architects, not usually working together but each picking up the work when the last one quit.

We have had other builders. Among those who came to us already experienced was Aaron, who had been a contractor. In-

---

*Rebar is steel reinforcing bar made to be buried in concrete.

stead of competing with Henry on domestic building, he tried to improve our income by getting the Community into building contracting as a business. This worked well for a couple of years and was in fact the first of the businesses to get us off outside work. Aaron and Henry were both good teachers. Between them they trained and inspired over a dozen members, some of whom later became professionals in the construction business.

This was by no means the end of the buildings or the stories about their construction. I interrupt it here, because this was the time when I personally left Twin Oaks. My relationship with Twin Oaks building process has typically been close and intense, so I will save the rest of the construction story until its proper chronological place.

By the time I left Twin Oaks in 1973, we had three large residences, two big shops, and a half-finished children's building. During my long absence the Community finished the children's building and then built two more big shops, two more large residences, and a warehouse.

Chapter 9

Why I Left Twin Oaks,
and Other Personal Things

People who have read *A Walden Two Experiment* have frequently said to me, "I don't see you in that book. What were you doing all that time?" The question surprised me at first. As far as I could see, I was all over every page of it. What was I doing those first five years? Building community. What did I think about? Building community. What did I feel? Elated by community successes, discouraged by community failures. Oh, I had a personal life of sorts. For one thing I was married for a while. But I thought of my husband in terms of his usefulness to the Community. My teenage daughter left us for a time to do some personal adventuring, and I was terribly upset about it, but I remember clearly that a major source of my emotion was my feeling that the Community needed her. I didn't go around saying " *La Comunité c'est moi,*" but I may as well have.

People used to ask me to list the basic requirements for community success, and I would answer, "One fanatic." I would say, "You have to want to do community more than you want anything else in the world."

These days I am less sure of the recipe, but then, these days I am less sure about a lot of things.

84

Getting back to my story, several things happened in 1970 and 1971 that changed my focus at Twin Oaks. For one thing both the number and the quality of people joining the Community at this period rose sharply, and Twin Oaks naturally needed me less than it had. The result of this was that other members felt freer than before to criticize me, especially since we institutionalized criticism in the Feedback sessions.

I fully approved of mutual criticism as a social control mechanism in our growing Community, and I was avidly interested in anything anyone said about me. But I could not accept the reiterated "You have too much power." In vain I tried to turn it around. I said, "I have no power except what you give me." I said, "That's not a criticism of me but of yourselves." They were not convinced. They wanted me to take the initiative to empower other people, and they wanted me to step down. I didn't see why I should. Nevertheless some members held me responsible for their feelings of inadequacy, and as a result they became hostile to me. Of course I felt it, and of course it seriously affected my morale.

The next thing that happened was that I wrote a book. It was serialized by Psychology Today, and Twin Oaks was suddenly famous. I did not know when I wrote it that the wave of interest it created would wash me away from Twin Oaks. Here is what I had to say on the last page:

Quoted from A Walden Two Experiment, 1972

> Where do we go from here? We are back to the grow-split-grow-split theory. As long as we can continue to attract members, we expect to keep growing in size. What the optimal size is we do not know and maybe won't know until we reach it. When we get there, we'll send a core cadre from our Community to form a new one, this time with the security of Twin Oaks behind it, as well as our accumulated experience and skills.

> Or if such security seems to lack adventure, there is nothing to stop a splinter group from breaking off sooner and establishing a sister commune, perhaps with slightly different ideas. We might have a hard-line commune and a soft-line commune, an expansionist group and an exclusivist one. Maybe the next group can take consensus procedure seriously as a form of government. They will have their own set of problems, but they will avoid the ones we had.

> There is no end to where we can go from here. Dwight used to say that if the commune movement ever got big, the Government would close it down. That's his guess. Mine is that it won't. My guess is that

we can keep growing until we run out of people who would be better off than they are now if they went communal. That time is a long way off.

Twin Oaks Closes its Doors

A Walden Two Experiment ends on a bright hopeful note. What I confidently expected of the future was a constant stream of people wanting to share our community experience with us. After the book's publication this expectation began to be fulfilled in a big way. Our correspondence quadrupled, and we had to start sending out form letter replies.

What the form letters said, in essence, was, "Sorry, no vacancy." Twin Oaks closed its doors. It had as many people as it could comfortably hold. The number was forty-five at the time. We didn't have enough residential space, for starters. Twin Oakers were still living two-to-a-room and agitating for privacy. We also felt crowded at mealtime in Llano. Most pressing of all, we had not yet handled the sewage problems. More people would have meant more water use, and we didn't have anywhere for that water to go.

At least those are the reasons that were given. I did not believe those reasons. If we had wanted to, I strongly felt, we could have found ways to deal with housing and sewage. But we didn't want to.

Count me out of that "we." I would gladly have lived in a tent, eaten in shifts, and built sewage treatment on borrowed money, in order to see Twin Oaks answer the challenge of that supply of potential members. I saw that lineup at our front door, people eager to join, possibly hundreds of them but certainly dozens, and my response was a whole-hearted welcome—more than that, an excitement, a sense of grabbing history by the tail, a promise of future community on a scale approaching Walden Two.

Political Failure

I couldn't convince anybody. My credibility had been stretched as far as it would go. I was held responsible (correctly, I suppose) for both Twin Oaks' low standard of living and for the general sense of social chaos that some people articulated. We had grown too fast, they said. We had thrown up cheap buildings with unskilled labor and never really finished them. We had provided for new members but not for the crying need among longer-term members for private rooms, decent clothes, bigger allowances, vacation money. Worse than that, we didn't know who we were or where we were going. We didn't have a common goal, or a long-range plan. "I feel like I'm in a speeding car rolling downhill out of control, and I don't know who's driving," said one member, in a meeting we held on this subject. "Can't we please stop this headlong rush and at least finish the buildings?" begged another, on the point of tears. "Let's ask the builders," suggested a third, and in this emotional atmosphere we did a go-round of all the construction people and their supporters. Would we be willing to stop new construction in order to finish the houses we already had?

By the time the go-round came to me, I didn't feel I had any choice. I said "yes," because I could see that there was no point in saying anything else. Everybody was saying yes. But it was a moment of decision. They could stop progress and finish the buildings if they liked, but that left nothing interesting for me to do. I would have to leave, and try to build community some other way.

Finding Another Way

It took me several weeks to figure out my next steps, because of course I had no money. All I had to offer potential members was my history and my self-confidence—that and my urgent desire to get on with building community.

The rest of that story is the history of East Wind. I left Twin Oaks, taking two members and some visitors with me, and we set out to form another community which would be like Twin Oaks in every way except one: we would never close our doors! Some day maybe I'll write the story of my years with East Wind. It is just as interesting a community as Twin Oaks, and quite different, as it turned out, though, ironically, it never got to be as big. East Wind today has about sixty-five adult members, compared to Twin Oaks' eighty-five.

In response to the people who say to me, "But you said you would never leave Twin Oaks," I reply: I didn't mean to. I meant only to take a year off and get another group started, then come back home. But it didn't work out that way. I got caught up in the East Wind version of community and spent five years there.

Morale Disaster at East Wind

It was at East Wind in its fifth year that I lost my zeal—lost my faith, in fact. Though I had created another viable community, it was not what I had intended. The crowds at Twin Oaks' front door did not come to East Wind. They did not want to pioneer; they wanted to join a community that was already stable. Twin Oaks put their names on a waiting list. If they waited a year or so, they eventually got in. Most found something else to do. After a couple of years those crowds thinned and then disappeared. Twin Oaks' waiting list shrank to nothing. Within four years Twin Oaks had supplied all its members with private rooms and now had some of those standing empty. East Wind was having a hard time getting members. Both communities started putting out money for recruitment advertising. We were in for a long, dry spell.

This was bewildering to me. What had happened to people's interest in community? I used to go to colleges to give lectures and seminars on community. The invitations slowed and then stopped. Toward the end of that phase, I noticed that audiences were increasingly critical, even hostile. The eager enthusiasm was gone.

The Media announced that the Sixties were finished, its culture discredited, and the future delivered to the "Me Generation". I had never believed in these media-described mass phenomena before, but I was forced to take this one seriously.

East Wind had a very hard time finding suitable people. In an effort to survive, it had to accept many people of dubious quality, people who, as their numbers increased, made the community unpleasant for the more idealistic and productive members, many of whom left.

It is testimony to the strength of the communal plan that East Wind survived those grim years, recovered from its losses, found new people, and today is an attractive community.

I'm the one that didn't survive it. Oh, I know, I'm back at Twin Oaks now and doing fine, but that feels like a rebirth. During my last years at East Wind my belief in community died.

I Question the Fundamentals

Part of my disillusionment came from watching the worst aspects of communism in action. Some of my friends were able to overlook the glaring flaws rooted in the system itself and dismiss them as temporary aberrations, but I couldn't. I saw a larger and larger part of the community sitting around on the front steps of the dining hall smoking cigarettes and drinking their wake-up coffee at 11 in the morning, and heard them ridicule as "workaholics" the people who made the money and kept the organization together. It looked possible, even probable, that this once-promising community would be undermined and destroyed by its own people. Our communism wasn't working. There was gross exploitation, but in reverse. The proletariat was exploiting the managers.

I saw this as a dead end. The group would collapse if this situation continued, but there was no obvious way to put things right. I saw a direct connection between the communal system and the poverty and shiftlessness. This was exactly the kind of result that skeptics had predicted from the first. If this perceived connection was a true one, then the mess that East Wind had become was my doing. I had removed the incentive of personal gain through work, and behold, the people chose not to work!

The same people who didn't appreciate hard workers also didn't like experienced leaders. I was a major target for hostility. I suppose it is natural for a group to throw out its founding leadership as it matures, and I also remember that I wasn't at my best and wisest under the pressures of the time. Nevertheless, the people who wanted me out of their way were not the decent and responsible who deserved to succeed me but the immature and destructive who sought total daily guilt-free personal liberty.

I knew that this phenomenon was not happening at Twin Oaks, and the difference seemed to be that Twin Oaks selected its members with some care. East Wind was wide open. That, too, was my doing.

One would think that once I had seen my mistakes and admitted them, the decent thing to do would be to set about trying to reverse their effects. Unfortunately, I really did not have the power to do so. I made several abortive attempts to raise standards in different ways, but all of them failed. Partly I didn't have the necessary energy, and partly it was too late for me to be effective in that environment.

By 1978 I felt I had probed the depths of communal theory and practice, and found nothing worthwhile at the bottom. I began to look at the free enterprise system with some respect and to wonder if I could find a place in it.

More important, by then I felt I no longer had a function in terms of the ideals I had once held. I had been a supplier of community. Now nobody wanted my product. I had been proud to present to the world a genuinely egalitarian environment. The people who were joining didn't care a fig for equality and sought privileges for themselves. We weren't getting the idealists any more, the ones who wanted to create a new and better world right there on East Wind's one hundred sixty acres. We were getting people who didn't have any place else to go.

I could have returned to Twin Oaks, but my disillusionment went too deep for that. I went through several years of believing that I had wasted my efforts, that the communities I had helped

89

create were not worth much. In self disgust I turned my attention to finding an appropriate place in the Outside World. I left East Wind in 1978 and lived and worked in Boston for four years.

There's another story there, but it isn't interesting enough to publish. It's about an unhappy communitarian trying to fit into a capitalist world, trying to stay excited about building a career, trying to learn how to be a computer programmer (a task I had no real talent for), trying to channel a mind which had been accustomed to dealing with big questions into the narrow slot of job and apartment. It all failed. I wasn't a successful career woman. I couldn't even get excited about making money. I found some friends and lived easily enough, in a boring sort of way.

The Decision to Return

But one day some Twin Oakers came to visit me in Boston, and they brought with them the scent of community. They were full of indignation about the latest controversy, full of news about events at Twin Oaks. We talked for hours, and I heard myself arguing the merits of Twin Oaks issues with heated conviction. Never mind my supposed disillusionment with community. Forget the cynical conclusions in which I had trapped myself in my last year at East Wind. I set these things aside to think about later. What was obvious to me right then was that the conversations with Twin Oakers were making me feel alive in a way that I had not felt for four years. I stayed up late and woke up early. My mind sped at a pace I had forgotten it was capable of. I realized abruptly that I had made no mistake in choosing community as my vocation. I may have needed the break, but my heart was not in business or in Boston. I needed to go home.

That's what made me come back, those brief hours of vivid color inserted into my black-and-white Boston life. That, and the April visit.

Dear reader, if you don't want to be tempted to join a country commune, don't visit it in April! I did, and I think I am trapped forever. I walked down the wooded pathways, smelled the fresh country smells and listened to birds, and I knew I never again wanted to live in a city. No beer cans, gum wrappers, urine smells in concrete subway tunnels for me! I didn't even want to go home to pack.

I did, though. I quit my job, and then I packed a whole lot of things, which brings me to the next phase of my community life.

Chapter 10

A Lot Happens In Nine Years

Obviously Twin Oaks didn't remain in stasis during the years when I wasn't here to record its doings. For one thing, I left just before the birth of the first Degania-dwelling community child. The Community's initial adventures in communal child-rearing all happened while I was busy at East Wind. So did the commercial farming enterprise, and the Screamies movement, and the first death. All of these things are well chronicled in Ingrid Komar's *Living the Dream*, but I will brush over them briefly.

Children

Twin Oaks' communal child-rearing began* with a group of three babies born within months of each other. This event was perceived to be of such importance that the *Leaves of Twin Oaks* devoted pages and pages to the details of their feeding and care. One can still find in our archives conscientious accounts of the

---

*Not quite literally the beginning. During our first two years there were several children who lived at Twin Oaks for a while. Since they took a lot of our energy, and since they left anyway, we stopped admitting families and decided to be childless "until we are ready to have our own children." We expected "our own" fully acculturated communitarian parents to be more amenable to our communal childcare ideas than families from the outside had proved to be. The Community closed its doors to children from 1970 through 1972.

meals and bowel movements of those first children. Babies continued to be born here each year, but over time many of the families left Twin Oaks, leaving vacancies in the children's peer groups. To fill them, the Community began to accept outside families. By the time I returned, about half the children in Degania had been born here, and the other half had come later. All were under age seven.

The children were not coming out quite the way we had expected. In defiance of carefully androgenous training, the girls fixed their attention determinedly on dolls, ruffles, and weddings, and the boys on trucks and tractors. In spite of minor disappointments, however, the children were bright and charming, and most communitarians were proud of them. As long as they were small and lived in Degania, it was primarily the parents and childcare workers who dealt with them. The Community as a whole felt that communal child rearing was working fine.

The Spiritual Movement and the Screamies

Just about the time I left, Twin Oaks began to be affected by certain spiritual, semi-spiritual, and therapeutic movements. There was a rebellion against our supposedly sterile secularism. A guru or two came to visit. I have a photo of my daughter, Josie, wearing a white dress and sitting, with other members, at the feet of one of these, gazing at him with eager attention while he discoursed. This was the heyday of "The Farm," a large religious community in Tennessee led by Stephen Gaskin. Twin Oaks lost a couple of members to The Farm. I talked to one of them about her choice, and she answered me, "Kat, all my life I have wanted someone to tell me the truth. This man tells me the truth. . ." No one at Twin Oaks had ever presumed to know what truth was, and we could not hope to keep members with such yearnings.

Gaskin's influence spread to Twin Oaks. In particular I recall that he disapproved of whimsical name changes, feeling that they showed disrespect for parents and the last generation. Several Twin Oakers heard this and dropped their assumed names in favor of the names they had been born with. Biological family ties began at this point to be openly respected. Twin Oaks' initial anti-family sentiments were cast aside by all but a hard core of Walden Two adherents.

Another of Stephen's theories was that everyone should "get straight" with everyone else, which I suppose meant putting the relationships on a sound, truthful basis. This fit in with the Feedback and mutual criticism ideas already in vogue here. For a while there were so many people off in private corners getting straight that some complained that they didn't have time to get their work done.

Along with this came a semi-religious movement called "Arica." I don't remember what it was, but some members were joining it, or thinking of leaving the Community to pursue it somewhere else.

The most forceful of all these movements was what came to be known as "The Screamies." This was not a religion but a therapeutic technique. The general idea was to go off with other practitioners and try to relive the emotional traumas of one's childhood, crying and screaming and presumably getting rid of the bad influence of those early experiences. The Community didn't have very many good places to do this, but the root cellar wasn't being used for food at the time, so the adherents of this movement fixed it up for their own use. Since it was underground, people could feel free to scream without upsetting nonparticipants. There were only about half a dozen Screamies, but they were evangelical about their beliefs. They thought they had an important, basic answer to human problems and they wanted to share it. *The Leaves of Twin Oaks* of the time talks of almost nothing but the fresh illuminations being visited upon the Screamies.

What interests me in retrospect about all these movements is that there is almost no trace of them now in Twin Oaks culture. There is some screaming here and there associated with co-counseling, and there are certainly people with a variety of religious beliefs, but basically, when the Screamies left the Community, there was nothing here to show for all their efforts. Both they and the spiritual people offered their vision to anyone interested, but converts were few, and after they left, it was as if they had never been here.

Commercial Farming

Farming is another matter. The members who got the Community into farming commercial crops left a residue in the form of farm machinery and debt.

The idea was to use our farmland to grow crops for profit. Several members felt they knew enough to make a go of this, and the Community decided to take the risk. We got as far as borrowing money, buying the necessary farm equipment, putting in some crops, and harvesting them. We may have sold them, too, though I never heard that part of the story. What I did hear was that, far from making a profit, the farm operation had lost $10,000 in its first year and looked as though it would continue to do so for years to come. Then the farmers, for various reasons, left the Community. A group of new provisional members were eager to take over the operation, but the longer-term members were not at all convinced that the new group could do any better than their predecessors. The Board of Planners in the last year before I rejoined decided to cut the Community's losses and get out of attempting to farm for profit.

This was a difficult and in my opinion courageous decision to make. The disappointed provisional members and their friends tried to get the Planners overruled but could not muster the necessary votes of a majority of full members. Almost all of those provisional members left the Community out of disillusionment over the issue.

The First Deaths

The members who lived here during the drawn-out illness and death of Seth have a bond that the rest of us don't and can't share. I can sense it when I see them together. Even though most of them are no longer members, they visit Twin Oaks often, and part of what ties them to this place is the grave on the High South where Seth is buried.

Seth was young, happy, and well-loved. The Community knew when it accepted him that he had lung cancer and would probably die of it. They did everything they could to lengthen his life and help to make it count for something. When he died, they canceled their vacations and other activities and assembled here for the ending ceremonies. They did so again for Margaret, a member who committed suicide as a result of prolonged depression.

Those ceremonies were not mere rituals or duty. Those who attended and who spoke their memories of the dead did so out of love and pity and respect and regret.

I cannot write very well of what I did not experience. The nine years of my absence are somebody else's story. Since my return there have been other deaths, later agricultural experiments, other movements, more children.

One thing happened during my absence, though, that had a big effect on the Community of today. This was the change in our domestic housing arrangements. It took a year to make the change, but it has endured. I think it was important enough that it deserves a chapter of its own.

Chapter 11

Branch Experiments
and the Small Living Group

Assumptions Built into Twin Oaks' Early Architecture

To the extent that Twin Oaks was "designed" in the early years, the effect of that design was to express our unconscious assumptions about our social lives. Each of us was to have a room for sleeping, storing personal belongings, and privacy. All the rest of our lives was to be public. Public living rooms, bath rooms, shops, and dining rooms all were supposed to fill our needs. We did not recognize this as a concept. We just built what we felt we needed at the time. Perhaps if we had examined it analytically, we would have seen its flaws.

Looking at that design idea twenty-five years later, it strikes me as an appropriate living pattern for the young and unattached. A young person's life is usually centered around establishing relationships, either friendships or love. Living in a community is a good environment for this, because it happens organically in the course of eating, working, and playing. Having most activities take place in public spaces promotes these aims. This pattern ought to work fairly well also for the people in their fifties, who are likely to be once again seeking companionship.

Criticism of the Design

For the early marriage years or the child-rearing years this design does not work as well. The principal flaw is that it makes it difficult to be choosy about one's company. After members have been here a few years, they frequently tire of the excitement of new faces. They tend to commit themselves to friendships with people they've known for a while, people who don't need everything explained to them, who will give them the benefit of the doubt and not take offense at small things—in short, people whom they enjoy or even love. If they have children, they need enough privacy to maintain their family ties and also to deal with those children's behaviors without onlookers. The presence of new members doesn't add much to their lives beyond the economic advantages of large size, and the flow of visitors can become hard to endure.

The original "affinity group" vision, as it was then called, was the creation of surrogate families. The idea was to live with a small group, get to know and trust the members of it, and feel a kind of family connection within it. The big, loose Community was felt by some to be inadequate as a home.

The Branch Experiment—Merion

The branch experiment developed out of this yearning for family. When the idea of settling a branch of Twin Oakers on separate land was first suggested in 1971, I was against it. It was obvious to me that we were not strong enough yet to start splitting up into separate groups, and I didn't want us to spend money on land, either. But this was the time when I was trying in vain to figure out a way to expand the Community's population. It occurred to me that branching might provide an answer. Although it involved duplication of facilities and other complications, those facilities could well provide for a separate group, and the two groups together would be Twin Oaks. Suppose, I theorized, the new branch didn't want to be quite so large as the current group. Perhaps they would be only 25 members. There would be 45 people on the main property, and another 25 in the branch, for a total of 70. Now that's fast growth! I became intoxicated with the notion and reversed my position on branches. I spent a week churning out numbers to prove that branching could be economically feasible, and I managed to convince the Board of Planners of the time. The new group quickly formed and named itself "Merion."

Merion was made up of people with a very different point of view from mine. They had no interest in population expansion. They just wanted to pursue their dreams of rural living in a simple, old-fashioned way, raise a few goats, feed themselves principally from their own garden, have some semi-spiritual rituals, and make decisions around their dining room table. What they needed Twin Oaks for was economic stability. Twin Oaks would buy the land and build the housing; Twin Oaks had a business that provided income.

We worked out a long and complex agreement about how the two groups would relate. Merion wanted a good deal more autonomy than many people, including me, thought they should have. For one thing they wanted to keep their own children with them, rather than placing them in the children's house we were then building on the main property. At the time this was heresy. I forget how we worked this out, but somehow Merion ended up having children on its own land, so we must have compromised. What I do remember is that the compromise was a source of bitter anger for some time.

The major part of the story of Merion took place after my departure. Doing the political work to get it off the ground was just about the last thing I did before taking off to help found East Wind. The rumors that reached me there were mostly bad news. Friends at Merion told me that they were constantly being frustrated and insulted by people from the main property. Friends from the main group told me that Merion was seriously violating the spirit of the agreement. I think there was some truth in both statements.

The creation of the branch could not be economically justified without population growth. We hoped to give Merion enough domestic autonomy to make them happy while still making economic sense. We expected Merion people to come to the main property to make hammocks, work in the garden, care for children, and every other task that was not directly domestic. What Merion wanted instead was to stay on their own land, do their own garden, raise their own domestic livestock, and generally have control of their own lives to a greater extent than Twin Oakers normally did. If they had to make hammocks, they would set up a separate shop and make them on their own land. But they didn't really want to make hammocks. They would rather have gone into some independent business for themselves, but that wasn't part of the agreement.

Twin Oaks would not accept goat-raising as part of its agriculture, since it had plenty of cows already and didn't want to waste labor on small animals. Instead, it meant to send cans of milk every day. Since the Merion land was only a few miles away and on the road to town, this seemed practical. Unfortunately, the town tripper kept forgetting to take the milk. The Auto Manager issued Merion a vehicle, but grudgingly. Nearly every day there was an incident in which either Merion complained of neglect or the main branch got upset about Merion's desire for greater independence.

What it amounted to was that the agreement we had worked out was not acceptable to Merion. They had agreed to it because they couldn't get anything better, but they were never happy with it and kept pushing against its limits.

One part of the agreement was that Merion would receive, in cash, a per-person stipend for domestic expenses, which they could handle any way they chose. They chose not to spend it the same way the bigger branch did but to distribute a larger proportion of it to their own members as personal allowances. Envious members of the large branch were indignant. When Merion people came by and stayed for supper, some people would angrily accuse them of eating off the bigger group in order to save food and have more personal money. Someone even wrote a paper objecting to Merion members' saving toilet paper money by using the main branch's toilets!

Maybe all this would have worked itself out eventually, but it never got a chance. Merion, never a large group (about eight to ten people), decided not to grow! It turned out that being small was part of the simple life they were so attached to. In the course of time some of their members left, and those who remained found them hard to replace. Eventually they stopped trying. Merion went from eight people down to six, hovered there for a while, dropped to two or three. At the end (several years later) one person lived alone on the Merion land. When she left, Twin Oaks called the branch experiment a failure and put the land on the market.

Tupelo

About the time I was settling in with East Wind on its Missouri land, I got a letter from my daughter Josie, saying that she was involved in founding a second Twin Oaks branch. This one, she promised, would not have the same kind of problems as Merion, because the people in the new group were not back-to-the-land enthusiasts but regular Twin Oaks types who wanted to get into the Community. I was tickled to hear that Josie was following in my footsteps in this literal way and delighted that the branch idea was spreading. As it turned out, Josie realized within a few weeks that she did not want to be a community founder but a doctor. The new group, however, found other sponsors. Twin Oaks agreed to take them in under the kind of living conditions they volunteered for—crowded into a small, rotting house on neighboring land.

They called themselves "Tupelo," because they liked the sound of the word, even though there are no tupelo trees on the land. They cheerfully occupied the old house and did what they could to make it livable. Such difficulties as they had with the main branch were trivial in comparison with the Merion problems. There was petty bickering, of course. The Tupelo people were considered too loud by some, too hedonistic, too disrespectful. But the fact that they lived right next door to the main property made things easier. They didn't expect milk deliveries, and, more important, they didn't close their doors to new people.

Affinity Groups on the Home Premises

As time went on, other people began to envy Merion and Tupelo in one fundamental—the supposed group intimacy of the small group living together. The envy gradually coelesced into a proposal and the proposal into a process. Perhaps a dozen Twin Oakers wanted nothing to do with it and desired only be be allowed to live the same way they always had. Everybody else seemed to want a family.

Twin Oaks engaged in a process it called "social planning" to see if it could create small social units that would meet the expressed needs. This took months, but eventually they decided they could. One residence was set aside for the dissidents, and the rest were allocated to groups that chose to live together. The groups were dubbed "SLGs" (Small Living Groups). There were originally five SLGs, most with about ten members. This institution has continued to the present day. All of us live in one SLG or another.

Finding family intimacy has proved a more elusive matter. There is a lot working against it. Some groups put out the effort to eat together once a week, or have house meetings, or have some SLG event from time to time. Most of them cannot get full attendance when they try it. Everybody is busy. Most people have serious relationships with people outside the SLG. Scheduling conflicts are always a problem. Though every SLG has a living room where its members can gather informally, some of these living rooms remain empty most of the time and eventually become storage spaces for people's bulky belongings. In short, organizing people into little groups, even though the groups are self-selecting, did not produce the kind of feeling that was originally sought.

Generally speaking, the longest-term members of Twin Oaks have not been of the affinity-group type, but are people who always thrived on the original idea—a private room and a public life. They are the ones who did not feel an intense need for a group of peers to hang out with, and therefore are not devastated when their friends leave the Community. Josie, an intensely social person who could easily have been happy in an affinity group, chose a different path. She made a point of getting to know one or two newcomers every year, so that she would always have a friendship group left, even after turnover.

What has evolved instead of the affinity groups are what one member once scornfully called "tenants associations." By this she meant that the inhabitants of a building would require nothing more of each other than a courteous nod and perhaps a willingness to take a turn cleaning the bathrooms. This overstates it slightly, but essentially that is what the SLGs have become. When there is a vacancy in an SLG, the other members of that household choose among applicants to fill it. They choose on the basis of some sort of compatibility. Perhaps they want quiet people, or non-smokers, or "fun" people or old-timers. Applicants have sometimes been rejected because they are too new or too noisy or too needy or even too cheerful. Some SLGs, fortunately, make a point of not being very exclusive, so as to make sure every member finds welcome in one household or another.

The End of Branches

By the time it became apparent that Merion was failing, Twin Oaks decided to close Tupelo as well. Tupelo members were just as happy to be an SLG, and more than happy with the house the Community built for them on the main property. Since their separateness had never been a matter of major cultural differences, their absorption made only minor problems. The Community did give Tupelo a large kitchen and dining room, so that they could continue to cook and eat as a group if they wanted. Over the years we have found that, so far, one building of the type in which people cook and eat separately is sufficient. Most of us prefer the personal independence that the central dining facility gives us.

What we seem to have learned from the branch experiment is that Twin Oaks can't handle it. This is disappointing to me, because I had seen branching as a way to facilitate growth without building enormous institutional facilities. So far the only successful groups to come out of Twin Oaks are the independent communities that were inspired by it. There are several of those. We have varying degrees of cooperation with these other communities, but we don't attempt to share income or government.

103

Chapter 12

The Return To Twin Oaks

I returned to Twin Oaks, but I had changed in the intervening years. The Community that accepted my return in 1982 was not prepared for the differences that had been wrought by five years of East Wind and four of Boston. By then not many of the members knew me personally, but I had a reputation, and my behavior didn't match it. For one thing, I had been known as a fervent idealist, with scorn for material things. I came back with a U-Haul truck loaded with furniture and appliances and an attitude to match.

Plotting Small Changes

I was tired of poverty. Along with my general disillusionment in my last year of East Wind experience, I also had begun to see that Community as it must at that time have been seen by outsiders, and much of what I saw disgusted me.* It wasn't just the loungers with their cigarettes on the front stairs; it was the condition of the dining room behind them, a totally unnecessary condition approaching squalor—dirty floor, greasy tables, cob-webby walls, lank curtains, broken furniture. I felt a powerful need to separate myself from identification with this dirty environment. I needed to recover my self-respect.

---

*I must emphasize that these remarks do not describe the East Wind of today. This was simply a stage they went through.

During the Boston years dirt was not a problem. However, when I started thinking about returning to community, I carefully considered what actions I could take to lift the physical standard of the Twin Oaks environment. It was cleaner than East Wind had been, but there was nevertheless a lot there that I didn't like. I did not like the anti-technology atmosphere that had taken over in the years since I had left. I didn't like the accumulated clutter that members had ceased to notice, or the dinginess that prevailed in the public rooms. On the one hand, I was prepared to live with the set of tradeoffs that came with my decision to return. On the other hand, I didn't think every single little thing was a necessary part of that tradeoff. I plotted changes, small and large, from drinking glasses to computerization. To assist me in some of these changes, I shopped in Boston for things I wouldn't be able to afford on my allowance once I was a member.

When I arrived at Twin Oaks in September of 1982, friends helped me unload the truck. I had brought far more things than would fit in my tiny private room in Morningstar residence. We put my furniture in one of the living rooms. My couch and carpet were nothing special, but they were a lot better than what they replaced. Torn posters came down from the walls to make room for my framed prints. The hammock shop got the water cooler, and the kitchen the ice machine. Both of these I had bought especially for the Community, as I had the computer, an Apple II+ that I promised to put into general community use as soon as we could "go through process" on it.

The Automatic Dishwasher

Especially disconcerting was the used domestic dishwasher that my friends carried from the truck to the Morningstar kitchen. I still remember the cautious, hesitant looks on their faces. They weren't at all sure how the Community would react to a dishwasher, but they didn't want to spoil my first day by bringing up the subject.

Twin Oaks today has five auxiliary kitchens besides the central one, and all of them these days have dishwashers. My old Kitchen Aid was the first, and I believe it probably served as an entering wedge, as I intended.

There was indeed a skirmish over the dishwasher. Carrol, a deeply conservative man in the sense of disliking change, thought I hadn't gone through enough process. To Carrol, "process" meant asking everyone's permission and retreating if anyone stated an objection. Carrol and I had a long talk about middle-class kitchens and symbols, and he let go of this particular symbol, though his dislike of consumerism is as strong as ever.

Pinc, the Kitchen Manager, was another story. His objection, I inferred from his remarks, was that I was too new to be throwing my weight around. He resented my getting any mileage out of my previous history at Twin Oaks. He reasoned that since the Morningstar residents had theretofore washed their dishes by hand, there was no reason they should not continue to do so, and besides, there were residences that needed a dishwasher more than Morningstar. My reply (written; the debate was on the O&I Board by this time) was that I had donated the dishwasher to Twin Oaks outright, and Twin Oaks could, through its normal channels, place it anywhere it chose to place it, including the trash heap, without any protest from me. I went on to say that, although his anger seemed to be addressed to me, the burden of change is on those who want change. I invited him to initiate process to move the dishwasher wherever he wanted. He didn't, though. That poor old machine is still sitting where I put it in 1982, limping through what is probably its last year of use.

The Computer

My computer was the seed for a whole bushel of Apple IIs that brought modern accounting to Twin Oaks. I had brought it partly in hope of just such a result, and partly for personal reasons. I wanted to make sure there would be interesting work for me to do, and at the time I still thought of myself as a programmer. Other little things from my U-Haul truck made smaller but, for me, significant differences.

Glass Glasses

The one I remember best was my attempt to get the Community to drink out of glass tumblers. I disliked drinking from plastic, which at that time was Twin Oaks' only available option, so before my return I armed myself with several cases of heavy, durable drinking glasses. The first week after I arrived, I quietly set six of them on the shelf alongside the Community's plastic. A day later they were gone. I found them packed away in a box, where conscientious Ione had put them to keep them safe, perhaps to be brought out for a special occasion. I unpacked them and put them back. It took two days this time, but when they disappeared again, I unearthed them out at Tupelo, where the same well-meaning person had sent them. "I knew they would be broken in the main kitchen," Ione later told me. "I thought they had a better chance at Tupelo, so I took them out there." I told Ione I had lots more and meant them for the main kitchen. I put out a dozen, and this time they stayed put until a member named Dexter approached me. "We don't use glass," he told me. "We use plastic." "I know," I replied. "I am trying to change that." Dexter appealed to the Kitchen Manager, who said that he didn't care one way or another, so the glasses stayed. My supply lasted several months, and they were so popular with the members that the Kitchen Manager started buying more out of his budget, a procedure now considered normal.

Aha! Triumph! But a fall was due. A few months later my friend Velma tried the same trick with paper napkins, and it backfired. There was a major uproar about it, and the napkins had to be withdrawn. To this day most people wipe their hands on their jeans, and there isn't a thing I can do about it.

This was the period I already mentioned of getting a group together to use the Tradeoff Game to refocus the food program. No luck there.

Tuesday Group

It was also the time of the chicken supper club, an effort that was to have considerable impact on the course of events.

We called it Tuesday Group. It was made up of the people who happened to live in lower Morningstar, plus a couple of friends. Since that section of Morningstar was not a popular place to live, it happened that almost everybody in the group was fairly new to the Community. The gathering started innocently enough as a way to enhance the social life of the SLG by eating together one supper each week. I lived in upper Morningstar but the downstairs group invited me to eat with them one week, and I asked, "What are you having?" They replied, "If you'll come, we'll have chicken." At that point I was meat-starved, and I accepted the offer without delay.

Ultimately Tuesday Group wasn't about meat; it was about conversation. We talked, of course, about community. To be frank, we talked a lot about the Community's faults and absurdities. For me the focus was always "What can we do about it?" I was never interested in running on about hopeless causes. Our conversation became excited (and, I'm afraid, loud). These new members were somewhat astonished (but rather pleased) to find themselves talking about how they might help effect changes.

Word got around swiftly that I was hanging out with a group of dissidents, and several friends tried to get me to stop it. No fewer than five different well-established friendly communitarians urged me to desist. They said they had experienced such get-togethers of new members before, and the tragic result had been alienation and eventual departure. They said the group I was eating and talking with were not well socialized, did not yet fit in to Twin Oaks. I would get a bad reputation by being identified with them.

I got stubborn. I liked the group, and it excited me to stir them to action. I saw that they were indeed a motley bunch of disenfranchised members, and I figured I could teach them to empower themselves. Especially I wanted to change the then-current idea that talking "politics" was not quite polite for mealtimes or much of any other time. I thought and still think that the Community's directions, policies, and norms are highly interesting conversation topics. Tuesday Group kept meeting and talking, and my horrified friends kept worrying.

One day Rico, a Planner and a long-term, much respected member, approached me and asked, "How do I get an invitation to join Tuesday Group?" I was moved by this, because I assumed that Rico was offering us the mantle of his reputation in order to help incorporate us better into the Community. Months later he corrected this impression. "Oh no," he said, "on the contrary, I was risking my own reputation because Tuesday Group was the only place I could get any intellectual conversation about the Community, and I was starved for it." Rico attended our next dinner, and we spent the evening discussing alternative labor systems until nine or ten o'clock at night.

After Rico came Josie, I think, followed, as vacancies permitted, by six other well-respected members whom I thought of as "Establishment." Within a few months Tuesday Group had quite a different reputation. We were said to consist of the power-elite. This name clung not only to the established people who had joined us but also to the original "disenfranchised" new members. The group lasted more than two years, and nearly every person in it eventually became a Planner at some point.

Still, many people did not approve of us. We were too loud, too frank, too gossipy, too irreverent. Also, we appeared to be all of a certain type. I'm not sure what the type was, but it became quite clear what the type wasn't when Josie started an alternative supper club.

Josie had been stung by some of the comments from outsiders about Tuesday Group, and she determined to start a group that would carefully include members of opposite opinions—"half us and half them," as she expressed it. Unfortunately, all of "us" were already in Tuesday Group, so the other one ended up consisting of "them." It lasted only a few weeks. Even Josie, with all her sparkle, was unable to stimulate them to lively discourse. I think this was because that group was essentially contented with the communal status quo and was not trying to effect changes. This is not fertile ground for conversation.

I made a lot of social mistakes when I returned to Twin Oaks, mostly because I was impatient for action, but I have never regretted Tuesday Group. It was never quite socially acceptable, but it got a lot done. Perhaps its most enduring accomplishment was bringing political debate back into Twin Oaks' culture.

Tuesday Group dissolved shortly after I became a Planner in 1985. I don't know how the others felt, but by then I was discussing politics in a very serious way six to nine hours a week and getting labor credits for it. I didn't need it any more as an extracurricular activity.

Another way I stirred things up was by writing O&I papers on controversial topics. I once posted a paper outlining how a vegetarian cook could please the meat-eaters. I meant well, but unfortunately for my argument, I used the term "veggie fad foods" to refer to tofu, tempeh, and gluten, and the indignation roused over this phrase exploded all over the O&I Board and provided entertainment for Board readers for several days before mutual apologies calmed everybody down.

Questions About Motives

Thus little by little I created space for myself at Twin Oaks. It was by no means the same space I had vacated nine years before, and it fit oddly with my history.

Looking back over this tale of the way I handled myself in the first year after my return, I have to ask myself what I was trying to do and why I felt driven to upset so many people in the process of doing it. All I can remember is that I was perfectly sincere about each thing I attempted. I really don't think we should be restricted to plastic glasses, or spend time washing dishes by hand. As to Tuesday Group, I still think it was good for the Community.

But what excuse can I offer for keeping up a constant pressure of agitation on various fronts? Wasn't this a pretty stupid approach for somebody who wanted to be a Planner? Wouldn't it have made more sense all around to spend the time making friends instead of making waves? I can't answer the question. All I can think of to say is a feeble, "Well, I hadn't yet learned to care about other people's feeling of security." That came later.

110

Chapter 13

Problems and Progress
of Recent Years

I think I know now why it is that the early years, seen in retrospect, seem "simple." It isn't that we had fewer problems then, or that they were any easier than the ones we have now. It is that they were so overwhelming we knew we couldn't handle them, so we didn't try.

Our first major problem was housing, by which we meant getting out of winter weather into heated indoor space. We "solved" it by building a big barn-like structure with crude room separators and a half-finished concrete floor—no bathroom, no ceilings, no trim, no siding, no carpet, cheapest thin windows, mattresses laid directly on the concrete.

Then we turned our attention to the next biggest problem, namely a source of income. We "solved" that one by working in the city by turns and pooling our paychecks. Next?

Next we faced our first political problems, differences in goals and methods, such as whether we should mortgage our land to go into business, whether some people should be exempt from the city job rotation, whether the new member with the house trailer should be allowed to live in it, whether parents had any say about how their children should be raised, and other challenges to our initial principles. The "solution" to this one was membership turn-over. Those who couldn't stand the way we did things moved out, and the survivors defended a somewhat vague but deeply felt status quo of at least theoretical equality.

Then came sewage. We had to dispose of waste water, and it didn't turn out to be cheap. It took several years to do it, and in the meantime we formed new branches and communities to get around the waiting time.

All this time there were lots of other problems waiting for us to get to them. There they sat, and continue to sit, like a big pile of invoices in our collective in-box, waiting to be paid. The issues we are dealing with this year require just as much of our attention as the original ones did. They are different, but only because we got the top ones out of the way first.

We are now housed. Our housing standards vary somewhat from person so person, partly by personal desire and partly by circumstance. Personally, I live in a charming, cozy, comfortable room surrounded by all my favorite belongings and projects, con-venient to laundry, computer, and cooking facilities, and I lack nothing. Everyone has a private room, the smallest about six feet by twelve feet and the largest ten feet by sixteen feet. In the older buildings people have modified their rooms by adding extra win-dows and lofts and even one skylight. At a guess, 70 percent of the members enjoy their private rooms, and the rest are waiting for something better.

We now have a steady income, and none of it comes from city jobs any more.

We have had adequate sewage since 1974, and it no longer stands in the way of Community growth.

We still "solve" some of our disagreements by membership turnover, but not at anything like the rate in the days when I wrote proudly that the average length of stay was 6 months and rising. (It is now over four years and rising.)

Some smaller items in our in-box got taken care of along the way as well. For instance,

... The external environment, once an eyesore, is now beauti-ful. (The matter of cleanliness and order inside the buildings is still in the in-box.)

... We are no longer limited to our original one hundred twenty three acres, but have purchased three large adjoining tracts and a separate piece of farm land. We have about four hundred acres now.

... We don't live financially from month to month but keep enough savings in the bank to get us through economically slim times.

... We can no longer be accused, as in the old days, of being "too serious." We have holidays and parties and celebrations to the point of satiation.

... We have established a distinctly Twin Oaks culture, with its own rituals, humor, and language oddities.

... Membership turnover is not a threat to our continuance; we are not dependent upon any one person or any small group of people.

... We no longer argue about central dining versus family style. We have both.

I could go on, but lists are boring. What I started out to say is that the stack of stuff in our in-box looks to us now just about as high as it ever was, but in reality it isn't. What is true is that we can now look at some of those buried issues and consider them in depth, whereas in past years we simply didn't have the time, or the money, or the spare energy to get to them.

The problems of the current decade are numerous, troublesome, and interesting. I intend to devote the next several chapters to those issues that challenge us now. Since our success rate in dealing with them will probably match that of past years, I can see that this book will be in many ways out of date ten years from now. That makes me a little sad. I wish I could send out yearly updates that readers could add on to this volume, the way those firms do that send out the latest tax law information. But this isn't likely, so I write of what is currently on our minds and in our hearts.

114

Chapter 14

Grow A Tomato,
Eat A Tomato

The Importance of Natural Foods

A couple of years ago the Planners put out a survey for the purpose of finding out how members felt about our general directions. In the Agriculture section of the survey, they asked several questions about organic farming and gardening versus other options. Just how much, they wanted to know, were communitarians willing to spend in cash and in labor, over and above wholesale grocery prices, in order to eat produce that we raise ourselves? The response was overwhelming. By and large, the Community does not care how much it costs to raise our own food. The value the group places on freshness and organic growing methods is not measured in dollars and cents.

Enthusiasm for restricting our diet only to those items we can raise ourselves, however, is another matter. Our Garden Manager, in fact, complains that the cooks don't want to serve sweet potatoes or parsnips (for example) nearly as often as they could, based on the crop we produce. The Community's appetite for any particular vegetable does not always keep up with the potential supply. Also, we like a lot of foods that we cannot raise, such as rice, pasta, and oranges, not to mention salt, sugar, and chocolate.

Twin Oaks menus offer great variety, and most visitors comment favorably on the fresh vegetables, home-baked bread, tasty entrees, and so forth. Occasionally a visitor expresses indignation because we serve meat or desserts, but there isn't much we can do about it. Not only do our tastes vary, but so do our ideas. We do not cater solely to any one group. Our cooks stretch their energies to provide enough variety at every meal so that everybody may find something acceptable. Frequently they serve several varieties of the same main dish—with and without onions, or with and without dairy products. There are usually about five different dishes at every meal—except on pizza night, when there are five different varieties of pizza instead.

In our efforts to make varied meals for vegetarians, we have found many different ways to serve tofu, tempeh, and gluten, as well as vegetables and grains.

Children's Opinions About Our Food

An interesting negative comment on our meals comes from our children. With a few exceptions, our children do not generally like what's for dinner, even though they have been raised on our kind of food since birth. I once watched a parent guide a child through the steamtable line:

"Do you want some salad?"

"No, I don't like salad."

"It's quite good. It has chunks of apple in it."

"I said no, didn't I? I said I don't like salad."

"Well, how about a vegetable? There's broccoli, and there's mixed corn and peas."

"No, I don't like vegetables."

"You have to eat something fresh. Choose between the vegetables and a salad."

"Oh, all right. I'll take some corn, but pick out the peas. I don't like peas."

"Okay, how about the lasagne? It's good. There are two kinds, the meat kind and the tofu kind."

"Yuck. I hate tofu. Let me see the meaty kind." (Adult lifts child or pan so child can see.) "It has tofu in it. I can see it. I told you I don't want any tofu. I hate tofu. I want some of that apple cake."

"You have to eat something besides cake. If you want, I can make you a peanut butter sandwich or a quesadilla."

"No peanut butter. I just want a jelly sandwich."

"Well, maybe a jelly sandwich would be okay, as long as it's on whole wheat bread."

"No, not whole wheat bread. I want store-bought bread!"

"Oh, all right. At least have a glass of milk."

Nevertheless, our children appear healthy. Maybe it's because the apple cake is made from wholesome ingredients. And mercifully, most of them drink milk (dairy or soy; we have both kinds).

Two members, upon reading the manuscript for this book, complained that the steamtable conversation I reported above makes the parents sound stupid. I suppose it's only fair to admit that many parents exercise better control of children's diet than the one I was quoting. In the words of one of the protesters, "Our children don't live on jelly sandwiches. They live on yogurt and quesadillas." Either way, the point remains that they don't usually like what is served at meals, even though they've been raised on it.

Last year we had an interesting meeting with some of the young people who grew up here as children. We asked them to tell us what they remembered about their childhood and how they now evaluate it from their young adult perspective. Their memories were mostly happy ones of playing with other children under the loose control of indulgent adults. The one negative thing they all mentioned was that they hated tofu! A current member ventured to ask them what they had wanted to eat instead. "Well," admitted the most forthright among them, "at the time I believe I was interested mostly in candy bars."

By thoughtful adult standards, Twin Oaks food is frequently very good indeed. In any given year we have a few excellent cooks, several who are quite adequate, and one or two who are just learning but trying to please. Among them they produce a variety of meals both nutritious and tasty, mostly without mixes or prepared foods. Almost everything, including the bread, is made from scratch.

Food Wars

I see that the above paragraphs sound as if we (adults, at least) were in peaceful agreement about food. The truth is that we live perpetually on the brink of Food Wars.

The first Food War had to do with meat. Twin Oaks was founded as a meat-eating Community before vegetarianism was common. All the lunches in the first month of our communal existence consisted of bread and baloney and Kool-aid. All the suppers contained hamburger. Our first vegetarian (in 1969) had to look out for herself. Some time in the early seventies we started serving some meatless dishes at every meal, and it became standard practice to make sure there was vegetarian fare at all times. Cooking two separate meals, one for meaties and the other for veggies, nearly doubles the work for the cooks, and partly for this reason meat-eating tapered off at Twin Oaks in the late seventies. There were a few years when Twin Oaks served meat only three times a week.

The initial impetus for Tuesday group, in 1982, was a hunger for meat. We started this supper club with the promise that there would be chicken every Tuesday night. We pooled allowances and bought the chicken ourselves for a few months. Then one year the Food Manager got a bigger budget, and the whole Community had chicken. Since then, the amount of meat served has varied, depending on the supply of home-grown beef, the size of the food budget, and the energy of the cooks.

All that is okay, but every once in a while somebody upsets the balance. We'll go through a month when a major meat cook gets sick or goes on vacation, and suddenly, from a meatie point of view, no matter how hard the cooks try, meal after meal is tasteless. Meaties start taking steaks and wieners and bacon from the freezer and frying up their own entrees. Hard working veggie cooks find their efforts spurned and overhear unkind remarks at the steam table, like "There's nothing to eat here; shall we go out for pizza?" One memorable evening when there was a vegan meal (the latest in a series of vegan meals), a few meat-eaters raided the freezer for steaks and got together to broil them. The smell drew a crowd, and the crowd became a party, with twenty happy greasy diners. They weren't as happy the next day, when they learned that the cook who had prepared the rejected meal had been heard crying.

That's from a meatie standpoint. I'm trying to stretch myself to feel this from the other side. It seems to me likely that during weeks when the meaties are happy with the food, the veggies may find the steam table drab. They are always fed, but if the major cook is concentrating on the meat dish, the veggie dishes may not be skillfully prepared. So maybe the veggies, too, meet in little groups and grumble. Maybe from time to time they get together and pig out on rice and vegetables and tofu cheesecake. Maybe they even go out for pizza. I wouldn't blame them.

There are only a few people who don't care what they eat. The rest of us come to the steam table with an expectation of finding something good, and if we are disappointed several days in a row, it hurts morale and breeds rebellion.

Recently this problem has been complicated by a third major subdivision of eating preferences. Vegan vegetarians don't eat animal products at all, which means no milk, cheese, yogurt, or eggs (and therefore no mayonnaise, no cakes or hot breads except the special vegan varieties, no souffles or quiches). The number of vegans appears to be growing lately. A vegetarian cook is increasingly likely to be a vegan cook, and the old-fashioned lacto-ovo vegetarians are the latest group to feel at times not taken care of.

Giving in to one another and taking turns is not a Food War. Food Wars come when any one of these sectors dominates the diet, or controls the budget, or makes discriminatory food policy, and the steam-table offerings become the subject of grumpy conversation or even public controversy. For a while we had a Food Manager who decided that he "didn't have enough money" to buy white sugar. People got upset, but he ignored them. So individuals began to buy their own one-pound or five-pound containers of sugar out of their allowances, and a whole shelf had to be given over to the private sweet stashes.

We came close to a mini-Food War one day when Gerri was cooking and got into a mischievous mood. She decided she would serve a supper consisting entirely of desserts. Hungry communitarians came to the steam table and met chocolate pie, peach pie, chocolate chip cookies, and spice cake. No salad, vegetables or rice. Nothing except sweets. Most of us were disappointed but took it with the humor intended. I believe I filled up on cookies. But some didn't think it was funny. They marched into the kitchen and took out the leftovers from lunch. (Since lunch is usually made up of leftovers in the first place, this was a pretty desperate act.) They heated them up and brought them to the dining tables with clenched mouths and wrathful eyes. It was this incident that impressed most strongly on me the fundamental thing about supper. It is a high point of the day, and not to be trifled with.

I don't know for sure whether the movement from all-meat through meatie/veggie and now on to vegan diets is a clear trend. There are those who think so and rejoice, and there are others who think so and panic. Somehow it doesn't seem very Twin Oakish to go all the way in any one direction, so I don't expect any diet to sweep the polls.

121

122

Chapter 15

The Builders

Only at the beginning did we manage to put up buildings without arguing about it. I suppose this is because the needs were obvious, and because we were small enough then to have a generally shared vision of the Community's future. People began to dispute the value of new construction in 1972. By the time I returned in 1982, there was a veritable party of resistance to building.

To Build or Not

The general line of objection to putting up more buildings is that we "don't need them." We can get along with what we have. We do not need (or do not predict) a higher population. We do not need larger or more comfortable quarters for the people already here. We do not need amenities such as a recreation building. We can get by as we are. People sometimes feel that their sense of what Twin Oaks is and ought to be will be compromised or even destroyed if the physical plant changes from what it has been during their membership so far.

Also, buildings cost money and labor. Some people like to leave the money in the bank or give it away. Some prefer to earn less and use the hours for leisure.

A more recent line of argument is that buildings take up land, and it would be nice to leave the land the way it is. They do not want Twin Oaks to resemble suburbia. They like living in the woods.

I like it, too. I like it a great deal and would be sorry to see Twin Oaks trade its natural forested beauty for too many houses and parking lots. Our differences of opinion on this subject are matters of degree. I believe we need probably about ten more substantial buildings before we declare ourselves big enough and satisfied with our indoor spaces. Some people are ready to call a halt right now.

For both sides of the argument, buildings represent progress, but we feel very differently about the value of progress. For me it's tied in with accomplishing what I have so long envisioned. For others, "progress" is a word describing all that's wrong with America, from crime-infested cities to fast food.

Whether to give up four acres of woods for a handful of buildings seems to me a rather smaller question than whether to pave the earth with asphalt, but who am I to despise symbols? My visions for Twin Oaks are also largely symbolic of the world I would like to see. The satisfaction I feel as each new building gets approved, as each foundation is poured, and as each structure finally opens for occupancy is beyond the practical matter of meeting needs. It has powerful symbolic overtones. It means progress—not haphazard and irresponsible progress, but appropriate progress, toward a better world.

The Need for a New Kitchen and Dining Space

It used to be a maxim at Twin Oaks that every new building cost us a builder. That is, whoever had been the "honcho" (project manager) of the building would get burnt out by the project and leave the Community shortly after it was completed. I'd like to talk about this interesting phenomenon, but I wasn't here during the major period when it was true. The years since my return have seen us engaged in eight substantial construction projects, and only one of them caused the departure of the builder. I do want to talk about that one. It was a landmark project in the history· of Twin Oaks, but the course of its design and completion was marked by conflict throughout.

The project started, I am proud to say, with me. I returned home to Twin Oaks in the fall of 1982, ready to commit the rest of my life here but not entirely contented with some of the ruts the Community had settled into. In particular I became acutely conscious of dirt, disorder, and unnecessary inconvenience. From my point of view the kitchen and dining rooms of the time (Llano, the original farmhouse with some tacked-on porches) was the real and symbolic core of what was wrong.

This is what I saw: A kitchen impossible to clean. At the time I rejoined, the stove was so full of cockroaches that the breakfast cook had to wave at them with a dishcloth to get them off the burner handles before starting up the stove—this in a Community 15 years old and considered successful! Shortly after that we had an exterminator get rid of the roaches, but the fact that they had been there in the first place told me that those who struggled for cleanliness and sanitation were losing ground.

Near the kitchen was a much-used bathroom. Many members habitually left the bathroom door open while they used the toilet. I believe the general idea was that we were all supposed to be free of feelings of shame about our bodies and natural functions. About ten feet away from this open door was the snack counter where bread and peanut butter could be had between meals.

The steam table/serving counter crossed the kitchen in such a way that when we lined up for meals we necessarily walked past the open bathroom door (as did our visitors, fresh from the Outside). We then picked up our food and continued on into the various small dining spaces. These spaces had once been bedrooms, porch, and attic. Among them they held about 30 diners. The Community had 70 members, so we didn't all eat indoors at the same time. Rainy or cold weather made the dining rooms so crowded that some people sat on the floor with their plates in their laps, but in Virginia most of the year is warm enough that we usually took our plates outside to the picnic tables in the courtyard.

In the process of getting through the serving line, if we wanted any condiments, such as catsup, we'd have to bend down and reach under the serving counter, the only available storage space. This bending and searching process blocked the line and held up other hungry people. Getting ice for a cold drink involved going to a shed in the back yard, which was the only available space for the ice machine. As to having a hot drink with a meal, it was virtually impossible. Your dinner would be cold before you could work your way in toward the stove and heat the water.

Much of Llano felt dark. There was one window in each crowded room. Much of the year the light from these windows was blocked by fans, and the glass was so old it could not be made truly clear, even supposing somebody cleaned it. The building had never been designed for a crowd, and the windows weren't enough. Some people liked an intimate ambiance for dining, which they achieved with 30-watt light bulbs or candles. All together this produced a dim and gloomy feeling, which, with the crowding, caused me to write the building off as a place to eat.

The KDC Political Process

There had been talk of building a KDC (Kitchen-Dining Complex) since 1969, and I thought it had been postponed long enough. In all of this I had a strong partner in my daughter, Josie. Josie had been a member of Twin Oaks for 14 years, and she cared deeply about cleanliness and sanitation. Probably her influence might have been strong enough to get the project started sooner if she had not been in school, but she had been for several years in the process of studying for her medical degree, so she was rather out of the swing of political issues at Twin Oaks. When I came, however, she joined me in putting before the Community the arguments with which we hoped to persuade the group to take on the building of a new KDC. We made a good team, and Pinc, the Food Manager of the time, added his voice to ours.

I went to an experienced builder, a man named Will, and I said, "Tell me, Will, since the community hasn't built for awhile, what sort of process do you think we could go through to get one started?" He thought about it a minute and then said "I think I'd advertise for an ad hoc committee to put a proposal together, and then present the proposal to the Community in an open meeting." I probed to see whether he himself favored a KDC and whether he had an ambition to build it. The answer was yes to both questions. Will confided that he had become very impatient with the Community's slow-paced building program. He said, "I want to see the Community built before I die. I know we'll get the development we need eventually, but I'm not satisfied that it be just for future generations. I want to enjoy it, too." I fully agreed, and we happily became partners.

We called an open meeting on the subject, "What building should we build next?" It was well-attended. The assembled group made a list of possible projects, including, as I recall, a greenhouse, a schoolhouse, and a swimming pool. We expressed our feelings about the comparative needs for each structure. At the end of the meeting we had a go-round in which each person informally voted for a personal choice of building. The vote was overwhelmingly "KDC" or "Community Center." From that moment on there was no doubt in my mind that we had the necessary public support to bring the project off.

Objections to Building a KDC

This does not mean that there was no opposition. There was in fact very strong and determined opposition.

The first argument was that a new KDC would be unnecessarily expensive. If, argued McCune, we were really dissatisfied with Llano (and he could see that it had faults), we could remodel the old house and expand it satisfactorily for about $35,000. Will's original informal estimate for a new KDC was $250,000.

McCune presented us with some rough sketches of how Llano might be adapted. He begged us not to jump to the conclusion that we needed a new building but to consider how we might meet our needs for a much lower cost. The idea of remodeling Llano gathered some support, especially among people who just don't like to spend much money, but also from another quarter. These were the people who like what they called a "funky" atmosphere.

It took me a while to comprehend what was meant by "funky." Webster's dictionary says "having an earthy, unsophisticated style and feeling." I guess Llano had that all right. For its defenders, funk meant a homey feeling. The ideas that turned me on—light, air, space, order, design—do not enter into the idea of funk. The feeling for funk is not an argument; it's just a preference, and there is no way to argue people out of their preferences. All I could do about the funk-lovers was hope to outnumber them.

Related to this was the resistance to anything that represented the middle class. New construction in our price range unquestionably does look middle class when we first finish it. The doors close; the windows match; the sheetrock is properly hung; the floors are flat; the tile gleams. After a few years at the mercy of ordinary wear-and-tear, not to mention individualistic communitarians with saws and hammers, much of this changes, and bits of funkiness enter in. Lack of funk is a temporary problem. More permanent changes come with the unquestionably higher standard of living that each new building brings. Some people don't want that, either.

Against all this Josie and Will and Pinc and I argued that there was no way Llano could be remodeled to get enough light and space and fundamental cleanability into it, that the Community deserved a better standard of living, and that "middle-class" is not a swear-word. Josie also pointed out that if kitchens had been the traditional domain of men, we'd have had a new one long ago. I don't know that we won the arguments, but there were quite a few people who agreed, so we won the decision. The central core people never wavered. We kept pushing, and the project successfully got through the Tradeoff Games for 1984 and 1985.

We formed some committees, considered two designs, and chose one. We flew Henry (now an ex-member living in California) to Twin Oaks for design consultation. He gave us the fundamental ideas on which the eventual design was based, by explaining to us that the building would be quite big, and we had to find some way of getting daylight to the middle of it. Ordinary windows would not do it by themselves. From there Will took on the design work and created the three-part cupola-topped structure where we now cook and eat. Personally I like it a lot. A few people don't. It is definitely not funky—yet.

Will as KDC Honcho

The people who had opposed the construction of a KDC went right on opposing it after it was started, putting a strain on the morale of those involved. Planning and building the KDC was an enormous and complex project, and Will, always subject to migraine headaches, was under constant pressure. He was our general contractor. The hiring and coordinating of subcontractors was part of his job, but in addition he did a great deal of the actual construction. The KDC project absorbed his full attention for two years. He dedicated his energies to it in a way very few Twin Oakers ever do. Will was not "laid back." He didn't take a vacation every few months, as most members do. He was intense, self-driven, and, I'm afraid, boastful. He could see clearly the difference between himself and the average communitarian in terms of work standards, and he didn't hide his disdain for those who were either less capable or less driven.

In retrospect it occurs to me that Will may well have been near the end of his patience with many things at Twin Oaks before he even started the KDC. He had invested ten years of his life here, was married to Gerri, one of our longest-term members, and had a child with her. In many ways he loved the Community, but he didn't really care for people until they had been here a long time. He basically thought new members should be seen and not heard. New members cannot be counted on to accept such a role. They tend to have ideas, and they are not necessarily respectful of their "elders." From Will's point of view, most of the Community's members were too new to be expressing opinions.

The KDC project brought out this conflict with new people in a very sharp way. Although the Community could not afford much labor to work on the KDC, and had instructed Will to hire subcon-

128

tractors, there were members who wanted to have a part in the building of it, and Will often made it both difficult and unpleasant for them to do so. He used his budget to hire ex-members (frequently personal friends) to do things that current members wanted to do. Some people thought this was an abuse. Will thought the newer members incapable of good work. When he did allow them to work on the building, they complained that he assigned them the most boring or unpleasant tasks that happened to be available at the time. This did not seem to Will to be unfair. He said it was what all apprentices had to do. For the newer people, the notion of "apprenticing" did not sit well. They wanted to participate in framing, roofing, tiling, and other such tasks that make a big, obvious, immediate difference in the appearance of progress on the building. They did not want to clean up the site, move boards, nail in small pieces of extra blocking, or staple fiberglass insulation to the underside of the floor.

Will

Not only Will, but all the Construction Managers we have ever had, have complained exasperatedly about Twin Oakers' casual attitude toward building projects. People have the idea that they can take part in a personally growthful and fulfilling way without dedicating themselves to see the project through, including the parts that aren't any fun—and there are hundreds of such parts. They want to show up 2 or 3 days a week, work only mornings or only afternoons, be instructed by a professional, and come out of the experience with a feeling of having participated and helped, of having learned and grown and been appreciated.

I understand this, because I remember my own experience. That's exactly what I wanted when I worked under Henry's direction at Degania. Henry had a miraculous talent for that sort of thing, and he gave me what I wanted. He must have done the same thing for several dozen other people before he burned out. Will, however, had long ago exhausted his willingness to teach. He just wanted to be allowed to do a good job with a competent crew and be appreciated for it.

Although he got appreciation from a few of us, Will antagonized so many people with his contemptuous attitudes that they retaliated by withholding the admiration he needed and, I think, deserved.

The Big Budget Overrun

The open explosion of protests against Will's behavior came out over the issue of budget overexpenditure. It is perfectly true that Will overspent the budget by $70,000. The budget had not been realistic in the first place, and he was not careful. But it always seemed to me that it wasn't really the depleted bank account that made people angry. It was Will's attitude about it. He had a way of conveying that he enjoyed spending money. He used his judgment (rather than careful process) on several peripheral matters that got the Community's attention. For example, he seriously underestimated the cost of the slate chosen for the front entrance patio. When he learned its real cost, he bought it anyway and had it laid by a professional. He got a bargain on redwood and on his own initiative made the dining deck twice as large as the plan called for. He had a decorative flower garden circle made of imported rocks, rather than using the stones from our own property. He used oak, rather than the pine the plans called for, to make the wainscoting in the dining room. He bought expensive interior doors of solid oak that had to be attached with hinges costing $75 a set; he surprised the Community by installing fancy entrance doors with "beveled glass" insets. (Actually, it's a kind of plastic, but it looked like beveled glass, and that's what people took it for.)

Will defended every decision, and he didn't have any trouble convincing me. His basic argument was that he was building the Community's central facility, its public face, that it should endure for many, many years, that the cost was trivial in comparison to the use the building would get and the pleasure it would give to generations of communitarians. I agreed with him then, and I still do. We had the money, and I think we spent it well.

The people who didn't like Will or his building or his ways argued that it was irrelevant whether Will's judgment turned out to be right or wrong. The point was that he didn't have the right to make those decisions by himself. Those rights are reserved to the Community.

McCune's Point of View

There were several people who resented Will's style and said so, but I'll talk mostly about McCune, the one I heard most from. McCune and Will had been at odds with each other for years before the creation of the KDC. They just naturally didn't get along. This was partly because their priorities were very different. Will wanted to build the physical plant of the Community, and to build it soon and well. He wanted Twin Oaks to be a place he could be proud to live in, and he wanted to be professionally engaged in architecture and land planning.

McCune wanted to maintain the "alternative" spirit of the Community. Over the years he had dedicated himself to saving energy and keeping costs down. He enjoyed the Twin Oaks custom of working at one's own pace and was seldom in a hurry to get a project done, or even started, for that matter. He just could never see what the rush was. Will represented the lifestyle that McCune wanted to avoid. McCune thought Will wasteful in his spending and uncooperative in his attitudes.

McCune was by no means a new member or a dilettante. He was (and is) also a builder, practicing his own form of dedication. He sees his projects through to the end, and he does high quality work. (He too had at that time a history of overspending project budgets, but he was apologetic about it and easily forgiven.) Will respected McCune for his virtues but hated his parsimonious ways. They had agreed not to attempt to work together on this building. McCune tells me he tried to leave Will alone and not criticize him publicly for the numerous instances of what he considered frivolous spending. But a $70,000 overrun was more than he could stomach. The amount of the overrun alone was more than McCune had wanted spent on the whole project!

When the news about the overrun got out, there was widespread indignation, and we had a public meeting about it. I facilitated the meeting and tried to keep it under control by discouraging irrelevancies, etc. But people were in an angry mood and had not come to the meeting to be fair to Will. They had built up anger and wanted to let him know about it. In the end I could not prevent them. Will was exposed to the publicly expressed anger of people he did not respect, and he had to listen, because they were right about the central point. They had the right to determine the amount spent on the building.

Will made a form of apology for ignoring process. He admitted he hadn't had the right to double the deck size without asking, and a few other things, but many people didn't believe his apologies were sincere, and they continued to be resentful. Will probably had more migraines than usual, but he went back to work. He finished the KDC. By the end he probably did it more out of personal pride than out of love for the Community, but he did it, just the same.

131

Llano, the original farmhouse

Zhankoye, the KDC

Post-KDC Building Push

The rest of the morale costs of the KDC struggles were not paid until the year after the building was finished and occupied. We decided through the 1986 Tradeoff Game to go ahead and do five building projects at once (dairy barn, Llano remodel, greenhouse, Oneida bathroom, and visitor cottage.). Will proposed that all five be done under his central management, but the Planners turned him down. We gave him his choice of projects instead, and he chose Llano remodel.

Everywhere Will turned that year, trying to put his talents to good use for the Community, he was blocked. Repeatedly he offered himself for one responsible position after another, and repeatedly was frustrated. I'm afraid I must take responsibility for this. I was a Planner, and the Planner group had placed me in charge of the building projects. In my judgment the Community was at a point where it was other people's turn to feel the accomplishment of a major building project. In order to make way for them, and in order to quiet the Community's outrage at Will's attitudes, I used my position to try to keep him contained. It was my ambition to keep Will usefully employed but to prevent his having any sweeping authority, particularly authority to thwart and frustrate amateur builders. All I succeeded in doing, unfortunately, was to block him and turn him against me. My vision of Will contentedly turning out useful work alongside other Twin Oaks builders, all of them under the benign and gentle guidance of the board of Planners, was not to be realized. He quit the Llano remodel project when his budget projections were criticized, and he never built for us again. The KDC was Will's last Twin Oaks building and almost his last useful act. He virtually stopped working. He devoted quite a lot of his last year to revenge. His hatred of those who had blocked him was palpable. I did not enjoy the last six months of my Planner term.

The Visitor Cottage

Will was openly derisive of our next builder, a young, relatively inexperienced man named Keenan. We had called on Keenan to take on the construction of the proposed visitor cottage, a project orphaned by unexpected turnover. With some reluctance, he agreed to build it if we would simplify the design to bring it within his ability. We did so. Keenan found a building partner in a new member named Alexis, and the two of them devoted themselves to putting up this straightforward little house, asking advice from more experienced people, working with a hammer in one hand and *Modern Carpentry* in the other. Will called the visitor cottage "that piece of doo-doo" and would turn his head away every time he had to pass by it. He attempted to get progress stopped on the visitor cottage by persuading various members that it was a terrible mistake. People then came to me with the worries that he had put in their heads. Gerri begged me to divert the building labor into the hammock shop for the latest production push. Alta said the Community was working far too hard and needed to cut back on some project. Leslie asked if we could get somebody more competent to put up the visitor center, because Keenan just didn't have the experience. It wasn't any fun for me to ignore these pleas, because, generally speaking, Planners don't succeed by ignoring people. However, by that time I was seeing the situation in simple terms: either we were going to prove that ordinary communitarians can build buildings or we were going to vindicate Will's belief that only professionals could do it. He had chosen the visitor cottage as his dueling ground, and

Keenan

that's where the point was to be proven if it could be. So the Planners didn't back down, and the visitor cottage was finished (adequately, on time, and under budget) by Keenan and Alexis.

Could We Have Done it Better?

In making the choice to accept Will's resignation and to back less experienced builders, I knew that it meant Will and his much-beloved family would leave the Community. Will had reached the point where he would accept nothing less than complete vindication, and this was impossible. We've done a lot of second-guessing about how the whole KDC process might have been handled in order to have avoided the severe problems that came out of it, and the subsequent loss of Will and Gerri and their children. Some people conjecture that we needed a Budget Manager to keep track of expenditures and keep Will within the bounds of the plan. Some think the problems were just bad communication, and that Will needed a liaison. I think all this is naive, and that the outcome was inevitable. Will set his sights on doing the overall physical planning for the Community, and he maintained hopes, in the teeth of the evidence, that the Community was capable of changing its ways and permitting professionalism on that level.

Nothing is less likely. Amateurism is, I believe, at the core of what Twin Oaks is and is likely to remain for some time. It fits in with our ability to attract young and restless people and with the probability that they will leave after a few years. Those of us who remain for many years do become professional in certain areas, but they are not areas that exercise sweeping control over the Community's directions. Will longed for what could not be had.

Though I had my part in frustrating him, I still feel a degree of sympathy for Will's position. I, too, wish that Twin Oaks could develop sufficiently as a society to be able not only to handle proud professionals but also to cushion falls from power and to channel good ability and energy into new directions instead of using people up and letting them go.

Building After Will

By the way, I should mention that women have played a role in construction leadership since the construction of Morningstar in 1976. We have never had many female construction honchos at a time, but we generally have at least one.

It felt like riches to have three able people available to build our newest residence. We appointed two of them (Keenan and Donna) to the official honcho position, and McCune, not at all attached to the title, worked with them in the management of the project. It was a reasonably compatible team. They did not produce tension in the Community when they worked. They all have egos and all enjoy being appreciated, but this wasn't a problem.

Donna used to grit her teeth occasionally at the phenomenon of the casual worker who wants professional instruction in exchange for a piddling commitment, and McCune preferred to work alone or with a true peer, but both compromised. Keenan has the ability to get useful work even from drop-in labor, and if McCune and Donna hadn't stopped him, he could probably have completed most of the building with visitor help. Keenan, however, avoids detail work like plumbing, cabinetry, and trim, so presumably we will never see this experiment.

The last few months of the new residence construction showed us the usefulness of yet another kind of honcho. Remember the story about people begging us to "finish the buildings?" Dianne took this idea to new heights. After the rooms were all constructed and the plumbing was being installed, Dianne offered to coordinate the finishing details. She trimmed doorways and windows, installed doorknobs, painted floors, built a linen closet. She enlisted a dozen or more people with varying talents to do parts of these jobs. One made bathroom cabinets. Another created drapery rods. A third sewed curtains. Dianne herself built a bike rack and put up clotheslines. She got people to lug furniture and carpet in from various places. She helped new residents move in. Even then she didn't consider the building finished until she had purchased attractive shower curtains and the right kind of dish sponges. There was, of course, criticism. McCune murmured that the detail was overkill. Others said it was too luxurious. However, even with all its details, the residence did not use all its budget by a margin of several thousand dollars.

All our honchos these days (except maybe Dianne) take vacations when they feel they need them, and mostly feel free to quit a project if they're not enjoying it. Work on the residence was interrupted a few times, and once Keenan quit for a while in protest over having to listen to too much advice from too many people. Even so, ten people (including me) moved into our new rooms in the new residence only a year and a half after it was started. It's a fair-sized building (14 rooms), and that's considered a brisk pace.

In addition to the residence, we quickly built two shops, one for stretcher-making (Donna in charge) and one for tofu (honchoed by Alexis), which took only a couple of months each.

I no longer think we can build any building without hard feelings somewhere along the line. People who oppose building in general will frequently also oppose it in particular and be critical rather than encouraging of the builders. I do think, however, that this last big project provided a model for cooperative leadership worth emulating. Also, we got through it without losing anybody.

If I could have what I wanted, I'd like a building honcho with Henry's imagination and charisma, Will's vision and tireless commitment, McCune's knowledge and reasonableness, Keenan's ability to find and use willing workers, and Dianne's dogged attention to detail. As any grown-up knows, we don't get exactly what we want. Twin Oaks is unlikely to come across anybody with all those qualities in one person. Our buildings and building processes will vary with the personalities that come and go.

Chapter 16

The Serenity to Accept
the Things I Cannot Change

It seems to me that a great deal of the sense of empowerment in community comes from the knack of bowing gracefully to the inevitable. I recall the king in *The Little Prince* who commanded the sun to rise each morning, and I feel some sympathy with him. I have made myself comfortable many times by commanding our little suns to rise. It is harmless, and it makes me feel good. The only problem with it is that some observer may laugh at me, as they did at that king, but they might do better to consider doing as the king and I do. Personal empowerment is no mean accomplishment.

I should give you some examples. Here's a big one to start off with: I command the Community to produce a huge garden.

I suppose that if I had designed a rural Virginia community and had determined all its directions, my imaginary community would have been guaranteed only a much smaller garden, just enough for fresh use and frozen berries, and pickles. After that, the garden would have been subject to economic analysis. What is the cost of potatoes in winter when bought from the wholesale produce dealers? What is our labor cost for the same quantity of potatoes? Add in the cost of seed, tools, etc. How does it come out? If it came out even or in favor of buying, I'd have my imaginary utopians ask the next question: Do people prefer working in the potato patch to working for cash to buy the potatoes? If so, we'd grow them. If not, we'd buy them. Isn't that rational? Don't you wish you lived in my imaginary utopia?

If you don't, then you probably understand why I know I can never get anywhere with this line of argument at Twin Oaks. For one thing, some members worry about the chemicals used to produce commercially grown foods. It is almost an article of faith for some that capitalists of all stripes are entirely devoid of decency and good will, and will do anything at all for a profit. I haven't met a lot of big capitalists, but in this matter I give them the benefit of the doubt and don't worry about being poisoned.

The words "organic food" have no glow for me. I don't care if the nutrients that fed my potato were dropped from a chicken or produced in a factory.

Obviously, I am way out of step here. So what do I do? Do I carry on a campaign on the O&I Board trying to persuade others to my point of view? Failing this, do I sit around and grumble and feel disempowered? Do I cringe and snarl every time I see a potato, thinking about all the alternative uses for that wasted labor?

I certainly do not! I eat the potatoes, which are perfectly delicious, congratulate the garden people on the terrific harvest, and add the idea "Home garden is a basic necessity" to my concept of a happy community in the 1990s.

While I'm at it, I note that the garden is beautiful. Walking past its well-tended rows in late spring is a sensual delight. The barrow-loads of big fresh tomatoes in late summer are perfectly wonderful to behold. I am by no means immune to the romance of country living.

I also note that nobody is asking me to get dirt under my fingernails. The people who work in the garden like the work or they wouldn't do it.

While I'm out here in the garden, let me tell you about the strawberries. Did you ever have as many strawberries as you wanted, for weeks at a time? That's what we have every May. If you like them with real cream, we grow that, too. Just talk to Sunflower, our Jersey cow.

By the time I've added up the psychological importance of organic gardening, the freely-chosen outdoor labor, the beauty of the plants, the presumed recruitment value of all of the above, and the fact that the food is good, I have to take another look at the economic question, and it becomes "How much am I willing to pay for all these morale factors?" The answer is, "Quite a lot." I'll probably never know what the price is, because the Community doesn't do rigorous economic analysis of its agriculture. I assume this is because we don't really want to know, and more than that, because we don't care. We're going to garden anyway.

Somewhere along in here that garden becomes *my* garden. "We" grow all that food, and "we" do it organically. Give me another five years, and I'll be able to write that with a straight face without the quotation marks.

For the past several years I have made out my Tradeoff Game without giving a thought to cutting back the garden. I no longer think of this as political defeat. I think of it as part of the status quo that needs to be maintained in order for us all to feel secure. As to the change in myself, am I being ground down and made to knuckle under to the numerical superiority of the irrational? No. I am just growing wiser. Is it a source of irritation? No. It is a source of satisfaction.

To identify with a movement that is going to go ahead with or without me is empowering. Anything that helps me to say "we" (and mean it, after thinking about it), is empowering. At the very least it removes a source of irritation and allows me to put my energy into more profitable efforts. At best it increases my joy in life.

The garden isn't the only place around here where I've empowered myself simply by moving from a "they" to a "we." When I came back to Twin Oaks, for instance, I noticed that some of the men ("they") sometimes wore skirts, making themselves look rather silly in my eyes and making our recruitment among more socially conservative people a wasted effort. What I notice now is that "we" very rationally adapt to the climate by wearing appropriate clothing, and that we do not allow the conventions to tell us what we can and cannot wear. Part of me is still sorry about the effect on recruitment, because I frequently like socially conservative people. But after all, it is the people I live with who count most, and we like the sexy, comfortable, free-swinging skirt.

Then there is the children's program. If you've read *Walden Two* recently, you remember the scene where all the children come from the children's quarters and move into the dining hall, where they all eat together before the adult dining hours. They move along the hallway in a happy, buzzing group, neither boisterous nor suppressed, but simply intent upon their affairs. Some of the adults join them, but it does not occur to anybody that the children be allowed to join the adults. Walden Two, as Skinner imagined it, was a place where people with different interests hung out in different places and did not infringe on each other.

As far as our experience to date has gone, the influence of *Walden Two* on our children's program is minimal. Not only was behavioral engineering abandoned quite early, but anti-Skinner sentiment is accepted as part of our diversity. Our children are attractive, healthy, and socially precocious. Their learning environment is extremely rich, their childhood happy. Whether they differ in any remarkable way from the children of similar parents in other parts of the country is open to conjecture.

I am disappointed. This is not what I envisioned. I meant for behavioral engineering to be taken seriously. I meant for our children to learn self-control, genuine intellectual curiosity, pleasant manners, and other dazzling rarities, all before the age of 6, as *Walden Two* promised. But this was not something I could influence at any stage. These are not things determined in meetings or moved by O&I papers. No amount of politics will prevent a parent from determining the personality of his or her child.

Do I say, "We think that behaviorism was a naive ideology, and we now believe that parents know what is best?" No, this time I can't manage the "we." I'd rather have done Walden Two, and I can't persuade myself otherwise.

Thus there are places where accepting the things I cannot change is just that—acceptance. In some ways Twin Oaks is what it is, whether I like it or not. I can't do anything about certain issues, but I want to live here anyway, so I accept them. I can name a half dozen things of this kind, facts that bring my mood down on bad days and fade into the background on good ones. In such matters it doesn't work for me to command the sun to rise, because I can't kid myself quite that much. I just have to say, "Oh hell, I told that sun to stay in bed, but it rose anyway."

Chapter 17

Suffer the Little Children

From Living the Dream, by Ingrid Komar, (covering the years 1979-1983)

The Twin Oaks child program is the best of both worlds. It provides each child with an unusual amount of love and attention as well as the benefits of communal child care. Every child's day has at least one period when he or she is the sole focus of a one-to-one relationship with a parent or other caring adult, and other segments of time within the group under thoughtful adult teaching and guidance.

For participating adults the system provides the satisfaction of nurturing little people, the refreshing stimulation of seeing the world anew through the eyes of children, and much more, all the precious things children can give to grownups—all that, without being totally confined to a children's world. Twin Oaks childcare workers and teachers can easily earn part of their labor credits in any other area they choose, and all of them do just that. This not only nourishes the person involved with the children; it also gives the children the educational opportunity to relate to teachers and metas in their other roles. For the parent, the price of communal child care is the loss of a certain amount of direct control. A Twin Oaks parent inevitably shares the upbringing of cos child from infancy through adolescence with many other adults. By the end of my stay—and I reserved judgment for a while—I was convinced, however, that growing up at Twin Oaks is a plus for any child.

Ingrid Komar was at Twin Oaks writing *Living the Dream* during the last years of the Twin Oaks child program as it used to be, back when it was really based in Degania, the children's building, and most of our children were small.

In some ways I wish I could postpone this writing for another five years, because I have some confidence that by then we will once again have settled on a particular child program that works for this Community as it will then be.

But the fact is that I am writing during a period in which the child program is in flux, and we can't tell from here how anything is going to turn out. Just the same, I'll give you a general description, tell some stories, and make some predictions that will probably turn out to be wrong, but you never know.

General Description of Child Program

We have three general groups of children whom we designate as "metas," "midis," and "megas." The metas are children up to age five, midi means ages five through nine, and megas are age ten through the teen years.

The meta children theoretically live in Degania, as they always did. In actual fact, most of them sleep there about 3 or 4 nights a week and spend the other nights with their parents in adult quarters. They frequently eat breakfast and lunch at Degania, take naps there, and use the playroom and toys that are stored there. Newborns and adopted infants stay with their mothers for the first several months in rooms we have specially designed for this purpose.

Midis do not have their own house. They sleep in the same building as their parents, sometimes in a private room and sometimes sharing with another child. Since they have no play space of their own, they hang out either in one of the residences or in the main dining hall when they are not outdoors.

The mega age is rather mixed. We have two 10-year olds and two teenagers, all girls. They have private rooms in the same building as at least one parent. They, too, find play space wherever they can.

Academic Education

For years our children attended Oakley School, a private cooperative school run by Twin Oaks and a few liberal parents in the area who wanted something for their children that would be better, as they saw it, than the public school system. Twin Oaks had as a member a talented and dedicted teacher named Trisha, who ran Oakley and educated our children, along with their peers. She taught them values of cooperation, interracial understanding, and feminism, along with reading, writing, and arithmetic. Two things destroyed the school. Trisha moved away, and the local children outgrew the school, which was designed only for small children. Without Trisha, whose labor had been provided by Twin Oaks for a very small salary, and without the financial support of those other local families (many of them former Twin Oakers), Oakley could not afford a full-time teacher. The number of children attending from Twin Oaks was insufficient to hold a school together, and the teacher we hired was so underpaid she was forced to work elsewhere to sustain her family. So Oakley closed in 1990.

What to do? For some children, public school was the answer, but not all parents were willing to send their children there. As the children approached age six, some parents successfully lobbied for an experiment in home schooling. We did this for a year. The children were home-schooled in various parts of the Community by a variety of teachers. Some of them got private instruction, and others were taught in groups, depending on their needs.

This effort was not entirely successful, either. The children did not readily accept the new teacher-pupil relationship as different from the parent-child or buddy relationship they already had. Accustomed to years of saying "I don't want to play that anymore," they found they also didn't want to practice reading or writing right now, and they frequently refused to do so. After a few months it became obvious that we had some perfectly intelligent children who were not learning to read.

Some non-parents tried teaching, and found themselves bargaining with the children: "If you do these arithmetic problems for 15 minutes, I'll play ball with you when we're finished." This worked, in that the children learned the basic skills, but the more manipulative ones kept pushing at the barriers and punishing their teachers with tantrums when they encountered limits. This was extremely exhausting for the teachers.

At the end of the season some parents decided that the public schools could probably do as well as we could. Others asked the

Community to send their children to a Montessori school in Charlottesville. The Montessori school turned out to be very good, and now other parents, arguing for equality, would like their children to go there, too. That brings the cost so high that our current income will not cover it without sacrifice, and the results of the most recent Tradeoff Game have not been encouraging in that direction.

It is hard to predict what will happen next. All I know is that we have several toddlers who will be school-age before long, and we keep on having babies, so we'll have to come up with something satisfactory eventually.

The Original Conception of Communal Childcare

Our children are well cared for, appropriately educated, and generally happy, but very little of this can be attributed to the purely communal aspects of the program. The fact is that the communal child rearing experiment, as originally conceived, has failed, and we are in the process of figuring out what to put in its place.

It is hard to remember, or perhaps merely hard to credit, how very naive we founders were on the subject of child-rearing and parenthood. The best excuse I can find for myself is that I did not personally come from a close family. As to my co-founders, they were just barely out of adolescence and still in the process of getting away from the authority of their parents. Whatever our excuses, we believed with great confidence Skinner's recipe for child raising. Theory: Children belong to their society, not to their parents. Natural conclusion: Therefore society is totally responsible for their rearing, and their parents should have nothing to do with it. Application: Twin Oaks must take great care to provide expert child-educators, scientifically trained to make sure every child develops to his or her full potential and is not hindered by the shortcomings of any particular set of parents.

It all sounded good to me. God knows I would have preferred to be raised by intelligent experts, and the parental urge was not very strong in my own personality.

Some Reasons for its Failure

One of the reasons it didn't work was that we didn't happen to have any intelligent experts prepared to take full responsibility for the future of our children. All we had was a group of miscellaneous people, many of whom liked children and all of whom had theories. Another reason was that membership turnover in the Community threatened to leave our children drifting from one care-taker to another, with no firm center to their lives, and their natural parents were not willing to see their offspring emotionally abandoned. They stepped in and took basic responsibility when the Community failed to do so. The third reason is that parents are attached to their children, theory be damned, and their children become and remain attached to them, good parents or not.

To this day the residue of this early theory makes trouble for us. We wrote the theory into our basic documents, which clearly state that the Community has both full authority over the children's rearing and full responsibility for their care. However, when the parents found it necessary to brush the system aside for the sake of their children's needs and their own desires, they naturally assumed a decision-making role at the same time. One of the first shocks to our theory occurred when an early parent independently decided to have her child baptized in order to please the grandparents. I was morally outraged at the time, but it was only the beginning. Later, when the Community at large realized that the children did not really belong to the Community, nor did the institution have much real say in how they were raised, many people ceased to be willing to provide full labor credits for all child care. To this day some parents complain that they are not fully compensated for all the hours they put in, and some non-parents begrudge the hours that we do give to childcare.

Regardless of who took ultimate responsibility, we tried to take care of our children in groups, with their age peers, but this worked only as long as we had a long-term, strong-minded, dedicated professional childcare worker in Degania. Her name was Amri, and she was with us for many years. Her theories became Twin Oaks theories. Some parents resented her dominion, but she held the program together, a fact the Community as a whole did not recognize until she left in 1984 and the program fell into serious difficulties. At that point we had several new babies and a couple of new families joining from the outside. None of these people had experienced Amri's firm management. They all had their own ideas, and none of them had the leadership skills to attract the others to a single path of any sort. Two things happened: They quarreled among themselves so much that they could not get decisions made at their meetings, and individual parents began to pull their children out of the program.

The complaints varied. Some said that the adult metas (childcare workers) did not take good enough care of the babies' physical needs. For example, a plastic bag was found on the floor of Degania, or a child was allowed to go barefoot outdoors on a cold day, or a stairway was not fenced off, or insufficient care was taken to get rid of the mold, which was troubling one child's allergies, or the metas did not take the trouble to follow the diet regimen the parent had laid out.

For their part, the metas disliked being ordered about by parents and cited the bylaws in self-defense. They argued that their care was plenty good enough, and that parents were being possessive and hysterical.

Aggressive Behavior in Degania

Meanwhile there was disagreement on the appropriate handling of what some called children's violence. Twin Oaks had become used to little girls, or boys with naturally mild temperaments. When a couple of aggressive boys were added to the meta environment, their behavior was troublesome. These boys played at war, threatened each other with sticks, and exercised heavy domination over younger or weaker children. The metas spent a lot of their time and energy trying to keep little kids from getting hurt. The parents of the aggressive children argued that this behavior is normal and the metas were making too big a deal of it.

One particular father, who was also a meta, allowed the children to pound on him. He would pretend to be hurt, and the kids would strike him with their little fists and otherwise abuse him, while he dramatized being overpowered. His theory was that children need to feel powerful, and that it did him no harm to take the role of victim. Other metas were horrified, because they figured it gave out the wrong message—the message that violence is okay, that it is approved, and the victim doesn't really hurt, etc.

I am brushing over these conflicts in a sentence or two, as if they were petty disagreements in theory. But that's not the way it was. Each of them was a major clash, a trust-eroding incident, an incentive to leave the Community and take one's child out of this environment. Some parents did in fact leave, in order to have more control over child-rearing. Many are still here, and the disagreement and anger continue. Those children who were meta age when all this began are now midis. There is no longer a Degania for them, and there are no longer meetings which the childcare workers are required to attend and where they are expected to reach consensus. Instead, the conflicts have expanded to touch the whole Community, and the issue of how we raise children is from time to time a passion-raising and time-consuming one for us all.

Caroline and Her Recommendations

In 1988 the atmosphere around child issues became so unhappy that the Planners got involved. Not knowing what else to do, they decided to seek outside help to bring the Community together, so that decisions could be made and order restored to the child program. They asked Caroline Estes, an experienced facilitator from Alpha Farm, another egalitarian community, to help us out. Caroline came twice. She gave unsparingly of her energy to help us reach agreement. She listened to various segments of the Community in groups, and she interviewed dozens of individuals as well. Several of our own "process people" helped her organize the sessions and served as apprentices at the same time. Caroline has, among other skills, a warmly sympathetic manner, and people trusted her with their fears and angers and opinions. She took it all in. What she attempted to do was to show us that, underneath all the conflict, we had a considerable amount of agreement and common interest to build on. Then she attempted to point us in the direction of finding agreement on specific issues by doing more face-to-face talking and less sparring on the O&I Board.

But what the Community wanted from Caroline was answers. The group hungered to be told what to do. In response to this, Caroline made some tentative recommendations. As answers, her recommendations were no better or worse than any that might have come from one of the Planners or other experienced members. But the fact that they came from Caroline gave them power. The Community in fact adopted, or attempted to adopt, virtually every suggestion she made.

Caroline took sides on one of the outstanding issues of the day. She recommended that we not have children living in the courtyard residences (which had historically been without children) but get them all into the three buildings that had been designated child-friendly. This involved moving a particular family against its will. We did not literally force this family to move, by direct Planner directive, but enough pressure was put on and enough compensation offered that the family did change residences. This removed a particularly tempestuous child from an otherwise quiet environment and answered one major complaint.

Caroline firmly recommended that we reorganize and clearly empower the Child Board, so that we could break the logjam of decision-making and a have a channel through which Community dissent and discontent on child matters could be expressed and acted upon.

The Less-Involved

An unexpected consequence of Caroline's work was the organization of what came to be called the "Less-Involved." During her time with us, she talked to people from all segments of the Community and discovered a large group of concerned members who had no avenue through which to express their opinions, because they were not childcare workers or parents. Caroline got this group together in one room, and they were astonished at their numbers. Suddenly they were conscious of themselves as a group with some things in common, and it was obvious they had a certain amount of power to press for changes, if they could agree on the kind of changes they wanted.

The existence of this new organized force was extremely threatening to parents and other child-oriented people. They assumed that it was unified in its general hostility to the child program and its determination to step in and make changes. Once the Less-Involved started talking about its real agenda, however, it became clear that they weren't any more unified than any other group. There was really only one thing they agreed on. They wanted a halt to the influx of new families with children until the program could be brought under control. After they achieved legislation to this effect, the Less-Involved group faded away.

Child Behavior Problems

No decision-making body has yet been able to deal effectively with the Community's largest problem in child-rearing. This is the fact that many of us are dissatisfied with the behavior of our children, and many of the factors that control that behavior are not within our control.

How do our kids behave? How you describe it depends on your experience. My grandmother would have said they were all destined for a bad end. My mother would have called them sassy and spoiled. I say many of them are disrespectful and self-willed and undisciplined. Their parents say they are perfectly normal children. From what I have seen of other children raised in permissive environments, I suspect the parents are right, as far as that goes. Our children do not seem to me to be worse than the average kid in the liberal suburbs. I believe the nation is full of children just like them. From what I see and read, it seems to me that millions of parents have turned away from the idea of teaching respect at an early age, and when the fruits of this practice come ripe at the age of six or eight, they don't know what to do any more than we do.

This manuscript has taken so long to write that I feel I need to insert a paragraph here to talk about the real improvements in child behavior over the last year. Some of this may be simply a matter of the most aggressive children growing older and learning better social skills. Some credit is probably due to the STEP training we provided for parents. But I give most credit to the parents themselves. They admitted the problem and have worked hard to bring their own children under reasonable control, not without success.

I hope, and I even suppose, that as these children become adults, they will find niches for themselves in society. I personally have some doubt that they will become accountants or engineers, or any technical profession that requires strong habits of self-discipline. Perhaps the fields of education, psychology and sociology will attract some—they are certainly perceptive and articulate enough. "Socially precocious" is not too strong a description. The fact that our children without exception are deeply loved by their parents should give them the basic self-esteem they need to make a satisfactory life for themselves as adults.

Children in an Adult Environment

In the meantime, they are not living merely with their own parents. They are living with eighty-five adults, and most adults don't like being around children who are whining or demanding or having tantrums or even just running around wildly and shouting in the dining hall. Even the most innocent child activities can become annoying to an adult who wants peace and quiet.

My personal theory is that this is basically an architectural problem and should be handled by building appropriate facilities. For one thing, I think we should consider having some separate housing for families with young children. There is, however, considerable opposition to this idea, partly because some members still cling to the old communal child-rearing ideas, but mostly because the solution I propose is expensive. There are always so many things to do with money.

Parents do not have a bad life here, though it has its difficulties. Looking at their lives from a Less-Involved person's perspective, one sees that they are getting a great many advantages that they could not possibly match in the outside world. They get a certain amount of help in childcare—the equivalent of babysitters and day-care and some household help. They get partial labor credits for caring for their own children. The opportunities for fathers to participate actively in child-rearing are important to many people. Both parents can make freedom for themselves to take vacations, either with or without their children. Also, like all members, parents are free from financial anxieties. Perhaps some of these things account for the fact that turnover among families has been very low in the last few years. Nobody else is going to offer them—and this applies most forcefully to single parents— the amount of support and security that Twin Oaks gives.

However, from a parent's perspective, Twin Oaks life is not all strawberries and cream. Here's how it looks to some: They are restricted to one of two ghettos—Morningstar or Tupelo, where they have to live closely with other families whom they may or may not get along with, each family raising children according to different theories, and each having personal habits that get on other people's nerves. (Somebody left a dirty diaper on the kitchen counter!) They can take their children into public space, such as the main dining room, but when they do, they are under constant pressure to control the kids' behavior. If the children run around, make noise, or quarrel with each other, some Less-Involved person is going to radiate tension and disapproval. It is like living with a houseful of mothers-in-law, all looking at everything they do with (barely) suppressed disdain. In addition, childcare work is not, like other work, fully creditable. Unless it is done with groups of children, one gets only partial credit. Like housewives every-where, Twin Oaks mothers (and fathers, in our case) have to work harder than the rest of the population, simply because they have followed nature's imperative and produced the next generation. It might be reasonable to thank parents for taking on this task instead of punishing them for it! And so forth.

Almost all the advice Caroline gave us has had some benefit, but the basic problems are still with us and as troublesome as ever. The Less-Involved are not smarter or more capable than the parents, and their input serves chiefly to protect their own interests. The Child Board is more effective than it used to be, but it has no more idea how to control child behavior than anybody else.

Reaching agreement in community is not easy. Raising children is not easy. Reaching agreement on raising children in an egalitarian community is, so far as I can tell, impossible.

154

Chapter 18

Cows and Concrete

By the time I returned to Twin Oaks, fifteen years after its founding, the agriculture program was fairly well settled. We were past the failed experiment with commercial farming and had settled down contentedly doing it only for our own consumption. The garden was large, irrigated, and productive. The dairy kept us supplied with milk and beef.

Personally, I am very pleased with our dairy and meat program. For the last two decades we have been breeding our cows to some of the best bulls in the nation by means of artificial insemination. As a result, the herd is both productive and attractive. I almost think they are worth keeping just for their looks as they chew their cuds and graze in our pastures. But we have them for milk and meat, of course.

The only beef we eat is from our own steers and culled cows.* In fact, a large portion of Twin Oaks' agricultural activity relates to the dairy herd. We maintain fenced pastures for them, and the focus of our crop farming is to provide grain and hay. Naturally, as the trend toward vegetarianism gains momentum, the value and propriety of this work comes into question, but we have had cows

---

*A culled cow is one who is being butchered because she isn't a very good milk producer or can't get pregnant.

and dairy products for many years, and this part of our lives is well enough established that it resists efforts to do away with it.

Why We Built a New Dairy Barn

The dairy program provided the Community with one of the most troublesome controversies of recent years. In retrospect it is difficult to make people understand what the argument was about. "It is as if the Community hungers for something to argue about," said a friend of mine, "and if nothing comes conveniently to hand, some of you will make something up." If so, I wish nobody had made up the "Dairy Barn Controversy," as it is now called, because I was in the middle of it, and it was hard.

Years ago we planned to build a modern dairy barn, because the old tobacco barn we had been milking in was rotting, freezing cold, and had never been meant for dairy to begin with. We got as far as approving a design and a site for a new barn and putting in a foundation and slab. The chosen site was on the other side of Highway 697, which bisects our property, placed about eight hundred feet from the old barn. Then something happened to change the Community's priorities, and we decided it was time to build a residence instead. The dairy barn project got postponed, and year after year for about ten years some other building project would seem more important. The old barn where the cows were milked kept getting older and rottener. On cold winter mornings the milkers shivered and complained. In summer the flies had carnivals there. The plan for a heated, cleanable barn remained a dream.

Then in 1985 "Build dairy barn" became our top building priority, and we decided to go ahead and do it. By this time, of course, dairy management had changed. The man who was Manager at the time we decided to build wanted to sketch his own design, rather than accept the ten-year-old one, so we started the design process from scratch. The new plan was not substantially different from what previous Managers had wanted, but it was larger. In retrospect we know that we should have looked closely at those plans and asked some tough questions, but even an ambitious dairy barn is only a barn and doesn't cost a lot, so we went along with the Manager's plan with hardly a murmur. After several weeks of our usual process, which includes meetings and posted drawings and site planning, we decided to put the new barn in the same across-the-road spot we had previously chosen.

Conflict Over the Chosen Site

This was not an easy decision, because, in the meantime, the dairy managership had turned over several times. The current Manager was woman named Hildegard. Neither Hildegard nor the new milking crew liked the site. They had grown accustomed to a central location for their farm work, and they wanted another central location for the new barn. They argued that they didn't feel safe in a place so far from other people, and that the calves needed closer observation than they would get in the faraway location. The old barn was also well placed in relation to our major pastures. Predominant community opinion, however, was that animal agriculture needed to be removed from the center of the Community, so the new dairy crew was overruled. This did not seem a very big deal to me at the time. I expected them to accept the decision with grace, just as we all do from time to time. But I didn't reckon with Halcyon.

Halcyon was the most recent of our former Dairy Managers and a close friend of Hildegard's. He had been on an extended vacation, but when he returned, he heard the story of the site decision and sympathized with the dairy crew. How dare we Planners, who never went near a cow, make a decision that affected the essential working conditions of the milking crew? He fought the siting decision by a public petition to overrule the Planners. At first the Planners didn't take this very seriously. After all, if there hadn't been an obvious majority in the first place, the decision would have been different. Let Halcyon try. What we didn't predict was that Halcyon would go around buttonholing people at lunch time and bend their ears on the subject until they would agree to sign the petition. People who hadn't thought about the subject one way or another suddenly saw it his way, and the number of signatures grew.

The upshot was that the Planners backed down before the petition was completed and agreed to a compromise site choice, one on the near side of the highway, and only 400 feet from the main part of the Community. This brought peace—temporarily.

The Barn is Rejected by the Dairy Crew

Construction on this barn started in 1986, proceeded during 1987, stopped in 1988 because of a financial crisis, and resumed in 1989. The building was about eighty percent completed (a large concrete structure with an attached specialized milking parlor), when some new people joined the milking crew and decided to take up the issue afresh to try to get the site changed. They did not

157

like the placement of the barn, nor the fact that it was made of concrete. They predicted that the cows would be unwilling to enter the milking parlor via the broad concrete stairs (a standard feature of such barns) and they painted pitiful pictures of the cows being forced into the barn by electric cattle prods. This horrific vision of tortured cows was politically useful. People who knew nothing about cows were concerned.

The milking crew said they had no need for a modern barn, that people had been milking in chilly sheds for hundreds of years, and if one moved about briskly, one could stand the cold. Most of all they argued that we did not need a milking parlor for our small number of cows. At the time we were milking only three cows, and milking parlors are really intended for herds of fifty or more. It seemed to them ridiculous to spend so much money on what was and remains basically a home-sized, not commercial, dairy. Against the argument that the money had already been spent they countered merely that it shouldn't have been.

It became a feminist issue. They confidently declared that all the women of the crew had been against this plan from the start, and the only reason we were engaged in this project was that we had listened to men who had their heads full of visions of dairy grandeur. There was an O&I paper about the tendency of males to design high-tech facilities that were useless and expensive.

I didn't consider all their arguments specious. They had a lot of good points on their side, not least of which was their determination to quit the milking crew *en masse* if the program moved to the new site. They offered to stay forever in the old barn where the Community had milked for years. A little repair and a few sheds was all they needed, they said, to keep them happy. Some day, perhaps, we could build a newer wooden barn a few feet away from the old one, but they were in no hurry. The old barn had been improved a lot, and under Hildegard's able management they had raised the standard of cleanliness to the point where no one had any reason to complain of manure or flies.

Compromise Offered and Rejected

McCune, the beleaguered builder, offered to adapt the new structure to the needs of the current dairy crew, offered to scrap the use of the milking parlor if they hated it so much, and let them milk in the barn section itself, perhaps redoing some doors. (The doorways were concrete, but rather than waste the whole barn, he offered to tear the doorways out and redo them.) But he argued forcefully that a new barn was necessary. He pointed out the faults of the old structure, the reasons we had wanted to replace it all those years. He reminded us that the new design was merely a variation of the designs proposed by several Managers over the years, and that the current Manager and crew were the first ever to voice an objection to it.

We Planners listened to it all (several times) and discussed it among ourselves for hours. The Community at large was divided into three opinion sectors: those say-ing we had built a dairy barn and we should use it for what we had built it for; those saying we should put the structure to some other use and leave the milking crew in the old barn, ac-cording to their desires; and those who didn't care which way we decided, as long as we could get the argument over with.

McCune

The Planners Stick to the Plan

I was a Planner at the time we had to make this decision, and there are a couple of things I'd like to explain while I tell you that we went ahead and finished the barn, and are now us-ing the milking parlor for our handful of cows. The project cost $30,000, 8000 hours of work, and four years in elapsed time, but at least we are now happily using it.

The transition was not easy. Hildegard, a peaceful person who could not deal with conflict, resigned as soon as the issue became heated. Most of the crew also quit milking, and it would have been virtually impossible to effect the change if we had not had anyone to take their places.

However, one day when the Planners were puzzling over the problem, we got a note from a member named Shana, which said "I would be willing to manage the cows in the new dairy barn." That put a new face on the matter.

Shana Makes the Move Feasible

I remember the Community meeting we had about the barn question, when we announced that Shana had volunteered to man-age the dairy. There was a moment of stunned silence, and then

159

someone asked bluntly whether Shana was qualified for such a job. We so rarely ask for qualifications that I felt somewhat shocked at the question. I feared that Shana would be offended and show anger, making the situation worse, but that isn't Shana's way. She simply took the question at its face value and answered it.

"I have a degree in Agronomy," she began. "I majored in Field Crops with a minor in Animal Science, and I took courses in Pasture Ecology and Intercropping. I have not actually handled dairy cows before, but I have raised beef cows, dairy goats, sheep, and horses. I assume the same principles apply." There was another silence after this recital. It is very rare indeed that we have applicants for managerships with anything approaching this list of qualifications. Shana also told us that she had begun to seek opportunities to engage in Twin Oaks agriculture, since that is what she was trained for, and this seemed like a good time. "I would like to try the new barn," she said later. "I'd like to see if it works the way it was designed, using the milking parlor. If it doesn't, we could modify the barn later."

It was Shana who made the Planner decision possible. However, the basic reason we decided the way we did is that by the time we understood the faults of the new barn, we felt it was far too late to change our minds. The new barn, milking parlor and all, was already built. We did not think any of the proposed alternative uses for the structure made any sense. The Community as a whole wanted to protect our investment. Furthermore, dairy crews come and go regularly, and this was the first time over a ten-year period that we had heard any objections to a modern barn. Personally I think the crew was quite right about the barn's being more than we needed. If we had had the option of turning that project around and making something more modest, once we realized we were overbuilding for our needs, we would unquestionably have done so. But by the time we heard the objections, we were looking at many tons of specially engineered concrete. It might be overkill, but it is perfectly useful as a dairy facility.

Shana loves the new barn and says it is a wonderful place for a dairy operation. It is heatable, for one thing, and has hot and cold running water, big sinks, a refrigerator. There is plenty of storage space. It is all cleanable. The barn is sturdy and should last as long as the Community does. If we ever do decide we need a bigger operation, we're prepared for it, barnwise.

Twin Oaks tends to evaluate past controversies in terms of the number of members who left over them. That makes the Dairy Barn Controversy a big one, because we lost five members during and right after it. All five of them said they were leaving for some other reason, but all five had been active on the losing side of the debate, and the Community believes what it wants to believe.

Some Lessons in Politics and Architecture

This whole episode taught me a sharp lesson about politics and process. We paid a penalty for drawing out the barn construction over several years. At the time I had thought there was no particular hurry, because one can always wait for improvements. It wasn't like the building of a residence, when potential members might be turned away if the schedule is slowed. What I didn't predict was that turnover, both in the Community and in the dairy program, would bring the very desirability of the barn into question. With hindsight I can see that the change of focus was almost inevitable, given a four-year building schedule.

In the course of four years there is time for cautious new members to become confident old members. There is also time for lots of people to join. The probabilities are high that some of the newer people will become critical of plans made before their time. Circumstances may well have changed. For example, keeping the barnyard flies far away from the dining hall seemed a solid enough contributing reason for a siting decision, but by the time the barn was built, Hildegard had done away with the fly problem. We couldn't have predicted that.

Even if circumstances don't change, new people have a need to make their presence felt in decision-making, and it is easy for them to dismiss as irrelevant plans made before they got here. I would almost say that some of them feel a need to empower themselves by tearing down something they don't care for and replacing it with something they like. Certainly this was true for me. I spent the first two years after my return trying to make changes in the Community to match my agenda. In smaller ways I am still at it, but I remember the urge being much stronger when I was fresh from the Outside.

Another factor is that people remember things selectively. I remember clearly that nobody ever approached the Planners complaining about the design at any time before the barn was nearly finished. Other people, however, remember that they heard objections at very early stages and are certain the Planners must have heard them, too. I believe these people are truthful, and I know I am, so I have to conclude that some or all of us have our memories mixed up. It is highly predictable that five years will do that.

What I learned from the dairy barn controversy is that when we make a big change, particularly in the physical plant, we had better proceed full speed ahead and get it established, because if we don't, somebody will come along halfway down the road and want to turn it around or abandon it. One of the reasons the Planners ultimately decided to go ahead and move the dairy into the new barn was that we wanted to discourage people from attempting changes in the last stages of a project. We felt that there has to be a cutoff somewhere, after which a decision is firm. Otherwise its opponents will just keep on fighting against it until the Community begins to see them as an abused minority with right on their side, and all the careful process time of the original decision will be wasted. The more time elapses between the beginning and end of such a project, the more likely it is to become a disturbing controversy.

The other thing I learned is that Twin Oaks probably should not build extremely specialized buildings. It should build in a way that allows for changes in the use of the structure as the Community's priorities change over the years. There is nothing we can do with the milking parlor except milk cows in it. As I now see things, this piece of construction assumes too much. In the course of planning for future buildings, I think those of us who went through the dairy barn controversy will be considering alternative or backup uses for everything we build.

Old Dairy Barn

New Dairy Barn

SO LONG, RHEA (1983-93) AND THANKS FOR ALL THE MILK.

Chapter 19

Turnover

The good news is that there are now forty-two members who have lived at Twin Oaks for five years or more. Less cheerful is the fact that we haven't beaten the turnover problem yet. In case that word isn't part of your normal vocabulary, I should explain that in community "turnover" means members leaving. It also refers to new members coming in to take their places (numerically speaking), but that part of it isn't a big problem.

We don't know exactly how a turnover rate is supposed to be calculated, but until recently we called ours "twenty-five percent." By this we meant that about a quarter of our population leaves every year, and a similar number of new people join. That isn't as chaotic as it sounds, because about half of the comers and goers are the same people. That is, there are about ten people a year who join the Community and then leave it within a few months.

Why People Leave

Obviously, turnover means loss of knowledge and skill and a general feeling of instability that some people are sensitive to. But the biggest problem with turnover is the loss of personal friends. We have seen cases of people deciding to leave the Community, not because they expect a better life Outside, but simply because they are lonely when their close friends leave. "I am leaving the Community because it has too much turnover" has an ironic ring to it, but it is sometimes true.

It isn't easy to predict what a person will do after leaving Twin Oaks. We can't tell a lot from their leaving papers, that's for sure. Sometimes people who have complained about our not being simple and rustic enough end up moving to an apartment in the city. People who have urged the Community to have a lower material standard of living have frequently gone on to enroll in a university. People who say their main desire is to do more traveling go and get a job that gives only two weeks vacation per year.

Then members write on the O&I Board, "Why doesn't this Community do something about its turnover instead of...." (fill in the blank with anything the writer doesn't care for.) The answer is that the Community has been trying to reduce turnover for twenty-five years. To do that, we first try to find out why people leave. The answer is that people leave for a hundred different reasons.

Some leave to care for aging parents, some to escape the presence of a former lover, some to find a more spiritual atmosphere. I remember one who had had the flu all winter and figured her home town in Texas was a healthier place. Being turned down for a Managership or a room in a particular Small Living Group can be a trigger for leaving, if the person is on the verge anyway. A few have found the labor quota more than they want to do. Some just feel they don't fit in.

As a Community we look at all these reasons, and then try to fix whichever is within our reach at the time.

The Planners Try to Take Action

In 1985 the Planners decided to tackle the problem once again. They put out a survey asking members what features of their Community life would need to change in order to tempt them to remain Community members for an additional five years. The survey responses consisted mostly of protestations of commitment, along the lines of "Don't change a thing. I love it just the way it is." (Most of those people are gone now, of course.) But a few people got specific. Two of them said they wanted their residences to be free of visitors and other strangers. This didn't really seem fundamental, but at least it was specific, and it gave additional impetus to a suggestion that was coming from Keenan at the time, that we build a visitor cottage and move our most transient population out of the member residences and into their own quarters. So we did that. Did the turnover rate drop? No, not

166

enough to notice, but the project got one of the problems out of the way, and one of the people who had made the request did stay another several years before leaving for an unrelated reason.

The biggest complaint that surfaced from this survey was the lack of sufficient personal spending money. Several Boards of Planners in a row gave this matter a lot of attention. One Board created a bonus; another raised allowances; a third relaxed one of the restrictive rules against earning; a fourth created a way to get certain kinds of travel costs covered by doing extra work. Did this lower turnover?

Turnover Declines

Something did, because our turnover rate among long-term members has recently declined sharply. Whether it was the Planners' efforts that really paid off or whether some entirely unrelated factor made the difference we really can't tell. But it makes sense that if the Planners each year take steps to please the people, within the limits of our income, there ought to be progress.

Oddly enough, it turns out that there are also a few difficult and unsettling aspects of the decrease in turnover, particularly among long-term members. The first one is that we are beginning to have to face some of the social problems that used to solve themselves simply by someone's departure.

Suppose, let us say, that we have a child who is hard for us to handle. We now have to look at that problem and ask ourselves what we will do if that child's behavior has not changed before adolescence. A few years ago we could have assumed that we would never get that far.

In addition to the rising material standard, there are some other possible explanations for the recent downturn in turnover. For one, the average age of members is up. People in their forties do not move on as lightly as people in their twenties. For another, the outside economy is not doing very well. Jobs are hard to get, and desirable, interesting, socially worthwhile jobs even more so. I still think the fact that life gets better at Twin Oaks year by year is having an effect. There are many things about living here that would be hard to match on the Outside.

People Who "Outgrow" Twin Oaks

Such departures as we still experience are for reasons slightly different from the ones people used to give in the 1970s. There is a good deal less of the "I want to travel around and find myself" sort of motivation. These days a more likely reason is "I need to get started on a career path before I get too old." We have heard this regretful statement several times in the past ten years. What it says is that, though the Community is good in many ways, some members cannot take it seriously as a permanent home.

Well, why not? Some of us take it very seriously indeed. I do; McCune does; probably several others. What are they looking at, these people who leave us affectionately but with their faces turned to the Outside?

It is not a matter of impermanence. None of Twin Oaks' good friends and ex-members have said that they doubt the sheer physical continuance of Twin Oaks. On the contrary, what they seem to have concluded is that Twin Oaks will continue, more or less unchanged, though they themselves have changed and no longer fit in. In the years before they decide to leave, such members try to help steer Twin Oaks in a direction that would make their permanent membership more likely, but Twin Oaks is very hard to steer. The constant influx of new members who like the Community as it is, working together with the most conservative of the old hippies, hinders movements for change.

Josie

I see I need to give examples. Take Josie. When she first began her medical training, she intended to remain a Twin Oaker and practice medicine in local Louisa for no compensation other than labor credits. If any doctor could do this, Josie would have been an ideal candidate, because she had spent most of her life at Twin Oaks, knew it well, and loved it deeply. But in the course of her training she seriously needed a car in order to commute to Richmond to school. The Community was not at all prepared to let her use any of our cars (unprecedented privilege at that time), and so for five years she carpooled with a neighbor. Later in her studies her schedule made carpooling impossible, and Twin Oaks allowed her to borrow money from a bank against her presumed future income and buy a cheap used car, provided she drove it nowhere except to the hospital and back, and provided that the car would be made available to the Community on evenings and weekends. This arrangement was arrived at through long and difficult decision-making process, in which Josie came to feel personally the rigid and insensitive aspects of Community, to feel hurt by the envy, the distrust, the need to regulate her life by the same rules as people with radically different needs, all in the name of egalitarianism.

168

Josie got the transportation she needed, but was humiliated and angered by the process. By the time she left to do her Residency, she had developed a longing for a car that she could get into and drive anywhere without going through process or hearing criticism. Once she had the medical degree and the experience of financial independence, Josie was reluctant to give them up, though she missed Twin Oaks and longed for it in a dozen ways. Having some money, having the freedom to spend it as she saw fit, making small choices like brands of shampoo, all these were weighed as she made her decision. On the other side was Twin Oaks and all its love, its interest, its fun, its essential goodness.

These days Josie is trying to keep what she can of both worlds. She has settled five miles from Twin Oaks, practices in Louisa, and visits us regularly.

Joanie

Or take Joanie. When she left, Joanie scorned writing the usual "I love Twin Oaks but it's time for me to move on" leaving paper. Instead she posted on the O&I a clear statement that she was leaving because she was tired of waiting for a few ordinary amenities. After seven years of membership she felt entitled to a bigger room, and a sitting room where her child could play freely, where she wouldn't have to make sure to pick up every toy every day to avoid offending somebody. In addition, she was past tolerating any more "reinventing the wheel," by which she meant having to reevaluate the same decisions every few years and struggle continually to make points that had already been made, as new members came into power and wanted to make their own mark on the Community. What Joanie had longed for and striven for futilely in the last few years before her departure was for the Community to move on and grow up in the same way that she was moving on and growing up, to grow past ideology and get serious about providing a permanent home for members who wouldn't be young and idealistic forever.

Christopher, Joyce, and Rico

Christopher and Joyce were not far from this same position. Joyce wanted a house of her own, space that she could decorate as she pleased, where things would stay where she put them and not get dirty any faster than a small family would dirty them. Christopher was disillusioned with Community economics. He saw that we were not taking a road that would lead to prosperity. Instead, we were prioritizing other values, like leisure, personal scheduling freedom, frequent job changes, and dodging professional commitment. Twin Oaks gave him no way of making his personal effort pay off for him and his family. Anything he did to make Twin Oaks more prosperous would simply make it easier for other people to have more leisure and less responsibility.

Rico came to the same conclusion. In his case he used a theoretical route and decided he did not believe in the collective ideal after all and that free enterprise was probably, faults and all, a more reliable system. He went out and joined it.

Most of these people were of the party that the younger and newer members were calling "middle class." Those who despised the middle class were not entirely sorry for their departure, even if they liked them as people.

Twin Oaks Unlikely to Change Swiftly

If Twin Oaks had a looser economic system, if we made more serious compromises with our standards of equality, if we permitted people to earn money of their own for something more permanent than travel, we could quite possibly retain members like these. But movement in this direction has been at best very slow, and I think it will continue to be so. Here's why:

I think of it in terms of a biological metaphor. Species survive if they adapt to an environment well enough to reproduce themselves. The Twin Oaks "species" is that group that likes Twin Oaks the way it is, with fully-shared income, controlled spending, flexible work schedules, and so forth. This environment at the beginning selected for a few people who liked it. Over time, new people were attracted both by the environment and by the people who had created it. Each new wave of members (metaphorically a "generation") makes the deeply rooted rules and norms of the Community more likely to survive. However, there are people who like it at the beginning of their membership but then change (mutate?) somewhere along the line. These people may survive and "reproduce," but most mutations fail. Thus, our little society changes, but not quickly.

Like evolution elsewhere, this process doesn't happen very fast, because there are forces working against it. Once again, the number of new members has a noticeable effect. New people come to the Community, full of their own enlightenment, ambitious to see Twin Oaks reflect their ideals, and ready to commit their energies to this end. They try to make changes, and they meet resistance. Old members object to their presumption, maybe, or are simply not impressed and keep on doing things in the old ways. Some newcomers become quickly discouraged and move on to plant their vigorous enthusiasms in less stony soil. Others make some compromises and settle in. They may compromise, but they have a kind of "recessive gene" that waits to be matched up with someone in a future "generation" who may agree with them.

Members who wish for more financial autonomy cannot usually wait long enough for Twin Oaks to evolve in their direction.

Twin Oaks is certainly more prosperous than it was ten years ago, so the materialists among us have had some effect. I'd even predict that the current trend toward a simpler life will not be able to stop the natural human desire to improve things, and ten years from now will see us with a higher material standard of living than we have now. The improvement won't be fast enough for some, will feel too fast for others, and will probably leave us with the same mixture of members, old and new, patient and impatient, permanent and transient.

One can speculate all kinds of different futures on the basis of current trends. My speculation, for what it's worth, is that Twin Oaks will grow somewhat larger, gradually liberalize its rules in small ways, hold on to its members a little longer, but remain for the next ten years at least, basically unchanged.

Oops! Things are changing already

The above paragraphs were written in December of 1991. Right after that I interrupted the writing of the book for the task of calculating the Community's taxes. Now it's April 16, 1992. Taxes are done, and I'm free to return to the writing. But in the meantime things have changed! These last three months have been, from a membership and turnover perspective, the most astonishing in our history. We predicted an average membership of seventy-four members for this current year; we have eighty-five, with another thirty people in the pipeline. I thought we would grow a little, slowly. We have grown a lot, fast! Furthermore, we're not alone. Other communities of various kinds also report growth.

This sudden burst of growth has been very exciting, to say the least. For weeks we have talked of little else. As usual, we do not agree on what to do about it. Suggestions run along three general lines: (1) We could take in all the people who want to join and endure the resultant crowding and chaos as an acceptable tradeoff until we have time to build appropriate buildings. (2) We could shut our doors, maintain our comfortable elbow room, and put applicants on a waiting list. (3) We could grow slightly bigger and then form a splinter community from our own "excess" and pioneers from our visitor groups.

My guess is that, in Twin Oaks fashion, we will do a little of all of these—take in a few more people than all of us are comfortable with, maintain a waiting list, and take some steps toward helping another group to get started.

Why is This Happening?

In between urging our arguments about next steps, we also stop and ask each other "Where is this coming from?" After all, Twin Oaks has been here for twenty-five years, and for most of that time we have been both viable and attractive. It's true we've been improving all that time, but just the same, we doubt that our own virtues are the biggest root cause of this sudden interest in joining us. For explanation we look to the Outside.

The first thing we note is that there is a national recession. Employment is down by many thousands and due to get worse, as the military decreases its payroll. Corporations are getting, as they enjoy saying, "leaner and meaner." Is it possible that Twin Oaks is getting people who aren't lean and mean enough to get or hold a job?

The answer is no, at least not yet. Not a single one of our newer members admits to coming here for lack of employment. We have seen no interest from either blue-collar or white-collar people who have been laid off. That huge mainstream of society has not so much as glanced our way.

I ask some of our visitors to comment on the upsurge of interest in community. What attracted them to us at this time? The answers I get puzzle me, because they sound just exactly like what other visitors before them have been saying for the last 25 years. They speak of alienation, of commercialism, of the overwhelming influence of television, of crime in the cities, of ecological disasters, of a search for meaning, a desire to live close to nature, a need to explore their own potential as humans in touch with the planet, and so on. It's a litany of cliches, but they speak them with sincerity. "It's crazy out there," they say.

It's true there's a lot of craziness in the world, and it's true that Twin Oaks, for all its absurdities, is fundamentally sane. But how come people are only now coming to notice?

Some people point to the new *Directory of Intentional Communities*. This reference book guide to alternative lifestyles, which the Fellowship for Intentional Community published recently, is selling a great deal better than many of us expected it to. It is reasonably up-to-date, informative, and useful. But which came first? Did the *Directory* cause the interest, or was there a movement out there that explains the success of the *Directory*?

Trying to Predict the Course of this Growth Phenomenon

If there's a movement, and it's anything like the movement in the Sixties, then maybe it will last about as long as that one did, which for our purposes was about three or four years. It's obvious that Twin Oaks cannot stretch itself to take in three or four years' worth of enthusiastic newcomers. We couldn't possibly move fast enough. No stable, happy group could. We'll take some action, absorb a fistful of new people, try to help establish others in new or existing Communities, and put the rest on a waiting list. If they wait long enough, they'll get in. It's all we can do.

If our communal history is any guide, then we should expect another long, dry spell following the current surge of interest. If so, the current growth climate should put Twin Oaks in a good position to absorb at that future time the bruised but determined refugees from the communes that predictably will rise and unfortunately fall within this decade.

History, however, is rarely a reliable guide to the future. There are factors that make this period different from the Sixties. At that time, established communities willing to take in new people were very, very scarce, so people who wanted communal living had to create it for themselves. Now there are dozens, if not hundreds, of communities that made it through the last drought and are fairly stable and organized. We also have associations that new groups can join. I'm not sure what kinds of help we would be willing to give to forming groups, but at the very least we can serve as examples of how various theories have worked out over time. People can visit, examine, and then copy or not, according to their own inspiration.

I find myself stirred once again with the longing to escape Twin Oaks' deliberate and wearying process and to step out independently to start yet another community along Twin Oaks lines. What I have done twice, could I not do again? I bang on my shield with my sword. "To me, future communitarians!" I shout, and they come running with eager expressions, ready for hardship and glory.

But I am laughing at myself before I can even get the fantasy in focus. No, I can't do it again. Twice was enough.

Chapter 20

Sex, Love, and Jealousy

I wrote these paragraphs in 1972 to describe the Community as I saw it in its fifth year:

> The biggest bulwark against jealousy is our heavy communal disapproval of it. This is why sexual freedom is easier in community than it is on the Outside. Here we stand behind it as a group. Nobody gets group reinforcement for feeling or expressing jealousy. A surprising amount of it is wiped out by that fact alone.

> What can't be accounted for by public pressure can be attributed to personal idealism. Strange as it may seem to our parents and to most of the world, the stand against personal possessiveness is a moral stand, and most of us here do not approve of our bad feelings when we have them. Just as a person with a Puritan conscience can often control erotic impulses by reference to religious beliefs, so a person with a communitarian conscience can control possessive impulses by remembering basic moral principles.

> Twin Oaks has taken a firm stand in favor of sexual freedom and nonpossessiveness, and that brings its problems with it. Problems notwithstanding, we did not have any real choice about taking this stand. Any group that settles on monogamy as a norm has to figure out

how to defend it. Without a heavy Puritan religious bias this is very difficult. Philosophy isn't the only problem with monogamy, either. Sexual rules are hard to enforce in any society, and more so among free-thinking communitarians. The closer people live together, the higher will be the opportunity for attraction. A commune has to take the choice between dealing with jealousy in an open way or dealing with complicated questions of sin, dalliance, adultery. I conjecture that a group norm of free choice in sexual matters is not only philosophically consistent but literally easier to manage than any compromises would be.

In any case we are rather pleased with our progress in this area. We are managing fairly well to live what we believe. Members do whatever seems right for them, and wrong choices do not shake the Community itself at all. A good many unconventional sexual arrangements have worked out perfectly smoothly and successfully here, probably because the individuals involved were prepared for them.

When I first completed my original manuscript of *A Walden Two Experiment* in 1972, I omitted all references to Twin Oaks' sexual norms and practices. I thought that our sex lives were our own business, and that the Community, as a community, could do its experimenting, such as it was, more intelligently without the public peeking into the bedrooms. But when the manuscript was accepted by William Morrow & Company, their editor told me gently, "Kat, you're going to have to say something about sex. We can't publish a book about a commune and not even mention the subject!" Of course I understood. The public mind at that time connected the idea of communal living with "free" (i.e., available, uncommitted) sex, and they were not likely to believe or accept a picture of a commune where, by implication, monogamy and celibacy were the norm. So with reluctance I wrote the chapter I've just quoted from, and with that inclusion we went to press.

Today, in 1992, I find I have even less to say than I did then. If I had my way entirely, I'd just say, "We don't do anything special. Our sex lives are pretty much like yours—private." But even without the guiding hand of an editor this time around, I know that it is foolish to talk about the Good Life without mentioning sex, and besides, *A Walden Two Experiment* opened up questions that need to be addressed.

Patterns of Personal Relationships

Very well, then, here's a brief description of this part of Community life in 1992. Legal marriage, lifelong monogamy, and celibacy are not dominant patterns of relationships at Twin Oaks, though we have some of all of those. Both serious love affairs and casual sex are treated as normal and usual. Homosexuality for both sexes is accepted without great question or much excitement. "Coming out" as gay is a matter of interest mostly to those directly concerned. Legal marriage is uncommon but still done occasionally, sometimes with great fun and fancy dress. All of the above are matters of personal choice.

The usual pattern is pairing up and breaking up, with their attendant euphoria and misery. A frequent reason for breaking up is the temptation of an attractive third party. Thus I describe and dismiss, in two sentences, the most important thing that happens in most people's lives, the events that take the most energy, cause the most membership turnover, most profoundly affect each individual's future.

It is not that there are no stories to tell. The grapevine can supply me with enough gossip to people a soap opera. But the stories are the stories of love affairs everywhere. The impact of community on these relationships is not always obvious, and it is always mixed up with the characters of the people involved.

Nevertheless, living here is different from living elsewhere. Community affects several aspects of love relationships. First of all, there's the matter of availability of partners.

The Search for a Partner

What are one's chances of finding a soul mate in a group of eighty-five adults? Since some of that number are people outside of one's preferred age range, and some of them have different sexual orientations, and some are happily coupled already, it would seem that chances aren't too good. But considering that we spend most of our time in this same small group and can get a sense of compatibility long before committing ourselves, the atmosphere for mating improves beyond the sheer statistical likelihood.

Furthermore, members frequently travel, or have friends who travel, or attend various conferences and festivals, all places for possibly meeting someone special. Add to that the fact that there are still some people who experiment with multiple relationships, and I'd say that Twin Oaks is a better environment for mating than most others.

Beyond the actual membership, there is a stream of visitors that flows through the Community all the time. The visitors are usually not reluctant to get to know the members, and many good relationships get their start during the visitor period.

Some members have found they can maintain better relationships if they choose their lovers from outside the Community. Unfortunately this arrangement entails traveling, which the average member can hardly afford. In addition, such couples often go through the strain of deciding whether they really would rather live together, and if so, which home to choose. For those who weather these two problems, however, long-distance relationships have proved quite satisfactory.

Twin Oakers older than prime mating age are more likely to find some romance here than in many other places. The group is not prejudiced against mixed-age matings, regardless of which partner is older. (Oh sure, there is gossip, and even some criticism, but the gossip is seldom vicious, or the criticism harsh.) This doesn't mean that older people find mating as easy as young ones do, or are as likely to find life partners. But most people who want a sexual and/or loving relationship can find one if they aren't too fussy.

Add to this the preselection factor. People who join Twin Oaks probably have some basic values in common. The person you're digging potatoes or washing dishes with is much more likely to be stirred by environmental or feminist issues than by entrepreneurial ambitions or television. Not too many people sit around discussing the Rose Bowl or the Red Sox. A person can count on having lunch without having to hear what kind of car somebody is thinking of buying. Twin Oakers may have a hundred different interests, but here, more than Outside, we feel respect or curiosity about the interests of others, because these interests are in some ways like our own.

It isn't a good idea to join the Community just in hopes of finding a mate, however. Neediness repels, and pushiness is punished by emphatic rejection. To be successful in love at Twin Oaks requires some self-confidence and probably some patience.

Finding someone is only the first step. Living in community affects all aspects of a love relationship.

How Living in Community Helps Relationships

I asked some people the other day to list some positive aspects of love affairs in the community environment. They found the question unsettling at first, because they were primed to explain the difficulties instead, but with a little prodding they came up with the following ideas:

Twin Oaks itself is a romantic environment. When people have dates, they are likely to choose canoeing on the river, walking in the woods, or swimming in a secluded spot. A more serious date might take place out in the tipi or the retreat cabin, or possibly in the big double bathtub with its curtain drawn and candles lit.

Relationships here develop faster than they do in most places, because there is time for them. Our jobs do not necessarily interfere with this, since we tend to work short shifts and can often choose our own company, or even take some days off at will. A hot new romance therefore tends to be fully and immediately satisfied. This is wonderful while it lasts.

The opportunity to work with a loved one is as commonplace in community as it is rare elsewhere, and it can be a rewarding experience, but it has its own difficulties. Take the question of unequal skills. Suppose a skilled male carpenter and an inexperienced female apprentice carpenter become lovers in the process of building something together. The man naturally gives directions. In many cases the woman, though acknowledging the need for training, finds herself resenting something about the situation. Maybe it's his tone of voice, or the low level of tasks she gets assigned, or the lack of appropriately spaced compliments and encouragement, or the suspicion that he thinks she lacks the basic talent for the job. Whatever the reason, this common situation is potentially explosive. A man I know, placed in this position and feeling its threat to his relationship with the woman, once protested, "Look, I'm just barely learning how to teach. Give me a break!"

Physical Appearance

A wholesome aspect of relationships in community is that the impact of physical appearance is much reduced from what it was before we joined. I brought this up a few days ago with some friends while I was fishing for material for this chapter, and the response was skeptical. They pointed out that the standard here is subtler than on the Outside, but it is still there. The prettiest women are pursued more than plainer ones, here as elsewhere. Handsome men don't do too badly either. Just what constitutes attractiveness is only slightly different from the Outside standard. There are some differences, however. Nobody (except the teenagers) wears makeup or high heels. Both sexes may use jewelry or occasionally scent. Though striking and original clothing is not unusual, it cer-

179

tainly does not conform to the Outside idea of style. (Actually, I'm never sure about this. The other day I saw a member dressed in a classic sundress that I admired, and I asked her, "Do you know if the dress you are wearing is considered in style on the Outside?" She looked down at the dress, fingered its fabric speculatively, thought about it a minute, and finally replied, "Gee, I don't think so.")

We do not dress specifically to attract a mate, except perhaps on a special occasion. There is certainly no competition to look sexy. Few would want to be indiscriminately pursued, anyway. Being "popular" isn't really the point at Twin Oaks. Finding someone special is the point, and physical attraction may not have much to do with it. We don't have to worry about first impressions. After all, we see each other every day, in our grubbiest work clothes, faces smudged with grease or mud or ink, clothing stained in the processes of cooking or gardening or baby care. These working hours are often the times when attraction happens. What's the point of emphasizing looks? What we're searching for is a mutual spark in which appearance plays a minor role.

An undeniable plus for community love relationships is that, if there are children, their lives need not be much disrupted if their parents break up but both stay in community. The parents may be going through private hell, but the child's life remains in many ways much the same as it always was—"primary time" with each parent on separate evenings, playing or learning with the same peer group, probably living in the same quarters as before.

"One positive aspect," said a friend of mine, "if you want to call it that, is that we have a lot of opportunity for personal growth through dealing with our jealousy." There's no denying that one. Life is full of "growth opportunities" of this kind. A few determined people go ahead and do this growing and come out richer for the experience, capable of loving more than one person, or capable of sharing a love without resentment. We don't see a lot of this, but it does happen, and when it works, the Community tends to applaud (enviously, while skeptically watching for cracks in the relationships).

There is one kind of sexual liaison that is not common in community at all, and that is the secret affair. It is almost impossible to keep an interesting secret. It is not that people necessarily judge harshly, but simply that they are interested in each other's lives and like to talk about them. In addition, most of us honor truthfulness as a basic value. We lie badly and avoid it when possible. Add to that the general feeling that sex is natural and need not be hidden, and what you get is a little village where everybody knows everything.

Negative Aspects of Community for Love Affairs

In community there are ways of getting hurt that are different from what we met before joining. I don't think they're worse, but they're unexpected. Take this situation: Last night you slept with a man you think you may be falling in love with. The experience was lovely, and you go around all morning with a half smile on your face. You dreamily make hammocks and look forward to lunch, when you will naturally see him in the dining room. Lunch comes, and so does he, but does he smile significantly at you or come up and touch you in some way? He does not. He waves at you briefly as if nothing had happened last night at all, and he spends lunch with two other people, discussing laser printers. All the joy drains from your life. What went wrong?

From his point of view, nothing at all went wrong. He simply does not spend all his time thinking about love, and at the moment he is fascinated by laser printers. His romantic interest will revive, but right now in the dining room he is being made uncomfortable by the hurt look he perceives on your face, the eyes that follow him wherever he moves. He isn't stupid, so he recognizes that you want more attention from him than he wants to give. That makes him feel guilty.

Is this incompatibility? Probably not. It's just overexposure. Not many people on the Outside run into this problem in this form, because most people don't have the option of seeing each other several times a day. They have to earn a living in separate places, and this necessity prevents, or at least postpones, the overexposure problem.

In community this situation has to be faced in many relationships, and not merely those that include sex. The central meeting places of the Community (dining hall, hammock shop, offices) offer no place to hide from another member who seeks one's company. It is frequently necessary to express in sometimes painful words exactly what one wants or does not want from another person. This is one form of what we call "working it out," and sometimes requires the services of a third person acting as a facilitator. I am curious whether people on the Outside are trying to better their relationships by similar working out, and whether they use facilitators. I've been here so long I'm out of touch, but I suspect we do more of it here, simply because our lives interrelate so much.

Community Life Without Intimacy

One way to live in community without much emotional pain is to stay out of love. This good advice has been easier for me to follow since I passed my 60th birthday. There are some people over 60 here, however, who seek and enjoy love relationships when they come along, regardless of age, and I observe they have pretty much the same problems that the young people do.

There are, however, other things to live for, and community is rich in potential friendships, if one stops short of requiring physical intimacy. In Skinner's imaginary Walden Two, there was supposedly an atmosphere of "seduction not expected," which cleared a path for friendship between the sexes. This is one prediction of Skinner's that was right on the mark. I know people who go so far as to sleep together, limiting their physical contact to cuddling. In fact, I understand this is fairly common. Why not? Cuddling is comforting. Falling asleep and waking up with a friend sounds like a good idea. It doesn't make any difference what sex the other person is. It's just a privilege of certain close friendships.

If you're of my generation, you probably raise your eyebrows at this and say that this asks a lot of human nature, puts too much temptation in the way, etc. So it may, but if giving in to this temptation is what both people decide they want, so what?

Well, there may be a good deal of "working it out" to do the next day, that's so what.

In this and other ways, I notice the changes in sexual mores over the past 40 years. One thing for sure hasn't changed, though. People still like to talk about sex. Sexual innuendo is as funny in 1992 as it was in 1952. What's new is getting together in formal groups explicitly to "talk about relationships." There are conferences at which this topic is the subject of workshops. I never went to one, but I understand people sit around and talk about how love relationships ought ideally to proceed. Indeed, there are whole books on the subject. The latest enthusiasm as I write is a book that recommends forgetting about relationships and spending your life doing things that are less frustrating. Everybody is reading it, but I don't expect the idea to catch on, really. Falling in love is too much fun.

Breaking up isn't any fun at all. Everybody over the age of ten knows that losing someone you love is awful. Most people over the age of thirty know that it is virtually inevitable. But they still take the risk. If they didn't, the human race would have come to an end some time ago.

Forces that Discourage Long-term Monogamy

At Twin Oaks, the chances in favor of a lifetime commitment to a single partner are not very good. I have known quite a few cases in which a couple, having found each other at Twin Oaks, quickly leave the Community and go live somewhere else together. Some of them have said bluntly that they are doing so in order to protect their commitment to each other. They fear that if they stay in Community, their relationship may not be strong enough to survive. This interests me because it is a rare but clear case of people deliberately choosing to be less free, because there is something they want more than they want freedom.

The first and most obvious enemy of mutual commitment is what we call the "candy store" phenomenon. A couple moves to Twin Oaks, and one or both of them see themselves surrounded by people who appear to be both interesting and interested. Who is going to walk out of the store without spending a penny? The truth may be that this availability is more evident than real, but the urge to find out is very strong.

In addition to the temptations of alternative (or additional) partners, the couple find themselves without cultural support for a monogamous life. Few couples, it seems, are committed to struggling together through the hard places and sticking to each other. People who bounce from one relationship to another every year or so meet little disapproval. We aren't a society that gives much respect or support to marriage or marriage-like arrangements. Here, as in other aspects of our lives, the emphasis is on doing what you really want to do, when you want to do it. If two people happen to want the same thing at the same time, that's happiness. When one of them wants something else, that's life.

In recent years yet another influence has made long-term mates feel even less supported than before. This is feminist theory and rhetoric. A woman is encouraged to feel complete in herself and not dependent upon a man. She is urged not to arrange her life to suit her partner's, nor subordinate her other interests to the success of her relationship. Regardless of the rights or wrongs of these attitudes, a woman living at Twin Oaks, where these ideas are strong and frequently repeated, will think about them, and they will affect her commitment to her husband or lover.

Besides all this, there is an atmosphere here (not an overt statement but just a feeling) that everybody is fair game. This leaves everyone who is in an unbalanced relationship feeling threatened a lot of the time. For a person who feels (theory notwithstanding) a need for or dependence on a partner, there is no safety. Even marriage is no protection.

Breaking up in Community

Here, as everywhere, perhaps more than most places, couples break up. It is at this point that living in community shows a serious disadvantage. We call it the "In Your Face" phenomenon.

When a couple breaks up, the usual reason is that one of the pair finds some new attraction and pursues it. Chances are good that the left-out person feels rejected, regardless of the "facts" of the matter. It may be that the rejected one deserves no sympathy, having broken a number of hearts on other occasions. It may very well be that the breakup was fully mutual or even initiated by the person now feeling hurt. It doesn't seem to matter what the background was. The fact is that if one partner moves smoothly and excitedly into a new affair, the other partner gets hurt, and the hurt is five times worse than it would otherwise be, because the new affection is displayed in public. There they are, the old love and his or her new flame, holding hands, sitting snugly together on the couch, furtively nuzzling, looking into each other's eyes, signing up for work shifts together, going on trips together. There is no being rational about a thing like this. It simply can't be borne.

No, we didn't conquer jealousy in 1970, or 1975 or 1985 either, and 1995 isn't going to be any different, as far as I can see. All efforts along those lines were failures. What we once took for progress turns out to apply only to certain rare personalities that do well in multiple relationships. We have a few groupings of this kind from time to time that work very well, but it is neither the norm nor is it any particular credit to the Community. Some people can do it, and some people just can't.

We sometimes lose members because of the "In Your Face" phenomenon. People may leave because they find they cannot stand watching their old romances played out before them with an understudy taking their place in the lead role. Even if the new couple is courteous enough to avoid public affection, just being in the same environment as a loved one (or a once-loved one) causes some people more pain than they are willing to endure, and they occasionally solve the problem for themselves by packing up and living somewhere else. This is not usual, however. In nine out of ten painful breakups, both parties stay in Community and live through the aftermath. For most, Community continues to be a better way of life than their other choices, and they stick it out. To some degree, the In Your Face phenomenon is countered by the ready access to friends and support groups.

Is Sex a Community Problem?

Other communities avoid the pains of jealousy and breakups by one or more of the obvious solutions: marriage and fidelity; celibacy; group marriages; higher thoughts. None of these is going to work for Twin Oaks, because our very foundations depend on individual freedom of choice. It is a problem likely to remain on the unsolved list for a long time.

Unsolved list? Is romantic and sexual unhappiness then a Community problem that we are supposed to solve? Certainly I did not think so when we first founded Twin Oaks. I thought it was a private matter that each individual would have to handle.

The first time I met the notion that the Community should take care of individual sexual needs was very early in our history. One of the men in the Community made a public complaint that he wasn't getting any sex, and suggested that communal theory ought to include sharing of that commodity. In other words, the women of the Community ought to take turns sleeping with him to satisfy his "needs." He was shouted down. The women did not care to be thought of as commodities and didn't like him anyway.

The complaint reemerged in a different form a few years later when another man complained that the gender ratio was too far out of balance, even though there were roughly as many women as men at the time. He told me, "Yes, but some of the women are too old, and all the young ones who aren't ugly are taken." He wanted us to stop the influx of males until there were "enough" women, by which he meant until he personally found a mate.* The Community didn't change its policies for him, either.

Both of these unpleasant men are long gone, and I remember them mostly because of the theory they unconsciously championed, that sexual dissatisfaction can or should be handled institutionally. The "system" should take care of them.

Periodically, throughout the Community's history, there have been O&I papers complaining about this problem, but they are usually veiled in more acceptable language and purport to be on loftier topics, such as "relationship imbalances at Twin Oaks." Such papers generally get more attention and attract more comments than any other topic.

As to our official response, our Planners and Membership Team have never come right out and declared that sex and love relationships do not come under their purview or that solutions to such

---

*This same argument was used in reverse in the early days of East Wind. A certain part of the group wanted us to stop taking new men until we had "enough" feminists and lesbians.

problems are beyond their ambitions. They just admit that they don't know what to do.

For all "utopian" communities there is an unspoken assumption that all problems have solutions. From that it follows that we ought to try to find them. I don't know how many of us actually would admit to believing this, if we stopped to think about it, but we act as if we did. We are very self-critical as a group, and we take on the guilt for non-solutions even though we never consciously took on the responsibility. Therefore, personal misery is "our" problem. It may even be "our" fault.

If we aim at happiness and don't quite make it, if people join the Community with high hopes and leave later with restless discontent, this is the biggest reason. Life offers nothing better than love, and people will seek it in spite of previous failure and in defiance of common sense.

Twin Oaks drops all its communistic idealism in this matter. We compete with each other for mates, and few acknowledge any rules in the competition. People do what they can for themselves, and government keeps its hands off. In this, at least, we behave like the rest of the world.

OH. OH, DANA. OH, THAT'S **WONDERFUL**. THAT FEELS SO **GOOD**. MMMMMM. OH, **WOW!** OH, **YES!** MMM, **YES!** OH, DANA, KEEP **GOING!** OH, YES, MMMMMMMM! **OHHHHH! DANA! OHHH!** OH, **YES! DANA! OH,OH, WOW!** OH, **LINDA, I LOVE** YOU! OHHH... HUH?

LINDA?

LINDA **!?** YOU JUST CALLED OUT THE NAME **LINDA!!** I... I'M STUNNED! I CAN'T EVEN **BELIEVE IT!** ALL OUR TIME TOGETHER AND WHAT DOES IT COME TO? YOU CALL OUT A NAME OTHER THAN **MINE** WHILE WE'RE MAKING **LOVE!**

SOB...

YOU... YOU DON'T LIKE MY NEW NAME, DO YOU?

OH, DANA, I **SWEAR:** THE NAME LINDA DOESN'T MEAN **ANYTHING** TO ME ANYMORE! WILL YOU **EVER** FOR- GIVE ME?

188

Chapter 21

Living in a Diverse Community

The Ideology of Diversity

The diversity of Twin Oaks membership, in the sense of ideological differences, has been at times a major concern and at other times our chief pride. In the early seventies we worried a lot about these differences, acknowledged that they were serious, and made efforts to bring the whole group to basic agreement. This was a complete failure. We all had our own ideas, and we stuck to them.

Despairing of agreement, Twin Oaks began to see ideological diversity as a virtue. The idea is that, because we don't get whole group agreement on any one direction, and therefore have to compromise virtually every decision we make, we avoid all the dangers of going off any deep ends. It is true. The most extreme decisions this Community ever made came from the initial founders, who were either few enough to agree or else strong enough to ignore those who didn't. In present day Twin Oaks nobody could create such sweeping policies as our strict financial rules, the prohibition of television, or full communal authority in child raising.

Over the years this kind of diversity has effectively prevented our treading any straight and narrow path. One might even say it keeps us on a highway so broad that we're not sure where the pavement ends. Is this good? I'm assuming it's good, because

192

we're obviously a viable community. We have prospered where many other communities have crumbled. So hooray for diversity. (I guess. But I wish there were more people like me.)

Race and Class

In the last few years the Community has turned its attention to another kind of diversity. We have begun to ask ourselves whether we are sufficiently diverse from a sociological point of view. In plain words, why do we have so few Black people, so few blue-collar men, so few gay men? We certainly do not deliberately discriminate along such lines. Minority group members usually meet friendliness and welcome when they visit. You could even say they are courted for membership. Yet they seldom join, and when they do, they frequently leave after a short time.

Let me introduce Ira, who has a lot of opinions on this subject. Ira is a Black woman about 43 years old who has been a member of three different communities, of which Twin Oaks is the most recent. Ira fits in easily with white society, and I would have forgotten her color years ago if she didn't keep talking about it. The reason she talks about it is that she thinks racial diversity is desirable, and she thinks Twin Oaks shoots itself in the foot as it tries to aim for it.

One built-in contradiction, says Ira, is that there are cultural norms at Twin Oaks that the Black people who might otherwise be interested in us cannot tolerate. She names them: nudity; stained and sloppy clothes; dirty houses; small families.

If Ira is right about the kind of Blacks who show interest in community and about their typical biases and standards, then it is obvious that we are accidentally keeping them out. Occasional nudity and habitually sloppy clothing are thoroughly entrenched in Twin Oaks culture. We don't treasure bad houeskeeping, but we tolerate it. Certainly we try to keep a lid on the number of children we have, considering that we haven't yet proved very adept at raising them. Under these conditions Ira doesn't feel that she can realistically extend her Black friends an invitation to try for membership. Does that make our norms and our caution about children a class or race issue? Ira thinks it does.

The Black candidates this Community is eager to accept are the ones who are just like the rest of us, only with darker faces—more people like Ira, in fact. If they like nice clothes, they can shop for them in thrift stores and rummage for them in Commie*

"Commie" here is for "community." The abbreviation is a joking reference to our supposed communistic beginnings. We also once had a garden we referred to as the "communist plot."

Clothes. We don't ask them to wear anything torn or stained. But we don't expect criticism from them if we wear what we please. As to nudity, there isn't enough of it at Twin Oaks to worry about, and some people theorize that anybody who can't tolerate that little bit is going to be too uptight to live here anyway. One thing is sure: We are unlikely to get agreement to change our ways in order to be acceptable to new people. They are expected to change their standards instead.

Are Good Manners Middle Class?

There are other issues of class that not only Ira but many thoughtful people see as boundaries we Twin Oakers unconsciously draw around ourselves and keep certain other people outside of. These are matters of behavior.

Twin Oaks is known in the community movement as a "middle-class commune." In some ways this is a fair description. Obviously the epithet doesn't refer to our income or the way we dress. In spite of the minor pockets of posh among our buildings and equipment, we qualify as "poor" by national standards, and even in the relatively poor town of Louisa we are thought of as people who might want to use old clothing or furniture when it is no longer good enough for local residents. The people who call us "middle class" usually mean something else. They are talking about behavior.

In spite of our diversity of opinion, we are surprisingly consistent in our way of talking to each other. We are considered "quiet." It is said of us that we don't shout, don't confront each other directly with hard words, and that if we have anything unpleasant to say to anyone else, we write a note. I can't deny any of this. I'll go further to say that even when we write notes to each other, most of us couch them in tactful language.

Now introduce into this environment a person who has grown up in a family where everybody shouts—probably has to shout in order to get heard—or where calling other people names is standard practice, and a daily exchange of half-humorous insults the norm. Call this lower-class or whatever you want to call it, it doesn't fit into Twin Oaks. We try to avoid belligerence, sarcasm, insults, aggressive stances, and any verbal behavior that might make another person feel afraid or abused. When anyone comes in from the Outside who does any of these things, we notice immediately, and if there is any question of applying for membership, warning flags go out all over the Community via the swift lines of gossip. Such a person's chances of being accepted by this Community border on zero.

Is this classism? Ira says it is, and she isn't alone. A substantial and growing contingent within the Community these days is saying, "Give them a chance. They weren't raised the same way some of us were." Giving a verbally aggressive visitor a chance means telling that person what the behaviors are that bother people, explaining Community norms, and suggesting changes in the way he or she talks. Since we don't have any central mechanism for doing this, what usually happens is that about 5 different people will approach the person and give essentially the same message, none of them knowing that it has already been delivered.

I imagine myself in this person's place, and I shudder. Would I be able to accept all that feedback and still want to join Twin Oaks? Only, perhaps, if I were desperate. Nevertheless, some people have in fact swallowed the criticism, figured out how to talk like a Twin Oaker, and been ultimately accepted for membership. Of such a person we say "He (or she) takes feedback well, and that's a good sign."

All this is clearly a filter that selects against a whole lot of people who were brought up differently and don't see why they should change. Calling it classism doesn't help anything. Most of us like our norms of courtesy. We have no intention of accepting a more aggressive standard. We expect members to conform.

This choice does not promote class diversity, and there are those who stoutly insist that Twin Oaks has no right to call itself a diverse community while expecting all applicants to conform to a standard that is easy only for those who were brought up that way. This fence we have built around ourselves is not unclimbable, but it is a fence, and those of us who are inside it tend to grow more and more alike in our speech.

The Refugee Family

A few years ago Twin Oaks got a practical demonstration of worrisome cultural diversity when we decided to host a Salvadoran family of political refugees. We took in a young couple with a baby, explained our systems to them in our inadequate Spanish, provided them with most of the privileges of membership, and tried to help them legalize their status in a friendly country. (We finally saw them settled in Canada, so the effort was a success, as far as that goes.) While they were with us, we got word that they were in the habit of getting into arguments and hitting each other. Embarrassed by having to teach and correct the morals of adults, we nevertheless felt compelled to tell them that we would not tolerate violence at Twin Oaks. They understood, but they didn't seem to be able to stop doing it.

Finally one day the husband announced that he was leaving and not taking his wife with him. He was furious with her and intended to punish her by stranding her at Twin Oaks. He said "You don't want me to hit her. If I don't hit her, I can't live with her. You don't know what she is like. Where I come from we hit each other from the time we are little children. Life is a series of blows. Everybody does it. I respect Twin Oaks, and I certainly appreciate everything you have done for us, but I cannot stay here where you won't let me hit my wife! I couldn't have any self respect if I can't control my own woman."

What could we say? Were we going to get across a whole lesson in fundamental feminism and nonviolence to this couple who had no interest in it? The wife did not fear his blows, and probably gave about as good as she got. All the time we were listening to the husband's explanation, she was wailing and begging him not to leave her.

What we did say was that we could not permit the violence, but we would take care of the woman and child and hope for his return. As I said, there was a happy ending, but somehow we didn't volunteer to host another refugee family after that.

Maintaining a Standard

Some thoughtful and experienced members believe that the concept of diversity ought not to be stretched to include bad manners, regardless of its class origin. What they mean by desirable diversity is a colorful collage of different races and sexual orientations, different music and art, a variety of interests and talents and even opinions, all under the general umbrella of clearly understood and accepted norms of social behavior. They—I should say "we," because I'm in this camp—envision Twin Oaks teaching its standards to any who are willing to learn them, but never lowering the standard.

I use the words "lowering the standard" deliberately, knowing that some eyebrows will go up and the word "ethnocentric" will be spoken chidingly (in a nice way, of course). There isn't much question that courtesy, sensitivity, and compassion, as cultural norms, are superior to angry outbursts, swaggering, and sarcasm. I don't think you have to be ethnocentric to acknowledge that being kissed on the cheek is more fun that being slugged on the jaw. I'm not claiming moral superiority for the class (whichever one it was) that first modeled such decencies, but I prefer pleasant interactions to hostile ones, and so does everybody else. Obviously, this means learning not only some self control but also the basic vocabularies of kindness. If some people come to us who haven't had a chance to learn them yet, it is up to us to be patient. It is not up to us to broaden our culture enough to be polluted by unpleasantness.

Class as a Personal Issue

Personally, I don't know what "class" I am. I was born to a poor family in the Depression, went to ordinary public schools, and lucked into two years of college. I was never taught how to dress, give parties, write thank-you notes, or eat a lobster, but reading and writing took me a long way. I suppose that makes me almost lower class. True to my origins, I entered adulthood with a smart-alecky tongue, and I took delight in clever and hurtful put-downs. Those old habits and nasty joys will probably never quite go away, but my speech has been much modified in the intervening years, particularly the Twin Oaks years. It turns out that it isn't necessary to be cruel in order to be witty. Kindly humor takes a little more work, but it's an art worth developing. I'm not claiming any great skill in the field of tact, even now, but my speech is not often intentionally hurtful any more, and this is because I'm a Twin Oaker.

I think that people who choose to live together need to treat each other well to the best of their ability. We can't afford the social penalties that come from doing less. If that interferes with our diversity, so be it.

Chapter 22

On Being Different

New Age Culture at Twin Oaks

For all our obvious and troublesome differences, there is nevertheless an obvious New Age cultural ambience at Twin Oaks. For instance, we eat a lot of beans, rice, and tofu. We have twenty kinds of herb tea in the snack kitchen. We subscribe to ten or fifteen radical leftist magazines. We wear used clothing made of natural fibers, and we don't throw it out when it becomes stained. When we buy new shoes, they are likely to be Birkenstocks. We have built geodesic domes, enjoy a rustic cabin and a tipi, and one of these days will probably get around to making a yurt. We depend on wood heat and cut our own firewood. We go in for. underwater births, mud pits, nude swimming, sweat huts, and pagan rituals. We think seriously about animal rights. Some people won't even kill flies.

A closer look, however, reveals that these surface features, though they may well represent the dominant culture at Twin Oaks at this time, do not command the loyalty of all of its members, not by a long shot. More than half of us do several of the following: eat meat, drink coffee, read Newsweek, go to regular AMA physicians, wear clean neat clothing, ignore the tipi, take rituals with a grain of salt, and kill flies with a clear conscience.

Unbelievers Who Don't Fit In—Namely Me

People join Twin Oaks for a great variety of reasons, which may or may not have anything to do with its New Age atmosphere. People whose beliefs and practices lie outside these norms may not feel as comfortable as those who embrace the New Age enthusiastically. I am a clear, if atypical, example.

In my unique position as only survivor of the original founding group, I create a puzzle for some who feel intuitively that I don't really belong here. They don't feel free to say so to a founder, but I can sometimes feel their irritation at my differences.

For instance: I don't much like vegetables or tofu; I am repelled by radical journalism and dubious about much of the political action my friends participate in; I rather like polyester and wear it when I feel like it; rituals make me either giggle or squirm; I wish we had automatic heat, and I appreciate air conditioning when I can get it; I don't think being sexually androgynous is an improvement over clearcut male and female; I don't think meat-eating is a moral issue; I don't think all morality is relative or that it's always wrong to be judgmental; I seriously doubt the superiority of the Native American culture over the European. I could go on.

Several questions come to mind. One: If I represent the thinking of the founding group, how did Twin Oaks get so far from its original intent? Two: How can I stand to live in a place where the majority of members do things and believe in things so contrary to my own opinions? Three: How can the more typical members tolerate my presence in their midst?

How Did We Get So Far From Walden Two?

I'll take these questions one at a time. First of all, how did it happen? How did Twin Oaks get so far from its origins?

When I tried to start a Walden Two community, I didn't expect it to turn away from the scientific and rational and embrace popular movements. But we did not have a lot of choice in member selection. Who was available to join the fledgling community of 1969-1972? Hippies, that's who. I know one group that was very serious about Walden Two and tried to build a community without any hippies in it. It failed for lack of people. At Twin Oaks we took the people we could find, regardless of their ideas and opinions. Most of them had never heard of behaviorism, or if they had, they didn't like it. What we see at Twin Oaks today is the natural result of that essential early choice. Half the community is still somewhat attracted by the original vision, the other half by the New Age theory and practice that overlie it like an ill-fitting coat.

But note: When I say "half" I don't mean half the people. Things are much more mixed up than that. I mean that the members themselves are half-and-half. True, a few of us would have been perfectly content in Walden Two, and a few are one hundred percent persuaded by New Age doctrines. But most Twin Oakers combine within themselves opinions and practices from many sources. We are not mutually hostile camps of opinion here. We are a jumble of often contradictory ideas. Even I don't claim to be entirely consistent.

My Adjustment to the Community

Question Two: How can I stand to live here, where I am obviously a misfit?

This was a very serious question to me when I considered whether to return to Twin Oaks in 1982 after a nine year absence. Did I really have the emotional stamina to live my life among people who disapproved of many of my favorite indulgences (modern appliances, bright lights, overstuffed chairs, air conditioning, sugary desserts)? Would I be content gently fending off suggestions that I try aerobics and brewer's yeast? Could I stand overhearing earnest conversations on topics I privately considered nonsense?

I was still drawn to my original community vision, and I knew very well that the dominant culture here was not going to be to my taste. There would be pressure to conform. However, when I thought about it, I realized that this pressure to conform in community is not really greater than what I normally experienced on the Outside. (Why didn't I wear makeup and color my hair? Why didn't I own a TV or a car?) What I decided was that Twin Oaks had so much to offer me that I could accept what I didn't like. The interesting outweighed the tiresome by a decisive amount. I took Twin Oaks for better or for worse, and I did it with my eyes open.

At the same time I knew it made sense for me to be reasonably considerate and not spend my life throwing around unwanted challenges. What this means in practice is that I don't often openly contradict people when they are speaking from beliefs that I don't share. I tend to avoid philosophical conversation. What I discuss instead are plans and proposals and predicted consequences for our particular Community for various courses of action.

Besides, in the years I spent in Boston, I noticed that the people I knew there were seldom more rationally directed than community people. My differences with them were of a different sort, but I had even less in common with them than I do now with New Age communitarians.

Furthermore, taken as a group, community people show a high standard of personal ethics. I see them as being kinder than the average human. They try harder to be good to one another, and to people different from themselves. They try to give the benefit of the doubt to strangers. Even their political stands, which I frequently consider mistaken, err in the right direction. They are always on the side of compassion for the poor or the weak. Since I seem to have to choose between living with strangers who believe in profit and success, and strangers who believe in love and peace, I picked the nicer bunch.

The Community's Adjustment to Me

Question Three: How can they stand to have me around?

My daughter Josie once told me that Twin Oaks considers me its mascot. They remember that I was a founder, and so feel obliged to tolerate my eccentricities. In addition, some Twin Oakers classify my opinions as typical of my generation, and they require themselves to be respectful of them, in the same sense that they respect people from a foreign culture. They do not feel threatened by my opinions, because they are secure in the midst of people who share their cultural assumptions. That is, they know that on certain subjects nobody is going to listen to me anyway.

I'd rather be a mascot than a pest, and I am touched by the earnest effort to understand another generation. However, my acceptance at Twin Oaks goes beyond tolerance. As long as I stay off the most politically sensitive topics, I'm as likely to be listened to as the next person. If I say, "There are studies that show that white bread is just as nutritious as whole wheat," people ignore me, because I'm out of line with current theory. But if I say "This sabbatical proposal has the following flaws," I can affect the outcome of that legislation.

The Microwave Story

This seems to be the right chapter to talk about the "Great Microwave Controversy," as it later came to be called. This is a personal story, all mixed up with high principles and other motives. I'm a little hesitant to write it down, because I think, "This book will still be hanging around twenty years from now. Do I want people still reading about this embarrassing incident in twenty years?" But it is a perfect specimen tale of exactly the kind of issue this chapter is concerned with, and I think its central questions will be relevant for a long time, so here goes:

The time was early 1987. I had been back at Twin Oaks for five years and had served a Planner term. I hadn't been politically active for a while. My main interest at that time was trying to learn to play the piano. The most efficient way for me to practice was to combine it with eating lunch, so I got in the habit of taking my plate to the basement, where the piano was housed, and chewing on mouthfuls of lunch while I practiced. Unfortunately the trip to the basement cooled the food and made it unappetizing. I like my food hot.

About this time Josie, who was in medical school, moved in with a housemate who already had appliances, so she offered me her microwave oven. I was delighted. I plugged it in near the piano and used it to bring my macaroni up to temperature.

The Community did not own a microwave oven. Todd, the Kitchen manager, had considered buying one for general use and had done research on their safety. He collected all the articles he could find on the subject and posted them for general information. I read them. Microwave ovens had passed all tests, even under the nit-picking scrutiny of people who were trying to find fault with them. The evidence seemed to be that they were safe. Then Todd did a straw poll on the O&I Board, and several people (perhaps seven or eight) said they definitely did not want microwaves. They were not asked if they had read the material, and they were not asked to give reasons. Todd, not wanting to upset people, backed off.

The question that was asked later was, "Did I not know that introducing the microwave oven would cause an uproar?" The answer is that I thought it might, but no more so than the dishwasher or the glass tumblers or Tuesday Group. I had found that people quickly got used to new things once somebody dared to introduce them. Josie said to me, "Are you sure you want to go through with this?" and I answered, "Yes, I'm sure."

I wasn't sneaky about it. I posted a brief notice on the O&I Board, saying that I had acquired a microwave oven, and it was in the basement. Anybody could use it.

The response was immediate and ferocious. I remember in particular one comment that said, "Please remove it immediately!" Several people said that there hadn't been any process, and it was improper to make a major change in this way.

I responded by explaining that one doesn't need process to do something that isn't forbidden. There were no rules about microwaves. I went on at some length with my general theory that in free societies actions are considered acceptable until and unless they are outlawed, and that the opposite approach is tyranny.

The one person who addressed my argument said that there are some things that are so plainly wrong that a society doesn't have to make rules about them, and plugging in a microwave oven was obviously one of them. Others merely reiterated that they preferred not to live with microwaves. I asked if they had read the material provided by Todd. No, they hadn't, and they didn't need to. They already knew that microwaves were bad.

This "Don't bother me with facts, because I've already made up my mind" attitude infuriated me. What made it worse was that, as far as I could tell, it was shared by virtually the entire community. As soon as it became clear that the matter was controversial, nobody was willing to come out on my side of the argument. This made me feel entirely isolated.

Some people called me an anarchist, by which they meant one of those people who deliberately flout one of our laws in the hope of getting it changed. I have never respected this technique, and I was wounded by the accusation. I kept saying, "There are no rules against microwaves," and the reply was, "There are norms against them, and that's the same thing."

I thought these arguments not only mistaken but downright dangerous if taken as a principle. However, eventually the outpouring of indignation and the complete lack of support began to get to me. Even my closest friends and peers did not agree with me. I remember Velma saying, "It's just a matter of preference. You want microwaves and other people don't, and the Community can make any decision it wants. You're trying to make your desires into a principle, but that's just rationalizing." Velma was wrong about what I was feeling. By this time I cared very little about eating cold macaroni. As I saw it, I was battling for a free society.

I might not have backed down if I had not noticed something quite alarming. There were people who were experiencing distress because this act of anarchy (as they saw it) was coming from me, a founder, an old member, a person who had been looked to for certain kinds of leadership. They read my insistent arguments with dismay. I overheard remarks that told me they were seeing me as the latest in the series of old members who had exempted themselves from the rules that applied to other people and had moved beyond group control. They felt helpless against my determination. They felt that things were going wrong in a big, important way, and there was nothing they could do about it.

This would not do! Even though I was frustrated by people's unwillingness to look at either facts or arguments, such considerations became trivial by comparison with the effect the issue was having on the group's morale. Abruptly I realized that I had gone too far. I had in the past watched people feeling helpless at the hands of an old member turned arrogant, and I didn't relish the role. I felt a surge of "Oh no! Not me!" and realized that I had to find a way to undo the damage.

I once read a book called *Darkness at Noon* in which Stalinist police were trying to get a certain innocent person to confess to a crime. They kept after their prisoner and put a lot of pressure on him until he began to have a desire to be guilty, so that he could confess and get it over with. The only thing in his way was his personal integrity. He didn't want to lie. He got around the problem eventually by searching his soul to see if there was any way he could admit to a kind of guilt in principle. He hadn't literally done the thing he was accused of, but he allowed himself to be convinced that he could have done it, he had it in him to do it, if circumstances had been different. With this conclusion he obtained relief from the pressure, symbolically confessed, and was duly executed.

Without going so far as the execution, this is the kind of thing that happened to me at this point. I wanted to be accepted and liked by the group again. More important, I wanted them to feel confidently in control of their own Community and not dictated to by a strong-willed old-timer. They needed to win. Perhaps they even needed to triumph. I looked urgently for a way to convince myself that I was wrong enough about some aspect of the situation so that I could recant without hypocrisy and get both myself and the Community off the hook.

I couldn't very well say, "Oh, gee, I suddenly realize that microwaves are dangerous." But I could probably, with a little effort, take a different look at the process issue.

I found what I sought in an argument proffered by Scott and Gordon, which was that the commitment of a member is not merely to the rules of the Community but also to a general cooperation with other members. The application to my case was that I had already known that Twin Oaks did not want a microwave oven, and that I had violated the cooperative spirit by trying to take advantage of its lack of specific legislation. "Cooperation" would have meant going through the process of asking for group permission before using the oven. The spirit of cooperation had been presumably further violated by my reluctance to remove it once people had started kicking up a fuss.

On these grounds I found to my relief that I was guilty. I recanted. I said I had been uncooperative and was willing to hear feedback.

Before I could exercise much sincere humility, I needed to understand why it was that the more experienced thinkers of the Community had not supported my position. For this I went to Leslie, whom I respected as a Community peer and who I thought was closer to knowing how the Community felt than I was. I asked her to tell me why everybody was mad at me and why I could make no headway with my argument.

Her answer surprised me. She said that a lot of people didn't even follow my argument and didn't want to follow it. The very fact that I was trying to persuade them against their inclinations by using logic that went over their heads irritated them. If they were angry with me, it was because they felt I thought I was smarter than they were, and they didn't think my particular kind of smarts was the important kind.

This was bewildering, because it was obvious to me that I wouldn't have been using intellectual arguments in the first place if I didn't think the people I was writing to were able to understand them. Nevertheless, Leslie kept pounding on that same theme. People thought I was arrogant and disrespectful.

Right after the talk with Leslie I attended the public meeting where microwaves were to be discussed. The best way I could find to be unarrogant and respectful was to keep my mouth shut and listen to what other people said. It was truly awful, unquestionably the most unpleasant meeting I have ever attended. Some highlights: One person said that even if it could be proved scientifically that microwave ovens were harmless, the fact that some people feared them should be enough to keep them out of Twin Oaks. Another said he had read that if the U.S. Military devised a microwave rifle, it would literally scramble the brain of the person shot. A third opined that she didn't want to eat any food that had been microwaved, because she thought the microwaves got into the food and might radiate into her body. Another wanted to be sure that if there was a microwave oven anywhere in her building, she would be warned when it was used, so she could remove her children from the house.

I had such difficulty hearing these remarks without making caustic replies that I simply buried my face in my hands and did not look up. Let them think I did so out of shame and humiliation. Actually I did it so they could not read my thoughts through my facial expressions. I kept myself under control by saying to myself, over and over, "This is important. They need this. I asked for it. I have to take it. I mustn't talk back."

There were two people who said things I respected, and they helped to add reality to my contrition. One was Carrol, who said simply, "The process could have been gentler." The other was Paul, who said in a tired voice, "I am pro-microwave. It is energy-efficient and nutrient conserving. All I can say is I would guess Kat's unwise nonprocess has probably added at least two years to the time when we will have it here, and I wish she had used better sense." (Paul underestimated. Six years later the Community still doesn't have a microwave oven, and the main reason is that everyone who would otherwise favor it remembers the furor and is afraid to take the lead.)

The next day I unplugged the microwave oven and had someone (the one who had told us about the potential brain-scrambling rifle) triumphantly carry it out of the basement and store it away. I apologized on the O&I for causing so much trouble and said I would try to be more sensitive in the future.

Then everybody loved me. Some people even admired me. I felt the affection so strongly that I went around in a euphoric daze for weeks. Ultimately I got more pleasure out of the whole mess than out of a whole year's worth of hot lunches.

Post-Controversy Action About Microwaves

The Planners tried to set a policy about microwaves at this point and started off by circulating a survey. The results of the survey upset them. Two-thirds of the Community, given a secret ballot, voted to have the use of microwave ovens in one place or another for the use of people who wanted them. This result was so contrary to their expectations that the Planners simply shelved the issue. To this day there is still no decision. If I plugged a microwave oven into a basement socket today, I would be on as firm legal ground as I was in the first place. I am not likely to do so.

A couple of years later, when I was being interviewed for a second Planner term, one of the Planners asked me, "Do you intend to try to get microwave ovens into the Community while you are in office?" Startled, I replied, "Good Lord, no! Somebody else is going to have to do that one. If it even comes up, I'll stand aside from the decision." From time to time someone says to me, "A lot of people have changed their minds about microwaves. Maybe we could get it through now." Then they look at me expectantly, as if they think I might write a persuasive O&I paper. I say, "Good. Why don't you initiate the process?"

Looking back on this from a six-years-later perspective, I still think I was right in principle. Where I erred was in the importance I gave that particular symbol. Twin Oaks is not in danger of becoming a tyranny any time soon. Tolerance for differences is the norm, and the microwave issue was an aberration. Therefore the issue was never worth my digging in my heels in the first place.

Advice to Non-New-Age Potential Members

This last year I've been quietly approached by two different visitors and asked for advice on this confidential question: Should they join this community, though they do not have a counter-culture background and don't take for gospel a lot of New Age ideas? If they join us, will they make trouble for the Community by being different? Will they even be accepted? Can they carve out a peaceful and useful niche for themselves without giving up their intellectual independence?

My response has so far been to encourage them to try, even though I can predict there will be a certain amount of struggle and some feeling of loneliness. Twin Oaks is a good deal more accepting than it appears to be. All it really expects is conformity to decent behavior standards. We don't (officially) demand ideological adherence to much of anything, not even the Community's basic principles, much less the miscellaneous opinions that move the majority of members.

The very word "majority" is misleading. It may be true that there is a majority of opinion on any given topic, but it is not always the same majority. People who are very strong on feminism, for example, may or may not also feel strongly about animal rights. Serious concern for the environment does not always go together with enthusiasm for pagan rituals. A person who worries about America's role in the world does not necessarily care a great deal about health foods.

There are times when I get in a sour mood and feel surrounded by New-Age dogma, and at such times I imagine that everybody in the Community (except poor, beleaguered me) shares in this standard set of opinions. But this is nonsense. Probably no more than half a dozen people hold with the whole set of pet passions, from voluntary poverty to homeopathy. Probably half the people who live here feel, at one time or another, that they don't belong, because in their hearts they don't believe this or that (or despair of convincing others of important principles). But they do belong, and so do I. This is what Twin Oaks means when it says it is a diverse community. The cost of our diversity is that we argue a lot and don't find decision-making easy. The benefit is that we can and do accept a wide variety of personal opinion and conviction. The people who can relax and laugh in the midst of the struggle learn to identify with the Community as it is and make it their home.

Chapter 23

A Little Crime,
a Little Punishment

I'm not going to do any more television interviews. My agenda (telling people about community living) and the TV people's agenda (making news) are no longer compatible. In the Sixties, when communes were news, the TV hosts would lead me into saying things both truthful and interesting, but these days they need an angle. The last time I appeared on the tube was on some daytime show hosted by a woman named Sonia. Communes obviously bored her, and she needed an angle pretty badly. The one she decided on was, of all things, crime. A full half hour of national television, and we had to use it talking about people stealing other people's ice cream bars.

Crime in the Commune is a pretty narrow topic. It isn't exactly true that we never have any, but it sure isn't a major focus of our attention. Law infringement here generally means some form of cheating, like claiming labor credits for work never done, or padding an expense account on a business trip report. There isn't enough of this kind of thing to merit our appointing any kind of police officer or setting up a court. The Board of Planners, or perhaps the Process Team, stretches itself a little to handle what little crime does occur, and most of their function is to separate fact from rumor and calm the Community down.

212

The Cashbox

There is probably a noteworthy theft every four or five years. The first one was Simon, who took $400 because we ruined his car. (It was true. We did, but at the time we couldn't afford to fix it, and by Community rules it wasn't his anyway.) In later years the Community had to deal with Evan, who stole cash from the cash box. What made that case frustrating was that he was a close friend of one of our children. He wasn't the child's father, but he had taken an interest in her from birth and acted in many ways like a parent. Some wanted to expel Evan for theft, but we couldn't deprive the little girl of her surrogate father. What we did instead was to lock up the cash. That happened many years ago, and today we are accustomed to the locked cashbox. Before Evan we had never needed the lock.

The Inventory

Mel's jewelry theft was perhaps our most dramatic crime to date. Mel had been accepted for membership against the advice of some members who intuitively felt he was a sleazy person. Unfortunately the man was both unattractive and older than the average member at that time. Many members avoided his company because they didn't like him, but they questioned their own motives. They did not want to be guilty of ageism or even "looksism." Most Twin Oakers have not had enough experience to recognize a con-man, and in any case we tend to defend all manner of underdogs, so Mel became a member. He had been a jeweler, and he got Twin Oaks involved in the jewelry-making business. Before long we had an inventory in gold and silver and a few precious gems. One day the inventory, along with Mel, was gone. The Community drew various morals from this incident. For some it was "Trust your instincts. We knew there was something wrong with him." For others it was "Don't let one bad experience erode our basic trust." What I learned was "A community shouldn't go into any business that has a small, portable, expensive inventory."

It seems to me that we will lose some money to a thief every once in a while, as a natural consequence of our loose selection policies. Our losses have to date not been very serious. This is not because we are particularly careful, but because we normally attract honest people.

The Vehicles

Honest people may get very upset and do dishonest things. One day we couldn't find one of our cars, and discovered that a

213

new member had driven it away to Florida. He had been emotionally upset over a relationship breaking up, and he reverted to a pre-community solace—drinking. Once he got sufficiently drunk, his need to get away overcame his scruples. A few days later he was back, sober and contrite. But he didn't stay sober, and his drunken rages frightened some people. We were relieved when he decided to leave.

Town Trip Cash

Most troubling was the incident when the thief was a Black man. Twin Oaks is always yearning for a greater racial mixture, and D's application for membership was hailed with joy. He was a cheerful, pleasant person with enormous ability on the piano, a real asset at parties. True, he was 30 years old with no work history whatever and a previous residence in the "squats" of New York. But he got along well with people and was perfectly capable of working when motivated. He admitted to having at one time been strung out on cocaine, but he was obviously not addicted at the time we met him.

Unsurprisingly, D gravitated toward town trips as one of his jobs. A town-tripper is a member who drives into one of the nearby cities and does errands for the Community, mostly buying things. The Louisa tripper takes some shopping cash, does the errands, and brings home the change. When petty cash runs low, we have the tripper cash a check to replenish it. Obviously, the tripper has to account for the money spent, and for the first few weeks D did this with no difficulty.

There was one odd aspect of D's town-tripping behavior. Whenever he had to cash a large check for the cash box, he always came home right away and turned over the money to the office, saying, "I want to get this out of my hands." He then turned around and went back into town to finish the shopping. Most trippers could manage to work this check-cashing in with the rest of the errands, but D always made a special, extra, sixteen-mile round trip to do it. I thought this puzzling, but made allowances for individual idiosyncracies.

D spent more and more time doing Louisa trips. He had found friends among local Black musicians, who naturally welcomed him for his musical talent, and he was using the car to spend some time hanging out with them. We didn't think this was a problem, particularly since his friends started coming out to Twin Oaks to visit him sometimes too, which seemed natural and right.

214

Then there was a week when his trip accounting was very late. When he did turn it in, he couldn't account for all the money. He said, "I can't figure out what happened." We gave him the benefit of the doubt and wrote off the loss. The following month he didn't turn in any trip accounting for any of the four weeks. This came to light at the end of the month, and, with several hundred dollars missing, the Accounting Manager reluctantly had to fire him. Then the story came out. The money had gone for cocaine.

I ask myself why we didn't suspect sooner. There was the obvious, stereotypical connection—local Black friends, musicians, New York man with a history of drug addiction, then missing money. The conclusion, "D is using our money to buy drugs" wouldn't have been terribly hard to arrive at. But we resist stereotypes on principle. We give people the benefit of the doubt on principle. We give everybody a chance at a new, changed life as a matter of course. Add to this the fact that D was Black, and we wanted his membership to work, and what you end up with is functional blindness on the part of the Community.

We put D through a Community Feedback meeting and laid out certain conditions under which he could retain his membership, which he steadfastly claimed he wanted to do. He would have to work over quota in production areas in order to make up the missing money, and this would take a certain number of weeks to do. Meantime, he could take no vacation, and he couldn't be a town tripper any more, or handle cash. He would drop his local friends. D promised all this, and I think he meant it at the time. Promising is the easy part, however, and within a month he realized he couldn't do it. Much as he valued the Community, he couldn't make himself do even 47 hours a week of work or stay within $45 a month allowance. He had never learned self-discipline, and Twin Oaks certainly didn't know how to teach it.

So he went back to the squats, and we went back to an almost all-white population. This experience, and the borrowed car incident which immediately followed it, put the Community in a sour mood about accepting men from backgrounds of poverty. Some people bluntly said, "They don't work out here." Others said, "We don't handle street people very well." The only difference between those two interpretations is the placing of the blame. The stereotype set in in spite of ourselves.

Dealing with Theft

Although the Community has never written down a protocol for dealing with theft, we are gradually developing some customs.

The Board of Planners is informed right away, and they decide what to do. Perhaps they'll turn it over to the Process Team. One of the two groups writes an informative paper for the O&I board. This is to provide the Community with the facts. All attempts to hush up a theft have always failed, and in addition have stirred a great deal of anger. People feel they have a right to know when they've been stolen from. There is always somebody who will try to protect the thief, and will feel that withholding information or whitewashing the crime will be best for all concerned. These attempts have not been good for Community morale, as far as I can tell. Someone is bound to say "I want to know what is going on!" and the story will come out.

This is usually followed by a Feedback, and the people who attend it frequently set the tone for what is to follow. It may be couched in New Age terms, but the essence of what goes on at a mandatory Feedback is that the group expresses indignation at the theft and caring support for the person, the culprit promises not to do it again, and everybody goes away feeling mellow. I have known culprits who had previously fully intended to leave the Community come away from the Feedback with renewed determination to stay, because they were touched by the expressions of understanding and support they received. There are honest, hard-working communitarians who resent this phenomenon. They have sometimes accused the group of caring more for people who rip us off than for long-term members who have never done anything wrong. This is not true, of course, but it is true that wrongdoers get a good deal of attention for a while.

All this is much, much harder if the thief is a long-term member, or a child of the Community, or someone with a strong connection to another member. In such cases we have no customs, and I can't tell you what we do, except go through misery and ill-feeling and murky decision-making for a while. Such incidents are always clouded by the feeling, "This should not be happening!" It is easy to lose members at such times. To prevent this, the Process Team has tried calling people together in "circles" to share their feelings and clear the air. This seems to help some people. Almost any definite step we take is of some help. Mostly, time passes and the incidents sink into history.

Stealing Food

Then there is petty theft. I buy a package of ice cream bars from my allowance and put them in one of the freezers, clearly labeled with my name. A few days later, four of them are gone. I ate one. Three were stolen. Who took them? I have no idea. I will never find out. I'm just out three ice-cream bars. I go to the Planners and complain. I want my allowance reimbursed. Those things cost 45 cents apiece. The Planners say no. To reimburse for theft would encourage theft. I see the point, but I still feel frustrated and angry. Who are my fellow communitarians? Am I living with people I can't trust? They have as much allowance as I do. Why don't they buy their own ice cream?

I learn to buy my ice cream in half-gallon containers, which are usually safe, because it takes a long time to steal some, and presumably a potential thief fears being seen. But the people who buy private stashes of beer cannot do this. Beer stealing has happened often enough here that we have almost given up being indignant. Only the victim screams. The rest of us look at the announcement with glazed eyes and just want it not to be true. Some people even persuade themselves that it is not true. "You probably drank it yourself and then forgot," they say.

Most of us can be trusted. What is so frustrating is that at any given time there may be one or two people who cannot, and we never know who they are. One year, when Twin Oaks was serving mostly meatless meals, someone stole a private supply of fried chicken, and a few days later we found chicken bones hidden in a corner of the basement. The picture of some meat-desperate communitarian huddling in the dark, cold basement gnawing on stolen chicken made some people giggle. But it wasn't funny to the person who had bought it originally out of what was then a $10/month allowance.

Maybe the moral is that the Community should supply plenty of fried chicken, beer, and ice-cream bars. (I have never heard of a single case of any tofu being stolen.) Short of that, I don't see that we can do anything more than we already do, which is put up notes strenuously objecting to being stolen from.

Some of the petty stealing has been done by our children. We didn't find this out for years. Accusations were made, but they were usually met with indignant parental denials, and they died down. Only when our first batch of kids grew up and began to tell tales of their childhood did we have solid information. Out of naivete, we had thought that the beer would not interest them. On the contrary, confesses the Twin Oaks-raised child, the beer was the most interesting of all. These days we are more realistic, and parents no longer deny the possibility that their children may succumb to temptation from time to time. We are pretty sure that the children don't do all the petty stealing, however, so the problem remains unsolved, and probably unsolvable. It is one negative aspect of sharing refrigerators. The alternative, a refrigerator for every member, is too absurd to consider.

Political Corruption

What about so-called white-collar crime? I'm trying to remember if we have ever had to deal with embezzlement or bribery or fraud. The incident that comes to my memory goes back to 1969. The story, when I first heard it, made me frown with vexation. The recollection, considered as an example of community crime, makes me smile.

Twin Oaks had maybe sixteen members at the time. One was a man named Blues, who was Labor Manager. This was in the days when we used to assign most of our dishwashing chores to visitors. One evening Blues was hanging out in the kitchen and noticed that the visitor on dishwashing duty was wearing a shirt of a stunning blue color that Blues admired. He said to the visitor, "Hey, I really like that shirt." The visitor replied, "Yeah? Well, if you want to wash these dishes instead of me, I'll give it to you." Blues considered this and decided he could do better. "Wait a minute," he said, "and I'll see what I can do." Acting as Labor Manager, he then found another visitor, told him that we had an unexpected vacancy on a kitchen shift, and asked if he would be willing to fill in. With the usual good will most visitors exhibit, this one readily agreed. Exit first visitor, drying his hands. Enter second visitor, setting to work scrubbing pots. Exit Blues, with new shirt.

Corruption? Definitely. Blues accepted a bribe. The reason I smile is that the example is so petty, and—this is the point—it is the only example I can think of. Other than Blues and his shirt I have never heard of any Twin Oaks officer trading favors.

Verbal Violence

Twin Oaks bylaws contain a list of legitimate causes for expulsion, including theft, physical violence, and the like. They do not include any mention of offensive verbal behavior, and there are times when we wish they did. The member who becomes unhappy enough to be verbally abusive creates a bigger problem for the Community than the occasional thief.

Take this situation: Carl and Alice have been lovers, and Alice ends the relationship. Carl is hurt and angry. He wants to talk about it, to try to persuade her to change her mind. She is very uncomfortable in these talks and finally puts a stop to them, telling Carl the subject is finished. He keeps approaching her, and she is not getting any peace and privacy. He goes and knocks on the door of her room, stands there and imposes his presence on her. She asks him not to come to her room any more. So he stands in the middle of the path as she goes about her daily work, barring her passage from one place to another. It happens that Alice is a small woman and Carl is a large, muscular man. She becomes afraid of him and turns to the Community for protection.

The Community certainly wants to protect her! Members feel highly indignant. Not only do we recognize that Alice's privacy has been violated, but we feel violated ourselves. Carl's behavior is totally unacceptable, but we are not at all sure we know what to do about it. We feel that what he is doing is essentially violence, but he never physically touched her. The bylaws are not much help.

We can change the bylaws to make behavior like Carl's an expellable offense, but wording such a provision is very difficult. Specific language is useless, since no two cases are ever alike. General wording is threatening to other people, who feel it may someday be used against them or their friends for too little cause. The bylaws being difficult to change anyway, we go on from year to year depending on Feedback sessions, social pressure, good luck, and good will. (At bottom, even the Carls mean well.)

Mandatory Feedbacks

The mandatory Feedback is rare at Twin Oaks. I remember one time we had a member who had gotten hold of some LSD, and in the course of hallucinating decided there were demons in his bedroom that could only be exorcized by fire, so he set fire to his own mattress. The sight of the flames motivated him to vacate his room before he suffered any damage, and some nearby communitarian grabbed a fire extinguisher in time to prevent the flames from spreading to other rooms. However, the Community did not think the incident at all excusable, and we called a Feedback. The format was simply a "go-round," in which each member told the now very sober and repentant man (gently, of course) what we thought of him, drugs, arson, and unstable people living among us. We also gave our various opinions about what should happen next—expulsion, psychiatric help, etc. I don't quite remember what we recommended. I know he stayed a few more months, didn't take any more drugs, and then left the Community of his own volition. He got off easy, perhaps. So did we.

Expulsion a Rarity

The emotional cost of going through with an expulsion is so high that we rarely attempt it even when it is justified. The difficulty is the usual one—we don't agree. A decision to expel a member would divide the Community. So we are in the ridiculous situation of wishing for tougher laws to permit expulsion for verbal violence, while at the same time being unwilling to use the tough laws we already have for cases that clearly apply.

I remember sharply a member who, as I saw it, had stolen several thousand dollars from the Community. As she saw it, she had simply borrowed the money and meant to pay it back. She had no means of paying it back that I could see, nor had she had any permission to borrow it in the first place. But she had lived in the Community for many years and was very well liked. She was a good deal more popular than I could ever be, and I had a hard time persuading the Planners to act. I said she was stealing money; they said that since she didn't think of her actions as stealing, she wasn't really guilty. I said that Community morale would be negatively affected by letting one of our number get away with "borrowing" our money without permission. They said that nobody much knew about it, and we didn't really miss the money. I said it wasn't our business to shield her, that we needed to expose the scam and let the Community decide if it wanted to be lenient. They said we'd never get the money back if we put her back up. I said I had already written off the money but wanted to raise the general standard of expectation about financial behavior. I lost the argument. In the end one of the Planners talked her into borrowing from a lending institution in order to pay us the major part of what she owed us.

What I remember best about the incident is this: In the midst of it a good friend came to me and strongly advised me to soften the line I was taking and stop using plain language. She said, "Kat, the Community will resent you more for calling her a thief than they will her for being one."

My immediate emotional response to this is indignation. I say, "corruption and rottenness in high places", and such like. But on calmer reflection I notice that the people who ruled on this and the friend who advised me to modify my language did not do so for personal gain, which is what "corruption" usually means. They wanted only one thing: peace in the Community. We got it. Anybody who had heard rumors about the theft was told that it had been taken care of. Morale was not affected. The member who had taken the money was sufficiently angry about being accused that she left the Community a little while later. Life goes on.

That about sums it up for 25 years. Three or four thefts of money, some ice cream bars and fried chicken not accounted for, some children seeing what they can get away with, a temporarily crazed arsonist, a little minor cheating, and some angry words. The response: Locking up the cash, having some Feedbacks, some angry feelings, some worry. Not much.

Chapter 24

Movements and Causes

Political Agreement

Most Twin Oakers came here for two reasons. The first was to improve their own lives. Almost every fundamental flaw they see in society at large is conspicuously absent or at least toned down in this environment. The dominance of television, the emphasis on violence, the intense competitiveness (admired as a virtue), the sickening disparities between social classes, the environmental poisoning—all are left behind when we become Community members. Automatically we get the benefits of a rural environment, such as clean air and water and personal safety, at the same time keeping that part of city life we most enjoyed, the companionship of compatible people.

The second reason is related. We came here to be of help to the world. We want our lives to have a positive impact on the globe. Virtually every Twin Oaker will acknowledge both of these motives for being a communitarian.

How Much Sacrifice?

The agreement we do not have as a group is where to put the emphasis. For some, developing Twin Oaks as a viable lifestyle and modeling it for others is a major contribution to society already. People with this point of view do not feel obliged to be personally involved with outside movements and organizations. Just living here, conscientiously practicing conservation and nonviolence and pursuing peaceful happiness for themselves and their friends seems sufficient.

For others this is not enough. It even seems selfish. They see Twin Oakers as among the privileged. It does not matter that we earn very little cash money, wear thrift-store clothing, and share one toilet among five or ten people. It is obvious that in real values we are rich. They feel we need to be doing as much as we can to relieve the world's misery and improve its institutions. Twin Oaks can be a base for a wide-ranging effort to help the oppressed and fight oppression.

The Swimming Controversy

This difference in emphasis causes us to be at odds with each other even as we fundamentally agree on values. Take, for example, the purchasing of a luxury. Many of us find our river inadequate as a place to swim. It feels too far away and too difficult to get into. The Community can easily afford a swimming pool. Even a pond on one of our closer creeks might be enough. We once got so far as to set the money aside for a pond, but we couldn't get agreement on whether and how to spend it. One group felt strongly that having a good swimming place would make the Community more attractive and thus enhance the statement we are trying to make about the desirability of communal living. The other group argued variously (but heatedly) that a pond would destroy certain micro-environments, that a pool would waste water and involve the use of chlorine, and that it is not our business to spend money on luxuries but to use it to help other people who are less well off than we. The resulting decision was predictable. We got neither a pool nor a pond, nor did we give the money away. Some members still swim in the river; most don't swim. The money stayed in the bank pending future process.

Donations and Volunteer Labor

Every year's Tradeoff Game puts out a clear message of the limits of Community generosity and political commitment. We give away about $8,000 and 2,000 hours to various causes, but each year we also improve our standard of living.

Since we are all working for the money and the hours we give away, we all have a say in what kinds of efforts members make with group money and labor credits. This is expressed through the Tradeoff Game and will vary from year to year. This year we are putting a lot of effort into helping the local public schools and Headstart programs. We provide teacher aid without charge and do a substantial amount of private tutoring in reading and math.

The list of organizations we contribute to is long. Locally it includes the Rescue Squad and nursing homes. In nearby cities we sometimes provide meals for the homeless, in addition to money and labor for battered-women's shelters. We send small checks all over the nation to alleviate hunger, promote peace, assist Native Americans, and so forth.

Desert Storm

When the United States was engaged in Desert Storm, our Movement Support group sent a van to Washington, D.C. to protest. Kodiak was part of the group that kept George Bush awake all night by beating drums near the White House. Not everybody agreed with this tactic. I heard another politically active person say, "The last thing we need is a president who is strung out from lack of sleep!" All through that war, a vanload of Twin Oakers took part in a prayer vigil in our local County seat. They also wrote their anti-war opinions in letters to the local newspaper. Several were published, and roused the wrath of local patriots.

Those few Twin Oakers who sided with the President were afraid to open their mouths here at home. The feelings of indignation against President Bush and the military, and against the American TV-watching majority who backed them, ran so high that they caused general tension, because there was internal disagreement about an appropriate response. Somebody sprayed violently-worded anti-war graffiti on the outside of a building we had under construction at the time. The graffiti was in due time covered by siding, and no vandalism was intended, but some people objected to the violent language, even aimed harmlessly at people who would never be affected by it. This would have been a major issue for Twin Oaks if the war had not suddenly stopped. The end of the fighting left some members extremely frustrated, not because they wanted continued killing, but because they hadn't wanted the U.S. to win and crow about it. It took several more weeks for the anti-Administration sentiments to cool enough for the Community to get on to other topics.

Are We All Leftists?

Most Twin Oakers have pro-Choice views, and we have sent people to demonstrations. We supported a female candidate for Congress. I can't think of any Leftish or humanitarian cause that doesn't get some support from Twin Oaks.

I am not enthusiastic about this, because I wanted a community that could embrace people from a broad opinion spectrum, and that would have meant keeping the Community out of politics. After all, millions of people voted for Bush or even Nixon. Why don't we have any of them here? Other members tell me, though, that Twin Oaks by its very definition and organization is automatically Leftist, so my yearnings for balance are unrealistic.

Energy Use

In matters of ecology and energy conservation, the Community has a fair amount of fundamental agreement. (Actually, I remember a member we used to have who went around saying, "Nuke the Dolphins," but he didn't fit in very well.) We all favor making moderate sacrifices in order to help preserve the planet. Where we differ, and differ sharply, is in how far such sacrifices should go.

We encourage people to hang up their clothes to dry in the sun, for example, but we do not literally disconnect the gas-fueled clothes dryers. The result is that some people do one thing and some another. We encourage car-pooling, but we do not prohibit recreational travel. We have one, but only one, air-conditioned living room, and its use is governed by rules guaranteeing that it will not be wasted or used capriciously. We have battery-driven carts to assist the elderly or lame in getting around, but we do not permit anyone to joy-ride in them. We do not restrict the use of hot water for showers, but the choice of solar-heated water in warm weather is made convenient. We use energy-saving light bulbs in most public locations. In winter we keep the thermostats set at 68 where there is gas heat. Most buildings are heated with wood.

Much of our savings in energy can be attributed to the efforts McCune has made over his twenty years of membership. He became interested in this field many years ago. Each year he asks the Community through the Tradeoff Game for a little money and labor to build another solar water heater or other such device. His interest and his projects have encouraged others with similar interests to join the Community, and over time his priorities have become Community priorities. Since he is also a builder, each new structure he puts up has its own solar features. As the years have gone by, he has also led us to use more and heavier insulation. When the local building inspector looked at the insulation in our visitor cottage, he laughed and said, "You'll be able to heat this place by lighting a match."

Recycling

I have a memory of a conversation I had back in 1969 with Twin Oaks' then most prominent leader, Rudy. I said to him, "What do you think about encouraging people's interest in recycling? It's a good idea and it's cheap and it will give them a feeling that they're doing something significant." Rudy replied, "No, all this ecological stuff just distracts people from the main point, which is economic equality."

That's why the recycling movement at Twin Oaks didn't get started until later. Once it took hold, however, it became a permanent part of our organization and culture. At this point we recycle nearly everything, sometimes making some dubious trade-offs in the process. Since we live 50 miles from the nearest cardboard-recycling center, for example, we have to drive a heavy van there in order to participate, and whether the use of the vehicle can be justified ecologically we are not sure. From time to time somebody brings up the matter of the minimal effectiveness of some of our recycling efforts, but the Community isn't listening. As a group we feel that the good intent, the personal effort, the consciousness-raising, and the example are sufficient reasons to recycle everything we can, regardless of the actual effect.

Recycling is such an important part of our culture that we use half-broken and worn out furniture in our public rooms. This is not from poverty. I was once House Manager in charge of purchasing such things, and I could easily have kept our furniture in respectable condition simply by throwing out the worst of it and replacing it with other used (but not used up) items. When I tried to do this, people protested. They insisted they loved that couch with the broken springs and the faded cushions. The big chair, with its sagging upholstery and the marker-scribbles (contribution of some child) was still functional. Did we not believe in using things up? Mismatched dining room chairs that I had bought at an auction for $7 each and had intended to throw out when they broke were instead carted to the woodshop to be repaired. Some of them actually did get fixed, at an average of an hour's skilled work each. A lot of them are still there, ousted from the shop to make room for more important work and rotting quietly away in our yard instead of the dump. So be it. I guess I can sit on sprung upholstery and contemplate decaying wood for the sake of the feelings of the more politically correct members.

Feminism

Twin Oakers are certainly feminists. Partly this is a natural result of the Community's original egalitarian principles. There was never any question about women's being permitted to do "men's work." We were past such questions before the Community even started. As the movement gathered force in the nation as a whole, however, Twin Oaks refined its definitions of sexual equality to acknowledge a sort of affirmative action in the workplace. For several years the auto shop was run exclusively by women, and one season we had an all-female building crew. We no longer have to do this sort of thing. The point has been made.

Twin Oaks generally has at least one women's support group. Men's groups (of the kind that supports the women's movement) also arise from time to time. There was a skirmish when some women asked for a women-only residence. Eventually they got a compromised version of it which excluded men from actual residence and from visiting in the women's house after 6:00 P.M.

One noticeable impact of the women's movement is the effect on the male population. Men who exhibit obvious macho behavior are not usually accepted for membership, even if they apply, which they usually don't. Our men tend to be sensitive, reasonable, and well able to deal with women as equals. They seek relationships; they don't chase tail.

Notwithstanding all these efforts at political correctness, Twin Oaks is not by most standards extreme. This in itself frustrates those most deeply invested in the environmental or peace or feminist or other movements. We could do more. We could consume less. As usual, what we cannot do is get full agreement on any one direction.

229

230

Chapter 25

Power and Leadership

The subject of government and power in a community setting has been a dominant theme for me for 25 years. I see community through its government, and think a lot about directions and problem-solving. I'm acutely interested in how our law works, when it works, and whether we have too much of it or too little. I love crafting policy.

My own experience with power in community has been rich and intense. I have, within our little context, "risen to power" and "fallen from power" two or three times. (I use the quotation marks because, as anybody in a group with an egalitarian base knows, these phrases don't mean quite the same thing in community as they do on the Outside, but there is enough similarity so that we tend to use the same vocabulary.) Along the way I have formulated and discarded several theories, and I continue to refine the ones that stand up to experience.

Maybe I should explain what we do mean by the word "power." Mostly we equate it with "influence." We think a person who accomplishes something is powerful, or one who prevents action by somebody else. A persuasive person is said to yield power, or a person who tends to get his or her way a lot of the time. Any active person serving on the Board of Planners will be called powerful, because our system gives such a person the authority to interpret all the Community input and make decisions.

Power and the Plannership

Although there is power in the plannership, some Planners never use it. In various places in this narrative I mentioned times when a Board of Planners had to make a crossroads decision. Such occasions, however, are fairly rare. The biggest part of a Planner's job is administrative—gathering input and analyzing it, expressing the group's will if and when it can be determined.

In fact, one of the questions asked a prospective Planner these days is, "Do you have any agenda you would like to implement during your term of office?" God help the poor innocent who answers, "yes."

The plannership is not an easy spot from which to exercise free-wheeling influence. A Planner term is a year and a half of behaving circumspectly under close scrutiny and trying to keep some hold on the Community's purse strings in the face of a barrage of special requests, all without alienating too many people. The job does not attract people who just want to change the Community's directions. It has almost no scope for demagoguery, and it absolutely requires listening to everybody and trying to be fair. Power trippers and impatient direction-changers need not apply.

Why would anyone apply? There seem to be three main motives that keep us from literally running out of candidates. (1) People who haven't tried it yet want the experience, for personal growth; (2) People who see the need sometimes take it on as a duty; (3) A few people actually like the work. Thus we limp along.

It took us a while to learn that the actual usable power of the plannership is very limited. We've had several Planners who thought they were going to make major changes when they took office. They thought they represented a previously disenfranchised class of members, and they hoped to give power to those who had never had it before. They discovered, however, that decisions could not be reached and implemented swiftly and easily, no matter who was supposedly in power. If they wanted to put a new proposal on the table, such as doubling the allowance or changing the personal earning rules or loosening the video restrictions, they had to face the people who disagreed with them, hear the objections, weigh the arguments, debate the matter with the other Planners, and convince a lot of people. It was an eye-opening experience to find

233

that they were not in the majority. Some of them quit in disgust, saying, "It isn't what I thought it would be." Others adjusted and learned and became like other Planners. I remember one in particular who told me, "I can either be a good Planner and betray all my friends, or go back to my friends and quit the plannership. My friendships are more important, so I quit." What he meant, of course, is that his friends felt betrayed because he did not succeed in promoting their agenda, and they made him feel their disappointment.

We have had some oddly mixed plannerships. I remember one group made up of widely divergent personalities. One of them was less articulate than the other two but more determined, so when he wanted to make a point, he would jump to his feet and stomp and yell until he got his way. (Apparently the results didn't satisfy him, because he was one of those who quit the job before his term was up.)

During one of my terms I worked with a fellow Planner whom I enjoyed but frequently disagreed with. One time we were discussing air-conditioning, and I was arguing that the Community needed to have an air-conditioned retreat for those who felt a physical need for coolness in the hottest weather, particularly for old people. He argued that if those of us who claimed we required coolness would eat right, we wouldn't feel the need for air-conditioning. I replied that there was no medical evidence for such a connection. He said, "It doesn't make any difference if there is evidence or not, because I can get ten people to stand up and say they believe it."

This is probably the only time in my career at Twin Oaks that I ever heard anyone blatantly play power hardball. In a way, I respected it, because it was right out there in front, not hidden under any rationalizing layers. It made it easier, not harder, for me to work with him.

Special Difficulties of Strong Personalities in the Plannership

Talking of power and the plannership leads me to reminiscences of my own two terms, one in 1985-86 and the other in 1989-90. They were very different from each other, and both filled with interest. In both terms I started out with great vigor and enthusiasm, which lasted nearly a year, and both times I was glad to drop the job when the 18-month term expired.

I feared when I returned to Twin Oaks after my years away that I would not be permitted to be a Planner at all, precisely because my name was connected with the idea of power, which made a lot of people feel uneasy. Some people said that a person who understands how to be politically effective without being in office should not be put into office in addition, because it is dangerous for any one person to have too much influence. Others opined that people who seek public office should be denied it, because their motives are suspect.

This fear exasperated me. It was far from the mark. I never needed the plannership for power. Influence at Twin Oaks comes automatically as a result of doing good work in administration, writing sensible papers, paying attention and being cooperative at meetings, and, most important, having goals and directing one's energy toward them. I had all the influence I could use and always did have. What I wanted out of the plannership was the fun of being professionally engaged in politics. The job is interesting! I also thought I deserved to get labor credits for my political work. Everything I had accomplished up to then had been done on my own time. On another level I wanted to be a Planner so that I could prove to myself and the Community that I could handle it. I needed to erase the humiliation of the 1970 veto.

For these reasons I wanted the job, and I knew I wanted it. I also knew people generally preferred less decisive administrators, so I didn't set my heart on it. However, the day came when the need for fresh vigor in the job overcame the Community's hesitation, and I was asked to serve.

My First Term

The year preceding my first term had been a grueling one for the Planners. Heavy turnover had left Taylor all alone in the plannership for several weeks, during which time she had had to spend most of her time seeking partners to serve with her. It was Taylor's second term. During her first term, several years previous, she had worked with people who were her peers, people with experience and judgment. This time most of those people were gone, leaving her feeling stranded, without partners in the kind of leadership she understood and preferred.

Eventually she made up a board consisting of herself and two apprentices. She resigned herself to a teaching plannership. Both Novagene and Logan were willing to learn from her, and the team got successfully through the economic plan, including some innovative policy-making that we still use. However, some incident (I forget its exact nature) triggered a series of abusive O&I remarks aimed at Taylor, and she, tired of being scapegoated, resigned.

Logan and Novagene felt with some justice that her resignation left them holding a bigger job than they were quite ready for. They figured their first job was to find someone to fill Taylor's vacant spot, and while they were trying to do that, a Community emergency struck that needed someone of Taylor's experience in a guiding role. Taylor did not have the resilience to go back.

When Logan and Novagene approached me about being a Planner, I understood that what they wanted from me was strength. I have never been quite sure what people mean by the word "strength" in this sense, but at a minimum they meant they needed someone who would take on the job, put energy into it, and not quit if it got hard. I also knew that I was controversial.

There was a lot to do that year, and much of it was indeed controversial. Logan quit the plannership as soon as I took office. She had had too much tension to be comfortable with. Novagene stuck it out with me, and we recruited a series of stand-in Planners to work with us until one of them (Paula) got enough experience to become the third Planner. Paula and Novagene were both essentially apprentices, eager to learn and cooperative. I found myself being a sort of Chief Planner, showing the other two how I would approach problems. Certainly neither of the other two ever came up with a serious contrary argument. It used to anger Paula that people would say, "Kat is the Board of Planners." She was ready and willing to take her share of the criticism, to take a turn being blamed for the Community's problems, but she could never attract the fire, because the critics insisted on believing she was brainwashed.

When Novagene's term expired, we recruited Jake, who apparently took on the job for the novelty of the experience. Jake had no real interest in government. His heart was in the garden. He used to say, "Well, what do you think, Kat?" and when I told him, he'd say, "Sounds right to me." Throughout the warmer season he could barely endure Planner meetings. Instead of participating in discussion, he would flip through seed catalogs. When he started to speak up, Paula and I would turn our respectful attention to him, but most likely he would say something like, "I wonder how these seedless watermelons would do in this soil," or "Can we make a decision and get it over with, because this weather is perfect for being out in the garden."

I was tired at the end of my term, mostly because of the struggle with Will over who should or should not be permitted to do construction, as I have already told. Just the same, our group got a lot of work done, and I felt satisfied with my part in it.

My Second Term

Two and a half years later I served another term, and this one was a very different experience. For one thing I did not seek the job. It was offered to me by people who chose to work with me. It happened that I got a chance during my second term to get the kind of support that Taylor had longed to repeat—working with a group of peers. I was never Chief Planner during this term. Gordon and Juniee and Shal and I had among us more years of community experience than any group of Planners before or since, experience not only in living in Community but also in thinking about it. When we took on issues, we were likely to disagree somewhere along the line, and all our decision-making was the better for it. I learned as much as I taught, and the legislation we came up with bears clear marks of cooperative effort. We stepped up our meetings from two a week to three, and we got through an enormous pile of work. We fought a little among ourselves over personal irritations or points of process, but not over issues. Instead we debated the issues, then compromised or conceded or occasionally officially dissented, never losing our respect for each other and never interfering with our ability to get on with the next issue.

One thing I learned from working with peers and keeping up with our agenda was that it takes more than decision-making skills to be an ideal Planner. Somebody needs to be out there keeping in touch with the feelings of the less forthright people. I was never any good at that, and toward the end of my second term I recognized clearly that our Board, much as I loved it, lacked that element. We were not considered "approachable."

I suppose being approachable must mean that when people talk to you, they can count on a sympathetic ear. All four of us were willing to give the kind of attention we felt the job required, but evidently something in our personalities discouraged people from doing personal lobbying.

The Plannership as I See it Now

It feels strange to me, after all the years in which the plannership was an emotional issue for me, to realize that I no longer want to be a Planner. What has changed? I still care about the Community's directions. I still understand and relish decision-making about important issues. I still have confidence in myself. Saying, "I'm tired" doesn't get to the heart of it.

What has happened is that the job has changed, and in its present form it lacks interests for me. For the last several years the Planners have stepped back from the proactive approach to decision-making. These days their job seems to consist almost entirely of responding to various ideas and requests, seeking and analyzing input from the Community, and coming up with a decision that best approximates consensus, regardless of the quality of thinking behind that consensus. What I hear from Board after Board is, "Most people want...." When I do see an opinion paper from a Planner, it is always accompanied by the caveat, "This is from me as an individual, not a Planner." This is honorable, but it leaves me wondering whether the Board of Planners, operating as a group, has any opinions.

That is no job for me. What I liked about the plannership was the thinking and debating part. I enjoyed groping our way through the morass of irrelevancies, hidden agenda, and personal grievances and tackling the basic issue: Is such and such an idea good for the Community? Short run? Long run? Whom will it hurt? How much and why? Who will benefit? Is it just? Is it legal? Is it worth it? I enjoyed putting the results of all this thinking out on the O&I Board and seeing if people agreed, and if not, whether we could adjust our proposals enough to please them. I never expected consensus. A supporting majority was usually good enough as far as I was concerned.

It is not good enough for today's Planners, and they consider it their duty to try for an amalgam of public opinion, suppressing their own convictions in order not to be accused of abusing power. This is not merely a difference in style. It is a difference in theory. The way today's Planners operate makes most members comfortable. People criticize them less than they do bolder Planners.

The last proactive Planner we had was Keenan, who dared to interpret the results of a general survey and make a decision based on it, without querying specifically if his interpretation was acceptable. He got so much flack for this ("You're using the plannership to pursue your own agenda") that he quit in mid-term.

Balancing Power

There are people who think the Planner system cannot last much longer, because most people feel more burdened than challenged by the responsibilities of the job, and we have never found a way of supporting Planners through the periods when they are under attack. Others hope that we can hang on to the benefits of the system one way or another.

The truly powerful people in the Community are those who can communicate a vision. They may or may not hold office. Some of them write convincing papers; some speak effectively in meetings. Some simply talk about their ideas to their friends. By one means or another, their power consists of the ability to persuade. Over the years there have been many powerful people here, some of whom were fully conscious of that power, and others who never gave it a thought. They all have several things in common: They stayed for at least several years; they were willing to face controversy; they championed causes that served the needs of a substantial group; they didn't give up easily.

At no time in our history have we had Community-wide agreement on our major directions. Obviously, then, at no time has any one leader or group of leaders been all-powerful.

What saves Twin Oaks from its leaders is that we have so many of them, and none of them is all that competent. For a while some piper whistles a tune, and half the Community gets up and dances. Then someone else has a different song. Without having formed an intention of abandoning the first piper, the dancers now sway to a different rhythm. Meanwhile, the half of the Community that doesn't care for dancing will be interested in a dozen other things.

We have lots of leaders, and they tend to get in each other's way. That's why Twin Oaks proceeds so very slowly in any one direction and at the same time pops with energy in 20 places at once.

This is what I see, and what I take part in, and I'm not at all sure whether it's good or bad. Tugging at my mind all the time is a vision of what we could be if we would all go the same way for a change. But nobody will do that, so maybe this is the best we can do. Maybe it's the best anybody can do. Maybe it's utopia. Damned if I know.

I HOPE JERRY WORKS OUT, DON'T YOU?

YEAH, BUT **LOOK:** HE'S ALREADY 15 MINUTES LATE! DOESN'T HE KNOW THIS IS A **SERIOUS** INTERVIEW?

GOOD EVENING, MATRIARCHS AND PATRIARCHS, I'M GLAD YOU ALL COULD MAKE IT! SORRY I'M LATE, I WAS JUST AT THE LOCAL VEGETARIAN RESTAURANT AND I FOUND A **FLY** IN MY MISO SOUP! "WAIT-PERSON," I SAID, "THERE'S A..."

JONATHAN

STOP! WHAT'S THE **MEANING** OF THIS?! WE INVITE YOU HERE TO FILL THE POSITION OF **STAND-IN PLANNER**, AND YOU MAKE A **MOCKERY** OF THINGS! DO YOU HAVE AN **EXPLANATION**?

OH, SORRY, I MISUNDERSTOOD. I THOUGHT YOU WANTED ME TO BE A STAND-**UP** PLANNER!

YOU WON'T BE FORGOTTEN, BILBO (1977-1992)

Chapter 26

Some Leaders Who
Made a Difference

If we could take a poll of all the members who have ever lived here (over five hundred of them by now) and ask them to name the people they considered the most influential leaders of their time, I suspect we'd get a list of thirty or so frequently-mentioned names. After that, there'd be others who would be nominated occasionally, because there are so many different kinds of leadership and so many different areas to exercise it in. In selecting the people to write about, I chose from the last ten years some people who struck me as outstanding in fairly similar fields. The three I decided to write about have several things in common. All were young women from middle class Jewish families in large cities (Philadelphia, New York, and Washington, D.C., respectively). I don't know whether being Jewish has anything to do with it or not. Are Jewish girls taught to step in and take charge when they see the need? Certainly these three were.

GERRI, WHO RULED BY LOVE AND GUILT : 1970 - 1986

Gerri's entrance into Twin Oaks in 1970 seems to me typical, almost symbolic, of the kind of Twin Oaker she turned out to be. What I remember is that we had no decent space for visitors to

242

sleep, so she bedded down on a pad on the floor next to the furnace and—this is the symbolic part—didn't mind it. Throughout her 16 years as a Twin Oaker, she didn't think about her personal rights, never worried about empowering herself or finding support or getting enough air time. She was a puzzle to me, because she seemed to have no ego. She didn't like compliments and didn't even seem to need attention.

I didn't recognize her as a leader until 1975 or so. I excuse my blindness by remembering that she was nineteen when she first came and also that for the first several years she followed my lead with a reverence and dedication that would have embarrassed me if I had even noticed it. As it was, I thought she was a good communitarian and a nice girl. She didn't give the Community any trouble, and she smiled a whole lot.

Also, she stayed. When other, more obvious leaders made a two or three-year splash and then moved on, Gerri was still here, working steadily and happily.

Gerri

She went with me in 1973 to found East Wind Community. There we got to know each other well enough so that I began to appreciate her value and she began to see my faults. Pregnancy took her back to Twin Oaks while I stayed on at East Wind. We didn't live together for the next eight years, but I followed Twin Oaks events from a distance, and Gerri's name was prominent in the news.

Gerri as a Planner

Gerri became a Planner right after she returned from the East Wind expedition. She served with two other women, forming Twin Oaks' first and possibly only all-female plannership. Coincidentally, all three of them had recently had babies. The Community jokingly referred to them as "The Mothers," instead of "The Planners." They were the first group to avoid rapid or independent decision-making. They created the Council system and resolutely required the Councils to decide issues in their areas. Part of this came as a response to restive talk in the Community about "the

243

people" wanting a bigger voice in government, and part of it from Gerri's own personality. She hated conflict. She couldn't stand saying "no." Trying to be the "heavy" made her almost ill. Like me, she could always see at least two sides to every question. Unlike me, she hated being the one to make the choice. In spite of that, she accepted the planner job at least twice. During one of her terms her group (Gerri, Josie, and David of Merion) handled the crucial matter of Merion's wanting to become an autonomous community and take its per-capita share of resources when it split off. I remember reading the account of this issue as it was reported in detail in the Community's newsletter at the time. I became frightened as I read. Would Twin Oaks be stupid enough to set such a precedent? Would this be the end of the Community I had founded and thought safe? No, the close of the article assured me, it would not. The Planners said they felt the split idea was "not Twin Oaks." Merion rocked with indignation, but the Union was saved. Gerri was also on the Child Board when one of our adult members wanted to leave her child at Twin Oaks temporarily while she herself left the Community. The answer, after agonizing process, was no, but in this case the Planners absolutely refused to rule. They told the Child Board, "This is your decision. We will not handle it. We will uphold whatever you decide."

The Hammock Shop Boys

While I was an East Wind member I visited Twin Oaks several times for various reasons, and I was present when Gerri and her co-planners had to face the unpleasant business of an attempted expulsion.

Some background: It was the heyday of "The Boys," the Hammock Shop Managers who helped bring the hammock business out of its doldrums by making the shop a lively and efficient workplace, but unfortunately caused a great ruckus in doing so.

They were a jovial lot. The sound of their loud and frequent laughter could be heard across the Courtyard at almost any time of day. A lot of members thought the Boys laughed at the wrong things. For one, they laughed at the rules. Feeling that they had been the ones responsible for Twin Oaks' economic recovery and were entitled to some extra perks on that account, they began to have more liquor in their rooms than members could usually afford, and it was widely rumored that it had been paid for with Community money. One of the Boys was a town tripper, and our bookkeeper, Wrenn, questioned a highly suspicious discrepancy in his town trip accounting. The tripper disliked being suspected, and he and his friends turned their mockery on her, calling insults to her as she crossed the Courtyard.

The rule against earning vacation money within Louisa County also was laughed at when the Boys had an opportunity to make hammocks for a local fledgling community that was subcontracting from us! Instead of taking labor credits for their work and turning over the cash, they pocketed their earnings. By Community rules, this was theft, technically an expellable offense.

The biggest objection to the Boys' behavior, however, was not to the rule-breaking but to the very spirit that had successfully made the hammock shop a place of gaiety and high production. Early in the Boys' reign there, the high spirits ceased to be innocent by most people's standards. Hammock shop conversation came to consist mostly of pointed mockery of the Community, its traditions, its leaders, and its decencies. The hammock shop became a place where people who took the Community's standards seriously did not feel at home. In addition, the Boys decided they could work better without the presence of visitors, who cramped their style, so they used their managerial authority to bar visitors from the shop. This created a labor problem for the Community.

We had a member named Joshua, who had been at Twin Oaks since 1969 and was deeply attached to Twin Oaks' principles and institutions. Like many people, he was offended by the Boys' style. When they turned their mischievous malice against his friend and former lover, Wrenn, he lost patience and posted a paper entitled, "Throw the Bums Out." Actually expelling the Boys would have been exceedingly difficult, because they had the support of a large portion (perhaps a fourth?) of the Community's members. They stood for good times, loose spending, and the like, which tend to be popular policies the world over. Besides, they had become expert weavers and made a whole lot of hammocks.

Frustrated by lack of action on expulsion, Joshua then used his own authority as Vehicle Use Manager. He fired the town-tripper from his job on the grounds of misuse of Community money. I believe somebody appealed his decision. One way or another the Planners got involved. While I was visiting the Community, there was a meeting announced to discuss the whole issue. I got permission to attend, though I knew that I was at that point an outsider and could do nothing more than observe.

I found it a very frustrating meeting. There was a great deal of talk about feelings. People told how they felt about the atmosphere of the hammock shop. The Boys talked back. People mentioned the accusations of wrong-doing that had been made. The Boys said they didn't feel good about the accusations. I kept wondering if anybody would ever ask the plain question: Did you or did you not spend Community money on personal booze? Did you work for cash within Louisa County and keep the money or not? Will the accusers please give your evidence? Nobody asked these questions, so the Boys were not put on the spot to give any straight answers. From my point of view, as a "hearing" on a legal override, it wasn't fair to either side. But the Community at that time seemed to feel that the meeting was appropriate, and I kept my mouth shut—difficult but also appropriate.

The Planners then met privately and upheld Joshua's decision to bar the alleged booze-buyer from town-tripping. However, after making this decision, Gerri became unhappy with it. She could not sleep that night. The more she thought about it, the more wrong it seemed to her. Even if the man was guilty, was he so guilty that he had to be punished? Punishment is not usual at Twin Oaks. Troubled beyond endurance, she got out of bed in the middle of the night and went to talk to one (not both) of the other Planners. She talked him into changing his vote. The next morning they informed George, the third planner, that the decision had been changed. Joshua was overruled, and the tripper was vindicated.

Matters of justice are supposed to happen in a vacuum of personal involvement, but that isn't always possible in community. Gerri had been at one time in love with the accused, and George was at that time in love with Wrenn. Are these facts relevant? I'm afraid so.

The Boys stayed on at Twin Oaks for several months, only leaving when the Community went through its first Pier One crisis and the hammocks they were so justly proud of became (for an anxiety-filled period of several weeks) unsaleable lumps in a warehouse. Wrenn and George left the Community in anger over Gerri's action, and Joshua followed some while later.

The Protected Men

If Gerri had a fault (few could find her guilty of any), it was that she repeatedly defended men the Community was mad at. It was Gerri who stood between the cashbox thief and expulsion, by letting it be known via grapevine that she wasn't sure she would be comfortable living in a place where her daughter's good friend was not welcome. It was Gerri who backed Mel's getting Twin Oaks into the jewelry-making business. Her instincts did not tell her that Mel was a bad egg. They told her that Mel was a lonely, unhappy man who needed friendship and support. It was Gerri who successfully supported the acceptance of another man whom the Community didn't like much, and who a few years later caused immense grief by kidnapping his child away from its mother and suing for custody in a local court. If a man joined the Community who tended to macho swaggering, Gerri automatically took pity on him and tried to protect him from other people's disapproval. A few smiles and a half hour of warm, receptive listening from Gerri, and such men were instantly tamed and worshipful. With some justice, Gerri felt that these men were easily managed if one went about it right. The Community as a whole had neither the skill nor the motivation.

Gerri as Products Manager

Gerri's enduring fame is not for taming big bad men nor for her work on the various planner tasks she undertook over the years, but for being the Community's first Products General Manager.

Most of our responsible positions have, with the passage of time, evolved from a single manager to committee management. Products was the exception that went the other way. At one time the products area was handled by the Products Council, an unwieldy and unbusinesslike group made up of the production managers, office workers, and sales people, who would meet weekly and try to handle the business in the course of their meetings. Eventually this became untenable. The work load was too heavy and too technical for a group of a dozen people to manage. Gerri was at the time doing some products desk work bordering on management but was being hindered by disagreements with another office worker. Things came to a head and Gerri gave the Products Council two alternatives. They could do without her, or she would offer her services as a General Manager, provided the Community would give her full authority to run the business. With remarkable lack of fuss, for Twin Oaks, the Community accepted the offer, and created the Products General Manager job.

The job has enormous powers and even more enormous responsibilities. Gerri rose to the challenge. She subscribed to business magazines and read articles on sales, marketing, personnel management, and the like, constantly translating what she read into Twin Oaks terms. She sent out suitable advertising. She made policy. She talked capable people into accepting the various production managerships. She kept an eye on quality control. She managed credit and collection efforts. She worked with East Wind on the Joint Hammock Agreement. When she wasn't busy with managerial work, she stepped into the shop and made hammocks. For years she could be counted on to cheerlead every production push. She invented games and events, or recruited people to help her invent them, to make the shop attractive. Some of the "pushes" lasted for months at a stretch, with Gerri there most of the time inspiring the others to get out the big Pier One order. If the hammock shop event required costumes, Gerri would be dressed up for the occasion. If it needed edible goodies, Gerri got somebody to make them.

Through it all, Gerri managed to remain low key. She accomplished her tasks by being lovely to everybody and taking the worst on herself. Throughout the four years in which she held this job, nobody ever wanted her to quit, or envied her position. Very few even criticized her handling of the job. It was widely accepted that the Community would not normally let any single member have so much power, but Gerri was an exception, because she was Gerri.

"Wait a minute," said Velma, upon reading an early draft of this manuscript. "Gerri didn't accomplish what she did by being sweet and lovable; she did it by making everybody feel guilty!" Well, yes. There was that, too. Decent and sensitive people, seeing Gerri suffer because the Community was not responding quickly to her plea for more hammock production, or because she hadn't found anyone to manage the retail desk, tended to come to her aid by volunteering. Perhaps Velma herself was drawn to her first products job by the desire to help Gerri out.

Gerri and Will

Gerri married Will, of course. Besides being an able and attractive man, he was her type—proud and belligerent on the surface but capable of great warmth and sweetness. Throughout the difficulties of the KDC construction and especially the aftermath the following year, anyone who made things difficult for Will automatically had an enemy in Gerri as well.

Committing herself to Will made Gerri's life complicated and difficult, because in a sense she was already married—to the Community. For once her supreme self-confidence failed her. When Will's needs and the Community's became incompatible, Gerri could not handle them both. She had to choose, and she chose Will.

Realizing that she and Will would end up leaving the Community and that she would have to give up her beloved Products Managment job, Gerri took one last important step for the Community. The size of the Pier One order as their stores multiplied across the country became more than Twin Oaks and East Wind together could handle. Gerri negotiated a deal with a local sheltered workshop to make the hammocks that exceeded our limits, so that we could continue to meet the big orders, seek medium-sized accounts, and pursue other economic directions.

Choosing a Replacement

She did the best she could for us, and then faced the task of finding someone to replace her in the huge job that she had, over a four-year period, tailored to her own talents.

What happened next interests me a lot, because I think it is typical of situations where highly responsible managers attempt to replace themselves. They very frequently choose badly.

I remember that when I first left Twin Oaks to start East Wind, I turned my bookkeeping job over to a young apprentice. I had shown her how to keep the records, and she did a perfectly adequate job. However, within months of my departure the Community went broke, and I know this wouldn't have happened if I had been here to watch the numbers. The part of the "bookkeeping" job that had been of most value turned out to be my intuitive grasp of the Community's financial state and my ability to say, "We can't afford this" and be believed. Not only could I not pass this on to the apprentice; I didn't even know I needed to. People who fill crucial functions in a group don't always know how they do it, or even what those functions are. I didn't know in 1973, and Gerri, though less naive by 1986 than I had been, didn't get it right, either.

There was only one person in the Community who was at the time fully capable of taking on Gerri's job, and that was Velma. However, Velma's personality was radically different from Gerri's, and Gerri must have felt that Velma could not handle so much power with sufficient delicacy to satisfy the Community. I conjecture that Gerri examined her own history as a manager, analyzed how she had accomplished her work, and said to herself, "Velma cannot behave like that." This was unquestionably true. I know very few people who handle major responsibilities with the smiling, modest, behind-the-scenes style that Gerri was known for, and certainly not Velma! In addition, Velma was openly at odds with Will, and Gerri could not stomach working with one of Will's enemies long enough to get her trained.

Gerri turned instead to Paul, a pleasant, unassuming man who had filled the Community's Economic Planning job creditably for

249

several years. At first this seemed to work fine. The business had its own momentum, and Paul covered the basics without difficulty. This situation might have continued peaceably for several years if our hammock sales had continued on the projected path. Unfortunately, they did not. Like my bookkeeping apprentice of the previous decade, Gerri's apprentice turned out not to grasp one essential of business management, namely swift and effective response to a changed situation. Paul lacked executive ability, and Gerri probably didn't quite realize that she had it.

I'll tell the rest of this story when I get to the section on Velma. Right now I want to back up a few years. My tale of these three influential leaders with their radically different styles seems best told in roughly chronological order, and the next one on my list is Taylor.

TAYLOR, WHO TOOK THE COMMUNITY ON: 1977 - 1987

Difficulties in Joining

If Taylor had been allowed to join Twin Oaks when she first applied, in 1974, we might have had the use of her considerable gifts for three years longer than we did. Taylor originally applied to Twin Oaks when the Community had a long waiting list for incoming members. She joined the queue, number fourteen on the list, and set out to occupy herself for the number of months that it would take for her name to come to the top. For her this meant living in New York City in housing which didn't require a lease, working at part-time office and substitute teaching jobs, and in general keeping herself in readiness for the call from Twin Oaks. After a few months of this, she realized she couldn't endure living in limbo much longer. If she had to stay in the Outside World, she needed more roots—a job she could commit her energies to, an apartment she could make into a home, a circle of friends and some social activities that suited her. She felt strongly that it was Twin Oaks she had chosen as a career, but she wasn't sure how much longer she could wait for it.

To freshen her vision and help to make up her mind, she visited the Community again to check out the status of the waiting list. When she arrived for her visit, she found that the Community had grown by a dozen people or more, that there had been membership turnover and replacement in addition—but that none of the new members had come from the waiting list! That list showed Taylor's name still as number fourteen.

What had happened was that Twin Oaks in the intervening time had decided to grow by adding Tupelo branch. The people who formed Tupelo had organized at a conference. They had formed a social unit at the conference, and their offer to be a branch in a rundown, rented house on neighboring property was accepted by the Community. None of the Tupelo people were from the waiting list.

In addition, some new members had been admitted to Twin Oaks proper—had skipped to the top of the list—because they were lovers of current members. For these reasons the waiting list was stagnant.

Taylor

Taylor protested. She wrote an O&I paper saying that she strongly felt she belonged here, that she couldn't live in limbo much longer, and that she had been unfairly treated by the haphazard enforcement of admissions policy.

The Community's response was guilty acknowledgement but a firm refusal. Once the Membership Team or Planners took a hard look at what was happening with admissions, they realized they had to be firmer and fairer. From now on, they told Taylor, they would cease playing favorites, starting with her. To accept her would not, they said, be fair to the other thirteen people who had waited even longer than she had.

After her long visit, during which Taylor confirmed that Twin Oaks really was what she wanted but couldn't have within an acceptable time, she removed her name from the waiting list and set her sights on her second choice—a teaching career in New York.

Two years later Taylor came to one of those pausing places that occur in many people's lives. Her job had lost its savor. Her lease was expiring. A big love relationship was ending. Her thoughts returned to Twin Oaks once more, and this time she found that there was no more waiting list. All applicants had long ago been absorbed, and the Community now had space for her. She did another official visit and was accepted with no hesitation.

Getting Involved

The Community needed her badly. It was a period of high turnover, and Taylor took on her first managership (backpacker hammocks) within two months of joining. In addition, she was called upon for medical emergencies because she had EMT (Emergency Medical Technician) training. Her interest in this field landed her on the Health Team very quickly. As sometimes happens, the other people on the Health Team moved on to other things or left the Community, and Taylor found herself for a while alone in charge of the Community's health problems.

There was a sense in which Taylor never got out from under the Health job. She herself served a normal term, got a crew together, then resigned a year or two later, but the job would not let her go. For the entire course of her membership after that, people would go to her for medical guidance, just because she seemed to them to be the appropriate person.

Taylor was an appropriate person for a lot of things. She was shoved into the Plannership almost as soon as her provisional membership was over. There was about her a feeling of good sense, good will, and thorough reliability that made people want to give her responsibilities. One felt that she always knew the right thing to do.

Social Planning

It was early in Taylor's Twin Oaks career that she got involved in Social Planning.* This complicated process was really the brainchild of Henry and Gerri. Henry's interest in this project was an extension of the physical planning he was already engaged in. He could see how physical and social environments related to each other, and he suspected he could use some of the same techniques for both.

This was the time when the Community was deciding whether to divide itself into smaller units. As I have told, we had already settled Merion on a nearby piece of land, and had created Tupelo on rented propery. Merion and Tupelo had certain privileges as separate branches, and others were envying them their autonomy and presumed intimacy. The end result, dividing the main branch into small living groups, was something of a foregone conclusion from the start. The question was how the Community could handle all this without hurt and conflict.

---

*The social planning is described in full detail in Ingrid Komar's *Living the Dream.* Ingrid was visiting at the time it was going on. Like me, she thought it rather a lot of process to arrive at a foregone conclusion, but she recorded it faithfully anyway.

For her part, Gerri was stirred by what I can only call a political conviction. I think she got her idea partly from *Walden Two*, and partly from me (also influenced by *Walden Two*). It was essentially this: Do not ask the people what they think should happen. They do not know. They are short-sighted, tunnel-visioned, biased by their own immediate interests, and not prepared for leadership. Ask them what they feel. Ask them what they need, or what they want for themselves. Listen to their problems, but do not let them formulate solutions. They will botch the job. It is the job of leadership to put all this information together and come up with the solutions.

Taylor joined the Social Planning Team because she admired both of the people on it and believed she would learn a lot through working with them. The three of them collected data and made matrices and lists of criteria for several weeks. Taylor took an apprentice role, but after a while she realized that the other two didn't really know what they were doing, either. None of the three of them knew how to get from the analysis of the data to the conclusions they were attempting to reach. Somehow the expected pattern did not emerge by itself from the data. What had started out as a mess of petty disagreement ended up as nothing more than an organized mess of petty disagreement.

Taylor talked the others into taking the simple step of asking the members what they thought should happen. This was contrary to the doctrine they had been working from, but they didn't know what else to do, so they put out an ordinary survey. What they got back this time wasn't a whole lot closer to consensus, but it was at least a handful of concrete suggestions that had some backing from some of the people.

"What people really wanted," said Taylor later, "was something they couldn't have. They wanted a bunch of little branches, each with a lot of autonomy. We couldn't let that happen, for many reasons. For one thing, there was a group that was quite happy with Twin Oaks the way it had always been and did not want their lives disrupted by the desire for pseudo-families. So we settled on Small Living Groups as a half-way measure."

Taylor's basic agenda, she realized gradually over the months, was different from Gerri's. Gerri was aiming for a good solution to the problem. For Taylor it was more important that the members feel they "owned" the solution, that they had come up with it themselves, or assented to it, not merely in the technical sense of allowing their officers to do it, but in a direct way. Whether the solution was optimal, or even very good, mattered to Taylor only if the issue was a vital one. In matters loaded with more emotion than content, she tended to want to involve everybody and not let them delegate the decision-making.

What Gerri and Henry and Will (and I, for that matter) aimed at was government *for* the people, regardless of who did the governing. What Taylor thought more important was government *by* the people. Through all of her ten years as a Twin Oaks member, she prodded and guided the Community in that direction.

It's a popular direction, of course. It has an intuitive rightness about it. Who could possibly know better than the people how their government (and their industries, and domestic arrangements, and housing, and land planning, *ad infinitum*) should be run? Other theories stink of elitism and arrogance. Don't they?

In Taylor's hands this theory was not a revolution but a process of education. She saw a need for people to grow up and grow into responsible citizenship. Her only impatience was for that educational process to begin, with strong encouragement from the natural and delegated leaders. Heaven knows she did her part.

Like all of Twin Oaks' best leaders, she automatically asked, "What is best for the Community" whenever she made choices. She had a habit of filling in where someone was needed. She thought it was bad for the Community to come in for lunch and discover that there was no lunch cook. These days when this happens, there is just a big drain on the cheese and peanut-butter supplies, but when Taylor was with us, she would step in and cook lunch on short notice. "It's important," she used to say. "Not having lunch brings people down."

Why Taylor Left the Community

Everybody has faults, and leaders have them in capital letters, so I may as well tell you what Taylor's main one was. She was Overburdened. Of course she literally was over-extended and kept herself that way, out of a feeling of a desperate shortage of capable people to share responsibilities with, but that's not what I mean. I mean that she put out an aura of being always at the very end of her strength. She radiated exhaustion to the point of martyrdom. For a person like Taylor who accepts responsibility when she sees the need, living at Twin Oaks is a constant temptation to overextension. There is so very much to do.

When I rejoined the Community in 1982, Taylor had been a member for 5 years and had been through a lot. Most particularly she had stayed in the Community while helplessly watching all of her best friends and most trusted comrades leave. She explains now that it was not just the loss of friendships that affected her so deeply. It was the loss of partners in her view of what the Community needed. She saw that there were other leaders with fresh energy for the Community. Managerships would be covered. There would be progress. But she saw no one ready to give real help toward her essential dream, teaching people to take responsibility for their own actions and decisions, and intelligently taking control of their own government.

Instead she saw a capable but brash kind of leadership rising in the persons of me and Velma. I've talked a lot about myself, and I'll get to Velma in a minute. Taylor sized us up as useful to the Community but no help to her in what she believed in. If anything, being rather enamored of our own abilities, we were likely to take the Community back in the other direction, toward dependence on leaders.

Taylor accomplished a great deal in her ten years. She did a lot of it through committees, and it is easy to see her hand in the committee work—Membership policies, Health policies, Small Living Group policies, New Industries criteria. As a manager she handled Backpackers, Milk Processing, New Industries, Indexing, Health Team, Garden, Greenhouse construction, and probably others that I don't recall right now.

When turnover slowed down and other people could take her managerships, she went through brief periods when she wasn't being a full-time leader. She cherished these periods, which she filled with gardening, cooking, and construction. These infrequent intervals gave her the leisure to think about her life and the Community's. She meant to refresh herself and then reengage in leadership when she was ready. She rarely got the chance. Somebody would leave, and the vacancy called to her.

It was one of these periods of retreat and reflection that gave Taylor the time to decide to leave the Community. She could have stayed and worked out a fresh approach to her basic dream, and then reinvested her energies in her usual way, but she could see that it was going to be a while before she got any help. Instead, Taylor considered other paths for her life to take.

VELMA, THE EVERYTHING MANAGER: 1983 - 1990

At the beginning of her time with us, Velma did not have any intention of staying as long as she did. "A year or two," she thought. Instead, she fell in love with Twin Oaks and settled down for seven years. She wasn't really centered on communal living as an ideal. Before joining Twin Oaks she had spent several years traveling around the world, which gave her a breadth of focus that inoculated her against easy recipes for society. She wasn't at all sure that any one social pattern would work for the world. To the extent that she has a social philosophy, it can be summed up in the word "service." Wherever she is, she gives her energy to serve other people. Twin Oaks provides ample opportunity for such donations!

I think of Velma as being a kind of adventurer, thirsty for life, love, and whatever else could be had. As far as I could tell, Velma chose Twin Oaks almost as an extension of her travels. It was new and different and interesting, and she could see a role for herself here.

Velma

I don't literally remember Velma's first week, but it is safe to suppose that she started out right away being busy and useful, which is also what she was doing the day she left seven years later. She collected work, in much the same devouring way that she collected clothes and earrings and experiences and artwork and friends and lovers. She always wanted everything.

What is Community For?

One thing she lacked was a community ideology. She sensed that in order to be a successful communitarian one needed to believe in the Community in some way. She was perfectly willing to believe, if someone would show her what to believe in. She came to visit me in my room one evening and put the question to me. She said, "Kat, tell me what the Community means. I mean, I like Twin Oaks, but I don't know what it's for, really. Tell me what it means to you. Here I am, with a totally open mind ready to listen to you. Try to turn me on!"

I had no idea what to say to her. What, indeed, did it mean? Was Twin Oaks going to start a chain reaction of communalism that would in time do away with all the hate, violence, and competitive nastiness in the world? I doubted it. Were we a school of living, touching the lives of the hundreds of people as they came through, imparting a vision of cooperation and hope? Perhaps, but the notion didn't touch my emotions at all. Were we going to create a microcosm of utopian living that could be copied by other people to their advantage? That was closer, but it still wasn't really what motivated me personally. I admitted that this time around I was here for my own benefit, because I liked the place. To the extent that I still felt ideology, it was this: I wanted lots of other people to live here for their own benefit, too. To that end, I strove to improve—perhaps even to perfect—Twin Oaks. How can anybody explain the purpose of Utopia? It's like explaining the purpose of Heaven. It's just the place you want to be, that's all. Velma was left to find her own meaning, and I don't know what she finally came up with.

Managerships

Meaning or no meaning, she didn't have any difficulty finding work that needed to be done. She cooked, and the general standard of meal preparation went up. She made strawberry and peach jams. We hadn't had anything better than cheap, store-bought grape jelly for years. She became a milker, getting up at dawn and getting acquainted with the Holsteins. Through the dairy work she discovered that our fences needed repair, so she took that on.

Agriculture was not destined to hold her interest. With regret she had to let it go as she took on one job after another: Legal, Taxes, Computer Services, 20th Anniversary Coordinator, Craft Fairs. In addition there were some things she wasn't officially in charge of but did anyway, like phone system installation, and accounting. She didn't usually drop jobs to make room for the new ones. She just added each one on to her already full schedule.

None of these things were skills she brought in with her. She learned them all here, because they interested her. Her learning wasn't superficial, either. She read the law books and the tax regulations and absorbed as much as she could find time for. She studied accounting, admired it, and put it to work immediately. She learned about computer hardware by painstakingly soldering tiny components to circuit boards and asking questions while she worked.

She wasn't slow at political matters, either. It didn't take her long to figure out how various decisions are made here: which questions are actually dealt with by the committees assigned to them, which conclusions are reached by nebulous influences before they ever get to a committee, what kind of issues belong to the Planners, and which can be left in managerial hands. She became expert at process, in the legal sense of the word.

257

Bruised Egos

By anybody's standards, Velma was remarkable, and by Twin Oaks' necessarily looser ones, she was a miracle. Does it surprise you that a lot of people did not rejoice at her competence and that some people downright disliked her? Are you shocked when I admit that my own feelings toward her were at least as envious as they were admiring? Personally, I like to believe that I would have been able to regard Velma with a purer admiration if she had suppressed her delight with herself. But she could not. She greatly admired competence and high standards in other people, and she crowed with jubilation when she herself accomplished something that she could admire, which was fairly frequently.

As I got to know her well, I eventually realized that she was not trying to make other people feel inferior. In fact, she had a lot of respect for other people's work—in relation to their talents. She took her superiority so much for granted that she didn't even call it that. She said simply that she had standards for herself, that she was her own harshest critic, and that when she triumphed, the triumph was over herself or over the material at hand. She didn't compare herself to others unless they were serious competitors, in which case she relished the competition and was delighted to win or lose.

I remember at the beginning of her membership, when she was doing a lot of cooking, I said to her one day, "Ira will be here soon. She is also a wonderful cook. I wonder how you will feel about her." Her interest was immediately aroused. I predicted (silently) that she would find some real or imagined flaw in Ira's cooking and compare it unfavorably with her own. Wrong! It didn't take Velma more than one meal to notice Ira's ability and rejoice in it. The two of them cooked super-extravaganza meals for the Community once a month or so for years. They developed a friendship based on mutual respect that all started in the kitchen.

It was with this same zestful attitude that Velma approached the matter of power in Community. She realized, of course, that every managership she picked up and mastered gave her control in that area, and that the full house of jobs she had dealt herself amounted to enormous clout. With a few exceptions she used it with care and judgment.

Our personal friendship was turbulent. One week I would hate her for her superiority and self-confidence, and the next I would be overcome by the quality of her intelligence, her insight, and her compassion. I wasn't the only person to have difficulty adjusting to the amount of power that Velma exercised. Taylor also bridled from time to time, though mostly the two women worked in different areas.

Handling a Death

One area that Taylor had frequently handled, without anybody's ever calling it a managership, was birth and death. Expectant mothers frequently chose her for their birthing crews, and when tragedy occurred, the Community turned to Taylor with the sure instinct of children turning to their mothers. Taylor would take care of it. Taylor had been there for Twin Oaks' first death and for the three that followed it. She had handled funeral arrangements, created appropriate Community ceremonies, and talked with grieving families. She was just naturally good at it. Then came the first death of the post-Taylor period.

It was toward the very end of Twin Oaks' 20th Anniversary celebration, when Community members were sitting around the dinner table, Velma among them, relaxing with satisfaction at successfully bringing off the big weekend. The atmosphere suddenly changed as Twin Oakers Matthew and Denis strode toward the diners with expressions full of portent and awkwardly announced that they had found another member, Carl, dead in his room with a rope around his neck.

I don't know what other people were thinking, but what was going on in my head was this: "Oh shit, Taylor's leaving tomorrow, and I suppose I've got to handle this. But wait! I'll bet Velma will want to do it. I'm not going to compete with Velma for the privilege of dealing with a dead body. She's welcome to the job." I stood up and looked at Velma, who was looking at me. I said, "Are you going to handle this?" She replied, "Do you think I should?" I said, "I think that's probably best." She was off, viewing the body, getting someone to guard the door, calling the police, finding the phone numbers of the next-of-kin, collecting information, letting the Community know the facts as soon as she knew them. She was a natural. In fact, she behaved very much as Taylor would have done.

While all this was going on, other people were also preparing to take responsibility. They were Todd, who was serving as a Planner, and Leslie, who felt in many ways akin to Taylor in Community theory and in some respects would be following her footsteps. They were not as quick as Velma. (In truth, there is usually no rush in dealing with the dead.) What they did was to find Taylor (who had stayed for Anniversary but was leaving the next day), give her the news, and ask her advice. Taylor wisely refused to take charge but gave them some pointers. Leslie should get the Community members gathered in one place, preferably in a circle. Todd was to take on other tasks. It was confusing to both when they found that Velma had already taken over. They reported back to Taylor, who thought that Velma would not have the sensitivity to deal gently with the Community, and that Todd had the better manner for that job. Among them they decided that Velma should be relieved of some of the responsibilities she had assumed.

When Todd and Leslie tried to explain this to Velma, she told them in effect to get lost. Both backed off, and Velma finished the job, which took over a week, counting hosting Carl's family, who came over from Holland for the ceremonies, and explaining his death to them. This was ticklish, because the police told us that the death was not, as we had assumed, a suicide, but an accident. He had evidently been experimenting with auto-erotic techniques involving semisuffocation and had lost consciousness before he could loosen the rope. Try explaining that to a middle-aged, middle-class Dutch lady over a long-distance telephone line! Better Velma than me.

In the course of the Dutch family's visit, one of Carl's brothers said to Velma, "I do not like the way my brother died. I think it is disgusting." Recognizing this as an attempt to escape his sense of shame and wanting to lighten his embarrassment, Velma replied, "Oh, I don't know. Carl was a very creative guy. This was just a piece of his creativity that went wrong."

Taylor was mistaken about Velma in this case. I suspect that the reason she misjudged her is the same phenomenon I mentioned earlier about choosing one's replacements. Taylor must have expected the person who succeeded her in this function to resemble her in superficial ways—gentle, quiet-spoken, and the like. Velma's resemblance was not on the surface. She had what Taylor had—swift intelligence, good judgment, and sensitivity to the feelings of the bereaved, all in a high degree. Her faults, though grievous enough when they were on display, did not enter into this scene.

Can Powerful Leaders Coexist?

One question that has interested me for a long time is the matter of how many leaders a little community can tolerate at one time. I've seen times (mostly in early years at East Wind) when the answer was, "one and only one." Struggles for dominance, all carried out in the name of some principle or another, can make it impossible for two people to share leadership. I am reminded of those bull seals who take all the females and fight off all the young male competitors, who go slinking away to a celibate life. I've heard the evolutionary excuses for this, but I still feel sorry for the young, frustrated seals. I don't see why the seal population couldn't have evolved just as well if the leadership in their community had been split a little more happily.

Twin Oaks in the 1980s was long past the big bull seal stage. Multiple leadership had been going on successfully since the early 1970s. People like Gerri and Taylor worked in tandem with pleasure rather than problems. People like Velma and Will were another matter.

Velma and Will

At first I thought they would recognize what they had in common and each make room for the other. Velma did appreciate Will's work on the KDC, and, from a sufficient distance, Will could admit that Velma did many useful tasks. They clashed, however, as soon as their areas touched. Will was attempting to design office space for the remodeling of Llano. The old house was to be divided in two, half for certain kitchen functions and the other half for offices. The office half would contain space for bookkeeping, computers, labor accounting, photocopier, typewriter, the cash box and other front-desk functions, and a dozen or so file cabinets. What Will was working on was an interior arrangement allocating parts of the new space among its proposed functions. The job was ideal for the purposes of his theory of architectural services. He was one who believed that it is a mistake to ask users what they want, because they lack the experience to imagine more than one solution.

In pursuance of his theory, he asked all of us users what functions had to take place in the new space. Velma was Computer Services manager. Along with the rest of us, she submitted her written list of functions, and Will went to work. What he came up with was not acceptable to Velma. He had given Computers a lot of open space, some of which was to be shared with other functions. Velma said (politely at first) that open space wouldn't work for her area, because she needed wall space for the telephone electronics, plus storage. The rest of us also gave some feedback on the original sketches and passed them back to Will.

A few days later we had a new set of sketches to look at, a noticeable feature being that Computer Services still didn't have its wall. Velma lost her temper. She said she needed a wall, and nobody was going to deprive her of it. If Will didn't plan it in, she would build it with her own hands. (She might have, too.) Will kept saying that asking for a wall was asking for a particular solution, and it wasn't Velma's business to propose solutions. It was his business. Please allow him to explain that he had considered her needs along with other people's needs, and in all fairness, she had to admit he had allotted her more space, proportionally, than other areas got. In short, she couldn't have a wall, and that was that.

The users and Will had a meeting to talk this matter over. Before the meeting even started, Velma was trembling with rage. I was walking beside her on the way to the meeting, and she said to me, "I shouldn't be going to this meeting. I'm too angry." Will was also on edge. The meeting began with a short explanation by Will on the function of architectural planning, the essence of which was that architects know better than users. Velma would not even listen to the end of the speech. She completely lost her temper, told Will he was incompetent and had no business trying to plan something he knew nothing about. Will in turn tore his drawings from the board where they had been taped, crumpled them up, and threw them in the waste basket. Velma implied that was where they belonged.

There was no smoothing over this breach, ever. The upshot of that particular argument was that Will resigned the job and Velma took it on. From then on it was Velma's little sketches that the users considered, and it was Velma's design that was built and that we now use. I doubt that the two ever spoke to each other again.

Neither Will nor Velma sees this clash as a matter of two bulls who cannot coexist in the same herd. They simply each think the other has an exaggerated view of his or her own competence. For each of them, the limitations of the other are glaringly obvious, and it is not safe to praise either of them in the presence of the other.

Velma as Products Manager

This conflict may have been the main reason that Gerri didn't pass the Products General Manager job on to Velma when she and Will decided to leave the Community. In any case Velma was too busy for it and did not volunteer.

During Paul's one-year tenure as Products General Manager he did a great deal of useful work, but an unfortunate thing happened that overshadowed it. Pier One reneged on a purchase order, lowering sales predictions drastically. Paul did not act to funnel the bulk of the remaining business back to Twin Oaks, but continued to pass on the orders to the sheltered workshop. This meant that we put out many thousands of dollars to hire other people to make hammocks for which we did not have a certain or immediate market. Meantime we were enjoying a light production year here on the farm. Not until September did our economic situation come to light. Result: $100,000 loss in net income.

Within a few months Paul had decided to leave the Community, and the General Manager spot was open again. For a couple of weeks we considered committees of various kinds. One or two people said they would be willing to work on a managerial team along with Velma or other people, but Velma rejected the team idea. Her plainly spoken terms were that she would have full authority or none. She would be happy to have a consulting committee to bat things around with, but the decisions would remain hers. Otherwise she wouldn't do it at all. It was the same condition that Gerri had set, years before. Once again the Community meekly said yes, thank you, and once again it was probably the right decision.

During Velma's time as General Manager, she made it her business to keep in touch with each products area manager (woodshop, rope shop, varnish shop, pillow shop, and so forth). Whenever they had a problem, they went to her, and she helped them figure out what to do. Did they need a piece of equipment? She bought it for them. Were they having trouble with materials flow? She unstuck the bottleneck. Very much a hands-on manager, she spent most of her time talking to people, encouraging them and solving their problems. The people who worked for her liked her. Sometimes they called her "Boss," and they always smiled when they said it. There were people who bridled at this kind of relationship, but they solved their problem by not working for her. During Velma's time in this job, production in many areas was the highest in our history.

When Velma took on the General Manager job, she passed on one managership (Craft Fairs) out of the double-handful that she held. It was obvious to everyone, certainly including Velma, that she needed to lighten her load of responsibility in order to take on the big job, but she felt that she did not have the time to train anyone to take these tasks over.

The fact that she was competent at everything she set her hand to does not mean that she handled all her jobs well under these conditions. Velma was up against literal physical limits. There was not time enough in her life, even if she did nothing but work, to give the time and energy to each managership that it needed and still keep up with her paper work. This meant that in some areas some of the tasks simply went undone for weeks at a time. Large parts of our administrative work could not be done because they were under Velma's authority in one way or another, and she was either off on a business trip or too busy to do it.

At the time I criticized her for not delegating some of her work. Looking back on this, she says that she delegated as much of it as she could keep indirect control of, but she couldn't stand to pass a task on to someone who wouldn't take her direction. It was easier to do the work herself, even if the Community had to wait for it.

At one point she even advertised for a secretary—someone who would do whatever was needed, from dealing with membership agreements to emptying the waste baskets. I cringed when I saw the card advertising the job. I thought, "This is not done! Twin Oakers will not work for each other in this hierarchic way!" I was wrong. She got a very good assistant, and nobody said a word in protest.

When Velma left the Community in 1990 it was for personal reasons involving a painful love relationship. In other respects she was not really ready to go. She had really wanted to stay long enough to orchestrate the Pier One Strategy (freeing the Community from the domination of a single large account) and set Twin Oaks firmly on its economic feet. She worked hard to that end, but it didn't happen soon enough to fit in with her greater, personal priorities. Nevertheless, she left the business in good condition. She cut back sharply on the sheltered workshop's portion of the business and also added two new products to the line (stretcher-making and hammock pillows).

After Velma, the General Managership really did have to go to a committee of three. A total of eight communitarians these days handles the responsibility that was once under Velma's control in one way or another. This is not to say that Velma did the work of eight people. (She only did the work of about three people.) It means that the authority she once exercized is now spread quite widely. She has also made herself available by telephone, and her memory is so remarkable that she can literally guide us long distance step by step through a procedure or a computer program when we need her. Nevertheless there are gaps in places that she used to keep covered. The dependence was real enough.

Does the Community Really Need Leaders?

Twin Oakers do not like to think about leadership. They do not like to name, or have anyone else name, the people who move the Community. Some members don't believe that the Community's directions are really swayed by individuals. Some even think that we all have an equal part in making Twin Oaks what it is. Others feel that, regardless of the mix of influence, it is in bad taste to say in so many words that some people are more important than others.

I think the intuitions behind these opinions are sound. It is rarely a good idea to make people feel small. Besides, it's really true that everybody contributes, and that dozens of us exercise one or another kind of leadership.

In elevating the names Gerri, Will, Taylor, and Velma and calling them leaders, I do so for examination rather than for praise. To my mind these people clearly led. Now come the interesting questions. Is the Community better or worse for such leadership? If leadership makes us uncomfortable, why do we permit it? If it is so costly to the leaders, why do they get into it?

I think we get the leaders we need and deserve. Both Gerri and Taylor would have been content with smaller roles if there had been enough people in the Community willing to share the load of serious responsibility. Will would not have felt so abused by the Community-imposed limits if he had enjoyed the society of peers. Velma would not have gathered such a heap of authority if other people had not dropped it in her lap. What unites these four names is that all four prioritized the Community's needs above their own for long periods of time and at considerable personal cost. Eventually each of them had to stop doing this, but they kept it up for years at a stretch.

I believe that as long as Twin Oaks members continue to seek personal freedom, including freedom from responsibility, and to put this desire ahead of other priorities, we will have leaders of this kind, lean on them, exploit them, even abuse them.

Why do such people step forward, accept the burden, even accept the abuse? In the outside world this question scarcely has to be asked, because it is obvious that people hope for power, glory, and quite possibly money. At Twin Oaks the answer isn't as easy. Yes, there's a little prestige, but enough to pay such a price for? There certainly isn't any money!

Speaking personally, when I take leadership, I do it mostly for the excitement of it. It interests me. I can paddle along in still waters for just so long before I begin to get bored and want to try for the rapids. I know there are always social costs, but if I see some significant task I think I could do, and I don't think anybody else is likely to do it, I generally find the excitement worth the pain.

I have asked other leaders what they get out of the job, and they usually talk about duty—"Somebody's got to do this." Fishing a little deeper, though, nets me answers not dissimilar to my own. Taylor said: "Actually, I came into Twin Oaks very much wanting to lead, to have a chance to try my hand in designing a better society."

Then there's the other question—why do the members who are made uneasy by strong leadership continue to seek it and rely on it? Leslie tells a Woody Allen story on this subject that goes like this:

> A man once went to a psychiatrist on behalf of his friend. "Doc," he said, "you've got to do something for my friend. He thinks he's a chicken." The doctor said "I can try. Why don't you have him come in?" The man answered, "Well, the thing is, I need the eggs."

This seems to me an adequate answer to the question of why people unwillingly but predictably accept leadership from people who sometimes make them uncomfortable. They need the eggs. If the actual need for leadership is, as some people think, a delusion, then the people who seek it share in that delusion without necessarily admitting it.

The other possibility is that the friend really is a chicken, and the demand for eggs is perfectly reasonable. I tend to this opinion. When I'm in a leader role, I know I'm supposed to deliver something in exchange for the excitement of being in charge. When I'm following somebody else's lead, I try to remember to give respect and cooperation in exchange for what that leader is producing. Either way, I value the leadership function and wouldn't want to live in a community that rejected it completely.

But every once in a while a question sneaks into my mind that makes me nervous about the whole subject. It says "What would have happened if you (or Velma, or Taylor, or whoever) had not stepped forward to take the lead?" What if Shana had not been available to be dairy manager? What if Gerri had not found the sheltered workshop solution to the hammock labor problem? What if Velma had not been available to pull the Products area back together when it fell apart? What if we hadn't had Will to create the KDC? What if Henry had never come? My intuitive answer is, "Someone else would have stepped forward and done something else." It would be a different community, certainly, but not, I believe, one without leaders.

266

Chapter 27

Art, Music, and Theater

It used to irritate me when outsiders would criticize Twin Oaks for its shortage of artistic work. I don't know when they thought we were supposed to have the time to create a Golden Age when we were still struggling for basic income and living space. But all that, including the irritation, is history. These days we're so busy having fun and creating things and trying to make time to have even more fun and create even more things that I sometimes wonder how we manage to get the work done.

Take the visual arts. So far we haven't found the space to make a studio, but communitarians use whatever space they can find, and they produce an astounding variety of art work. Every year on one of the holidays we put some of this out for the whole community to see. Displays include paintings, carvings, drawings, photographs, sculpture, textiles, and handicrafts, and I think a lot of them are quite good. Some artists are too shy to display their work, so there is even more going on than we ever get a chance to see.

As to our writers, unless you consider O&I papers an art form, we have only one poet who puts his poems out for us to read.

Over the years we have had very few writers willing to show their work.

Music is another matter entirely.

Choir

There's a line in *Walden Two* that still has the power to stir me. It's where a woman who has been delayed is apologizing for her late appearance and explains that she has been at a choir practice, and "The Bach went badly, and Fergy kept us on and on." The vision of being part of a community choir which is good enough to perform a Bach mass, in a society disciplined enough so that the director had both the motivation and the power to "keep us on and on" at a rehearsal moves me to a wistfulness bordering on tears. The Bach that the Twin Oaks choir attempts is limited to straightforward chorales, which we find quite difficult enough, and as to being kept on and on, Twin Oakers wouldn't stand for it. They would simply get up and walk out.

Nevertheless we at least have a choir. Okay, maybe there are only two basses, and the tenor part is often sung by women; granted that we have no place to practice except the main dining room, where we have to compete with the loud tapes that are being played in the kitchen; and admitted that few communitarians really want to hear us perform more than about once a year. Just the same, it's the only choir I know about in the secular community movement, and there is a lot about it that makes it both valuable and enduring.

The reason the choir has lasted as long as it has (eight years so far) is that it is directed by a dedicated musician who is not a member. George, our neighbor and friend, describes himself as an "ant," in comparison to the average Twin Oaks "grasshopper." Not only is he steady and dependable, but he was taught as a small child to live his life for God and other people, and he never got over the lesson. We get the benefit.

Some of the most beautiful choir music in the world was written for the Christian church, and its lyrics are not comfortable for a group with a wide variety of beliefs and nonbeliefs. Rather than restrict ourselves to music with secular words, we have done some wholesale changing of the words to religious music. Thus, "Oh, sing ye to the Lord" became "O sing we in the morn," and "The watery worlds are all His own" became "The watery worlds are all our own," and the like.

Other Music

By no means all of Twin Oaks singers have joined the choir. A fair number of vocally talented people have explained that they do not like the sound of religious music, regardless of the words, and some people find the music too difficult as well.

For those who don't care for classical music, there is currently a band called the Flying Tomatoes. This is the most recent of many short-lived rock and folk ensembles. I think the first was in 1971, in which both the fiddler and the banjo player had to learn to play their respective instruments before they could get started. These days musicians tend to come into the community rather better prepared. The Flying Tomatoes musicians write a lot of their own music and lyrics. They play for us on holidays.

If you want to hear all the variety of Twin Oaks musical endeavor, you need to come to one of our coffee houses or "Talent/ No Talent Shows." At any given time we probably have a half dozen fledgling vocalists and an equal number of guitar players, many of whom make up their own songs. There are also people who play other instruments—anything from a saxophone to a pennywhistle. To date we have not had a serious attempt at a classical instrumental ensemble, and at our size an orchestra has remained beyond our reach.

Theater

But we are ambitious in other directions. We have an astonishingly large pool of acting talent, and over the last ten years we have had in-house performances of eighteen dramatic and comedy works. Twin Oaks is a lively audience, laughing at all jokes, even if only medium-funny, and awarding rave reviews to everybody.

My personal theater experience at Twin Oaks was in the field of musical comedy. Until I saw Leslie pull it off, it never occurred to me that Twin Oaks could do a musical. We have no orchestra, for starters. For that matter, we don't have a stage, either. Apart from the physical barriers, Broadway shows are usually on themes so far from our communal values that our actors are unwilling to spend the time memorizing the lines. They also are reluctant to sing songs with lyrics that are usually sexist if not worse.

Leslie solved the problem by choosing her favorite musical comedy, changing the male protagonist to a female one, then throwing out the original theme of the play and substituting a vigorous and amusing feminist one. She rewrote lines to suit the new idea, and molded new lyrics to the songs. Despite a certain amount of inevitable clumsiness, the amalgam worked in the Twin Oaks environment. The original music helped to carry it off, the voices accompanied by a piano, guitar, flute, and occasional drums. Clever costumes and props added a lot. The usual Twin Oaks audience was boosted by the attendance of neighbors and former members, who were all loudly delighted by everything, as usual.

I was inspired by Leslie's success and decided to write my own musical. I called it "Utopia," and based it on a rather old-fashioned theme, namely that home (in our case, Twin Oaks,) is better than other places. My protagonist was drawn from life, a young man who leaves the Community, experiences various setbacks in the Outside World, and eventually finds a way back home. I tossed in an angel and a demon, three romances, and 14 songs, depending once again upon piano and flute for accompaniment. Writing all the songs was beyond my skill, so I wrote a few and then raided Broadway and opera for the rest, changing the words as appropriate. My efforts met with the same heady success as Leslie's.

I'm not at all sure about the legality of what Leslie and I did, so I think I'd better not quote the takeoffs we wrote, even though we think them rather clever. But I think I can quote my own favorite, sung to the tune and in the spirit of Gilbert and Sullivan's "Modern Major General," which must surely be in the public domain by now. It went like this:

Good Communitarian

He is a perfect model of a Good Communitarian.
He tries to get consensus and is never a Contrarian.
He always reads the O&I but doesn't often write for it.
If he has an opinion, he is too polite to fight for it.

For listening and compromise he has a great affinity.
He never knocks the Planners, though they aren't the Holy Trinity.
He's humble, and he's modest, and he doesn't ever power-seek.
You find him in the hammock shop for every hundred-hour week.*

---

*100-hour week. When we need to make a lot of hammocks in a hurry, members will sometimes set a goal for themselves of working 100 hours, mostly in the hammock shop. This makes an extremely tiring week (seven 14-hour days in a row), but if a group makes this commitment together, the challenge may get them through.

271

If someone needs a volunteer, they have no trouble finding him.
He shows up for his kitchen shifts without someone reminding him.
He's done his share of milking shifts, and other things agrarian.
He is the very model of a Good Communitarian.

If he becomes a manager, the workers don't feel generaled.
He's quite efficient at machines he finds at City Emerald.*
He'll do by hand whatever we don't have the right equipment for.
He always does a year of what he's made a year's commitment for.

He's perfectly at home with matters officey and clerical.
He makes a calculator do its sorcery numerical.
He favors friendly nudity and sleeps without pajamas on.
He volunteered to act a minor role in Leslie's "Amazon."

He likes to be a primary and put the kiddies bed-a-bye.
He is a standard you can judge a midi-mega-meta by.
He celebrates on Halloween in costumes he looks scary in.
He is the very model of a Good Communitarian.

In Astrologic signs he knows the Libras from the Geminis.
He uses "co" and "person" and can tell which words to feminize.
If supper cooks have burned the beans, he isn't super critical.
He knows that what he eats is for the thinking man political.

He says "MT" and "STP" and all things alphabetical.
He knows what terms to use, and he eschews all views heretical.
He wears his very oldest jeans when dining in a restaurant.
He never puts a single thing that's made of polyester on.

He listens to his feelings and distrusts all facts empirical.
He'd never get through college short of some astounding miracle.
He's always liked the Courtyard more than Tupelo or Merion.
He is the very model of a Good Communitarian.

Twin Oaks' approach to theatrical productions is like almost everything else we do, by which I mean that half the people involved don't take it very seriously. Lines are frequently not fully memorized until the dress rehearsal. Attempts at directing are hampered by some members of the cast reading from a script, and one or two key actors or musicians not showing up for the rehearsal.

---

*Emerald City, so named because it is at the end of a rather long path, is a large woodshop with industrial woodworking equipment.

In addition, some people feel that directing a play should be a cooperative endeavor, and everybody's ideas are equally valuable. This means stopping for discussion, which takes a fair amount of time. I had a small role in Leslie's musical, and this style of cooperative directing made me frantic. Several times I just left the rehearsal, unwilling to wait for people to work it out, and so became, in my turn, part of the problem. In spite of or because of all this, Leslie's show was a tremendous success. Almost everybody who took part has wonderful memories of the whole process.

When I took my turn at trying to produce a show, I intended at first to emulate Leslie's method, because I could see what a joyous experience most of her actors had had. But it didn't work for me, and I abandoned the effort early on. It isn't in me to sit around and let a process meander on its own when I know where I want it to go. So I shared the directing with Colleen, a friend who is also a take-charge type. The actors accepted the direction and made their suggestions outside of rehearsal time. Our show was equally successful.

All I can make out of that is that we're a big, loose, tolerant community, ready to be amused and not attached to any one method of doing things. Our standards are not exacting, and we seldom produce art. We're more likely to produce fun. Part of me isn't satisfied with that, but since I don't want to go around being discontented, I'm back to commanding the sun to rise. Communitarians tend to be casual. Maybe they can be seriously committed to certain things some of the time. But it sure isn't going to be the theater.

As our population rises and we can afford to be generous with labor, we have taken steps in the direction of subsidizing some art. Weeds and Knots (committee created to ease personal money or labor problems) has given out labor credits for both play writing and music practice. Members contributed Personal Service Credits (from their own vacation balances) to be distributed after the fact to the actors and singers in both musical comedies. These credits were received gratefully, but the work was done without the expectation of compensation.

It is too soon to tell if this is a trend, if we are moving in the direction of paying our performers. I doubt it. Not all our homegrown music put together can match the popularity of professional performers and their high quality recordings. To a certain extent, the support musicians get from the rest of the members is in response to their intent and their effort, rather than to the quality of the product. People like the idea of having our own band, choir, instrumentalists, etc. When it comes to listening for pleasure, however, they use their radios, tape decks, and CD's to import the music. Twin Oakers gathering to hear their own musicians reminds me of fond parents at a class play. We do enjoy the show, yes, but the reasons for the enjoyment have to do with our relationship to the performers. That's all right with me. We didn't create Twin Oaks for the purpose of advancing the arts but for enhancing lives.

Recorder quartet. From left to right: Paula, me (Kat),
Sandy and George (choir director)

The Flying Tomatoes

276

WE AT SINCERITY WOULD LIKE TO THANK THE FINE FOLKS OF TWIN OAKS FOR SUPPORTING FURTHER COMMUNICATION BETWEEN OUR TWO COMMUNITIES. IT MUST HAVE BEEN DIFFICULT TO WEIGH THE RELATIVE MERITS OF ALL THE FINE OTRA REQUESTS THIS YEAR, AND WE ARE DULY IMPRESSED WITH YOUR CAREFULLY CONSIDERED JUDGEMENTS. IN MANY WAYS, SINCERITY WOULD BE NOTHING WITHOUT TWIN OAKS UNERRING ABILITY TO MAKE GOOD DECISIONS.

NOT TO MENTION THE MIND-CONTROLLING CHEMICALS WE PUMPED INTO THEIR WATER SUPPLY JUST PRIOR TO THE TRADE-OFF...

GUMMPPH!

THANK YOU AGAIN FOR YOUR FREELY CHOSEN SUPPORT!

AND REMEMBER TO KEEP DRINKING PLENTY OF H_2O !!

Chapter 28

Adventures with
Internal Revenue

I was going to start out by saying, "This is going to be a dull chapter, and you will probably want to skip it unless you're a bookkeeper or a community founder or an IRS agent." But the more I think about it, the less dull it seems to me. So I decided I'd put all the technical stuff in a box for the sake of the people who need the information, and tell some stories to fill out the chapter.

We are organized as an IRS Code 501(d) corporation. This means all taxable income, whether or not distributed, is taxed to the individual members, who are treated as partners. We file a Form 1065 as a community and a regular 1040 for each member, on which the appropriate share of the Community's income is declared under dividends (not wages).

We don't have to pay social security.

IRS has no forms to apply for 501(d) status. You write to them, and they tell you what information they want. If you're a community and need help, write to: Federation Desk, East Wind Community, Tecumseh, MO 65760, and ask for the Systems and Structures Packet.

When we started the Community we had a very puzzling time finding out how to file taxes. We figured there had to be some way to do it, but it wasn't at all obvious. We were incorporated, but corporate taxes didn't seem appropriate, because we had no employees at all but all kinds of "labor expense," namely the cost of supporting the members. We were sort of a partnership, but our "partners" came and went rapidly (like every three months, in the early years) and didn't bring in any capital with them or take any when they left. One glance at the partnership forms was enough to see that they had little to do with us. In some ways we seemed to be a not-for-profit organization, because our aims were personal spiritual growth and social reform, but the rules for not-for-profit organizations require that none of the profits go to the members. We couldn't claim that. We eat our profits.

And then we found it—a paragraph so obscure that IRS itself didn't seem to remember that it was there. It is Internal Revenue Code 501(d), and it was written long ago for the Shakers or somebody like that, who had a friend in Congress. However dissimilar we are in most ways to the Shakers, we have one thing in common, and it's the part that Internal Revenue cares about: Our finances are organized the same way.

What this paragraph basically says is that the corporation itself doesn't have to pay any taxes, but the members do. All we have to do is figure out how much money we make, divide that amount by the number of members, and tell each member to write that amount on his or her income tax return, as dividends.

We decided this was the status for us, but nobody could tell us how to qualify for it. Twin Oaks didn't get around to applying for several years. We just filed our taxes as if we already had the status, and for a long time we didn't hear any objections from the tax people.

However, when I lived at East Wind, that Community decided to make the effort to get its formal exemption. So I wrote to IRS, and they put my letter in their "When we have nothing better to do" pile. In the meantime, East Wind, like Twin Oaks, filed as a 501(d) organization without official permission.

Then one year IRS must have hired some college students to clean up the old correspondence, because they finally answered our question. No, there were no forms to fill out. The status was so rare that it hadn't seemed worth the bother. But if we wanted to, we could send them copies of our corporate documents, proof that we carried on our business pretty much like the prototype Shakers or whoever, and some financial statements. Financial statements? I wondered what a newly-organized group would do and was just as glad we hadn't tried earlier. By this time, however, East Wind had enough financial history to make up a financial statement, so we did as we were told.

It took months to get the exemption, but we got it. They have some very decent and careful people working for IRS, believe it or not. We lucked into a woman who made a point of understanding what we were and could then talk to us intelligently about what we needed to do. She shepherded our application through a couple of superior levels of administration, and eventually sent East Wind its exemption letter.

Once East Wind had its 501(d) status, we advised Twin Oaks to do the same, but Twin Oaks hadn't had any difficulties and didn't predict any. Rather than call IRS's attention to the Community's existence, after 7 years of a rather informal relationship, Twin Oaks decided to let well enough alone.

But one day Twin Oaks's number popped up somehow in IRS's mysterious system, and they came out to find out what we were up to. The man they sent was named Mr. Knicely, and that's the way he did things. We set Mr. Knicely up in the Compost Cafe* with all the ledgers he cared to see, and he studied us for several days.

Mr. Knicely and the friendly folks in his home office decided that Twin Oaks not only did not have a tax exemption, but wasn't entitled to one, because we were not their idea of communal. According to them, we didn't have a common treasury, because we permitted members to keep any savings accumulated before joining the Community. Mr. Knicely and company imagined that what Congress had meant by the original legislation was that we had to be exactly like those Shakers, donate all of our savings, and take a vow of poverty. However, IRS didn't take the trouble to study the Shakers, who in fact did not live under the strict rules that were imagined for them. Somebody pointed this out to IRS, and they argued (You won't believe this) that there was a high probability that the original members of Congress had gone by the same misunderstanding that the current IRS people had, that the legislation had been based on that misconception, and that it therefore applied only to groups organized the way that modern-day tax investigators thought that the long-ago Congress had imagined the Shakers to be organized.

---

*So called because, in the days before we got proper sewage disposal, this building was a posh, two-seater composting toilet. It didn't work very well, because we calculated the capacity wrong, so we revamped it into much needed auxiliary dining space. Today it serves as a smokers' retreat.

I know people who reason like that. I generally like them and have fun talking to them. It's a kind of game. But for ordinary people reading the plain language of the regulation, this sort of thing won't wash. Ultimately it didn't wash with the Tax Court, either, but that's getting ahead of the story.

Internal Revenue was friendly and courteous but stuck to its interpretation and handed us a bill for a quarter million dollars in back taxes, based on their denying us 501(d) status because we hadn't had, as they saw it, a communal treasury. Twin Oaks couldn't pay it, at least not right away.

So we did several things. We put up $50,000 for IRS to hold while we went to court. We hired a first-class firm of tax lawyers to handle our case, and with their aid we challenged the ruling through the Tax Court. We changed our bylaws to meet the stricter definition of "common treasury," so that at least in future years we would qualify, even if we lost the court case. (This was a messy business. We had to invent another category of membership, called "intermediate membership" for people who weren't yet prepared to take a vow of poverty, and we had to require that everybody actually donate all their savings when they had been in community for ten years. We lost two good members over it, too, who refused, when the ten-year mark approached, to let go of their financial security.) Then we assumed the worst and set about earning and saving the money to pay the back taxes if we ultimately had to—that and the legal fees, which would need to be paid, win or lose.

Four years later, our case came to the top of somebody's in-box and was looked at by a competent Tax Court judge. This judge studied the case and decided it on its merits. We won. In her comments on the case, she told IRS that 501(d) corporations, as far as she could tell, weren't getting such a big advantage that they should be required to make big sacrifices for it, since all the legislation does is transfer liability from the corporation to the individual members. She also remarked drily that she declined to read the minds of long-dead congressmen and would take the law as written, where there is no mention of a vow of poverty.

It cost us about $60,000 in legal fees to fight the case, and I sincerely hope there are other 501(d) groups out there who can get some benefit from it.

Of course, after that we had to go through the business of changing our bylaws back again, removing the "intermediate member" status, and doing away with the vow of poverty. But we did it cheerfully enough. We had a $50,000 refund coming! Not only that, but over the years that nest egg had earned another $40,000 in interest. This, together with the money we had been saving in case we had to pay the back taxes, built us two lovely buildings, with change left over.

Mr. Knicely, true to his name, congratulated us.

Actually doing Twin Oaks taxes is a complex process. First we figure out how many members we have, which isn't simple, because everybody who was a member at any time during the year is part of that number. If 20 people joined and 19 left during the year, and 65 were here all year, we have to produce 104 notices telling people how much to write on their tax returns.

In tax matters, as in other things, Twin Oaks is a law-abiding organization. It was obvious early on that it just didn't pay to try to be slippery. During the financially desperate first year I recall that we had cars with expired registrations driven by people with expired drivers' licenses, but not any more. You'd have a hard time finding a more cautious group on legal matters than Twin Oaks.

Since our businesses and our homes are all mixed up together, we have to estimate the amount of our expenses that can reasonably be deducted for the business. We have pages upon pages of these calculations. (Well, let's see, this shop is 1058 square feet, of which 650 square feet are dedicated to the machine shop, which in its turn is used approximately 50% of the time for business purposes. So you multiply . . .) The job is a lot of fun for us bookkeeping types who like keeping track of obscure things and coming up with numbers that are actually used for something. The whole job takes us about 300 hours each year.

284

Chapter 29

Whose Book is it, Anyway?—
The Chapters I Didn't Write

The process of writing and publishing this book about the Community has presented me and Twin Oaks with new territory to muddle through. First of all, whose book is it? I could say it is mine, because it was my idea, my work, and in many ways my story. Or I could say it belongs to Twin Oaks, because I'm a member, because I'm getting labor credits for the work, and because Twin Oaks' reputation will be affected by what I write.

The Washing Machine Conversation

The first time I wrote a book about Twin Oaks, when the Community was five years old, it did not occur to me to show it to anyone before I sent it off to potential publishers. I assumed, without thinking about it, that I spoke for the Community. Afterward, I got some feedback about that from a member named Daniel. I remember standing by the washing machine in the laundry room of Harmony. I remember exactly where I was standing, and where Daniel was standing, and what he looked like. (Negative feedback stamps the memory like that.) Daniel said, "I don't like your book, and I don't think it represents Twin Oaks." He went on to explain what should have been obvious to me, which was that he and his friends saw a different Twin Oaks from the one I described, and that they thought their vision just as legitimate as mine. To his mind, publishing my version and not his was twisting the truth.

Doing Better the Second Time Around

I thought a lot about the washing machine conversation over the years between that book and this one. Among other things I decided to present a more balanced view the second time around. Also, I determined to give the new book all the process that the group is by now accustomed to.

First I went to the Process Team and asked advice. They suggested I get the Outreach Council to sponsor the project. I talked to all the members of the Outreach Council, and they each said the same thing—"Write whatever you want. Our experience is that articles and books about the Community always turn out to be good for us, no matter what they say."

Even with this carte blanche permission I thought it would be a good idea to let the whole Community read the manuscript and suggest corrections and additions before it went to press. I put a draft in the lounge, circulated several private copies in addition, and invited anyone and everyone to make whatever comment they cared to. I gave them eight weeks to do it.

One response was a lot of copy-editing. Several people marked my typos and enlightened me on the spelling of "bureaucratic." Others corrected historical detail. A few asked me to change some phrase or other that seemed to them misleading or awkward or vague. One or two questioned my opinions and tried to convince me of a different point of view. Sometimes they succeeded. None of this was any problem beyond the drudgery of editing. I made dozens of little changes in response. When I just didn't agree with the correction or suggestion, I took the time to explain why I was sticking to my version.

Pam and Delancey Speak Up

Then at the very end, just as I was thinking with some satisfaction that I had handled the process well and that the washing machine conversation was behind me at last, I found two written comments that made me reconsider. One was from Pam, who simply asked for more account of the daily life. Another was from Delancey and read as follows:

> "I feel like you covered all the bases but I have some lingering disappointment. I think I wanted more juicy anecdotes, more account

of the life here rather than just the structure. How about a collection of some members' favorite memories (which you wouldn't have to write, just collect and edit)? My guess is I'm not alone in wanting more anecdotes and description of activities and flavor here.

"For example, I would say a favorite memory of mine is cooking for Freedom House one night when we had much more help than expected and a warm bustling jovial mood in the kitchen, a real feeling of camaraderie. And at the snack table Dianne was teaching of group of children and adults some Christmas carols in sign language.

"Another scene that warmed my heart was when I, as a midi, and Brenda and Ivy took all the midi and meta kids up to the graveyard on the High South, rolled and played on the hill and then the children went to each grave and asked questions about each person and about death in general, but didn't seem perturbed, only respectful and curious. It was a stretch for us adults to explain it—very poignant. I think such a collection of poignant memories would say a lot about the Community."

I think so, too. I think that it is just such scenes of comrade-ship and emotion that account for the attachment both current and former members develop and retain for this Community. I look over my chapter headings, and I see what she means. There are all my major interests: Government, politics, and power; systems and structures and theories. I have documented all the unpleasantness well enough, the conflict, the tense issues, the ego battles, even the petty crime. Where is the account of daily life? Where have I mentioned the sense of community?

The problem, of course, is that this is a personal account, not a documentary. My personal daily life is largely clerical and admin-istrative. My mental furniture is made up mostly of the sorts of things I've been writing about—systems and politics and growth and so forth. Pam's and Delancey's Twin Oaks is quite different, and so, I'm willing to bet, is the way they feel about it.

I Process Some Tomatoes

Both Pam and Delancey mentioned food processing. Every once in a while I have an impulse to do some mildly physical task like food processing, and I'll join the people sitting around the big tub under an oak tree. Here's what it feels like to me:

There I am, sorting tomatoes into categories for immediate eating, canning, or juice, and cutting out the bad parts. I have tomato juice running down my arms to my elbows, and I am trying to brush an insect off my cheek by rubbing my face against my shoulder, because my hands are full of tomato goo. The insect flies right back. My behind is getting sore from sitting on the wooden bench. The tree shade we started under shifts away as the afternoon progresses, and I feel hot and uncomfortable. The conversation is mostly stuff like, "Do we have another of those white buckets, because this one is almost full."

I have never been able to tell myself that I don't mind tomato juice on my elbows and insects on my face. I glance at Pam and wonder what she feels. She is up to her elbows in tomatoes, too, and her face is bright red from the sun, but she is smiling. I think she likes this whole scene. I am grateful to Pam and all her kind who feel cheerful about a thousand pounds of ripe tomatoes, and I am deeply grateful that I don't really have to do this kind of work regularly. Normally Twin Oaks lets me earn my living in the office, where I sit on a padded chair, and the worst thing I get on my hands is copier toner.

A Sense of Community

For Pam and Delancey, food processing is a significant part of daily life, and I wonder if, over all, and in spite of the heat and goo and insects, they get a sense of community out of it. I sure hope so. Do I feel anything like that in the office? What I feel is that I am doing a job that matters for people who matter, all living together in a Community that matters. That is quite sufficient for me, but I'm not sure I'll have poignant memories of changing a printer ribbon to carry into my old age.

Life here isn't all work, of course, and if I were a more social person, I'd regale you with anecdotes about what happened one evening in a bridge game, or Dungeons and Dragons, or Wednesday night Star Trek videos, or some of the encounter, therapy, or support groups. Since I don't attend any of these events, any description I gave you would be about as convincing as an advertisement for an ocean cruise.

I know what Delancey is talking about. There are moments in a happy person's life when one suddenly feels that one is in the right place, doing the right thing at the right time in the right way, taking part with other people in something greater than one's self. This experience is a central one for many communitarians, and some people have left us because they didn't feel it often enough. Taylor in her time and Leslie in later years have understood this need and have tried to create it purposely by organizing campfires, sings, sharing circles, and the like. I imagine this works for

288

some people. I avoid such ceremonies, because I'm pretty sure I'm not going to feel anything except silly.

Even though I draw the line at anthologizing group memoirs, I think Delancey's complaint is legitimate. I haven't communicated the emotional essence of belonging to Twin Oaks, and I wish I could have.

Incomplete Portraits

Another grumble I heard about this manuscript was that I have whitewashed certain characters the knowledgable reader thinks were obnoxious. Well, yes. Some people would rather have seen my first drafts, in which I was more critical and in some ways more truthful. By the time I got to final editing, I had exorcized some old angers just by writing things down. I have had time to distinguish between portraits that explain Twin Oaks and those that merely vent my personal feelings, and I deleted the latter.

On the other hand, I didn't see any good reason to tone down my compliments. Some readers found the results somewhat lop-sided. I see their point, but those are the kinds of decisions a writer has to make.

Process

I need to explain why there isn't a chapter devoted to "process." I tried to write one. In fact I wrote it, edited, rewrote, worried about it, edited again, and finally threw it out. What Twin Oaks calls "process" is so complex and at the same time so nebulous that I had a hard time explaining it briefly. My efforts to do it justice went on for pages and pages, unrelieved by anecdotes. I tried to shorten it, but it was still boring.

Anyone trying to understand Twin Oaks or any of today's intentional communities should know that we do a lot of what we call "process," and that we find it very important. The way Twin Oaks uses the word, it generally means a lot of structured meetings to talk things over and try to soothe feelings and resolve problems. Quite likely the reason I don't write about it well is that I have a hard time sitting through the meetings. The more we try as a group to make sure every member gets a chance to speak, the more I wish I were somewhere else.

Process is a difficult subject for me also because I tend to emphasize individuals and their accomplishments, and process isn't about individuals. It's about the group as a whole finding ways to get along together. I recognize that this is valuable, but I can't find a way to make it entertaining.

Now have I discharged my obligation to Process? Have I responded adequately to the gentle requests that my book about Twin Oaks have more facets of Twin Oaks in it, and not just the parts that fascinate me? Probably not. It remains unbalanced, analytical, and personal.

What all this comes down to is that in the long run the washing machine conversation didn't do a whole lot of good after all. I'd like to please other communitarians, but on some basic level I guess I think this is my book, process notwithstanding.

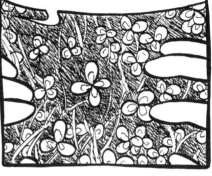

Chapter 30

Demographics and Some
Remarks About Aging

Recently I was in an SLG meeting of people of mixed ages, doing "check-ins." (That is, we were each telling the others how our lives were going, what problems we were dealing with, and so forth.) Sharon, age twenty, reported that she had been to a Twin Oaks party recently but had found it unsatisfactory, because there were so many people there who were older than she is. She felt inhibited, didn't feel that she could let go and be giddy and silly. "I'm feeling the need to have some serious fun!" she said.

Serious fun is a quantity also desired by the people who unintentionally spoiled the party for Sharon. Being in a majority, they are in a better position to get it. The desire of the middle-aged to retain as much of their youth as possible has prevented the development of a separate youth culture at Twin Oaks. The young accept the principle that age is not an issue and learn to treat their elders as equals.

Although we recognize that there are rough age groupings at Twin Oaks, we try to avoid classifying people according to age. Not long ago one of our teen-age girls asked permission to give a party for her high school friends and begged the adult Twin Oakers to stay away. The request was granted, but not graciously. Several adults resented the exclusion and said so. They called it "ageism."

On the other hand, the oldest Twin Oakers once organized a monthly supper group (The Wise Crackers), to which only those over age forty were invited. I didn't hear of any resentment, but there were requests from thirty-nine-year-olds to be included. "I'm in my fortieth year. Doesn't that count?"

For the most part, there is a general assumption that everybody is invited to everything except private parties. I have observed birthday parties for four-year olds at which most of the ice cream and cake was consumed by adults.

The real disadvantages of aging are those imposed by nature. The first one to hit, here as elsewhere, is the deterioration in personal appearance. Hair grays or falls out. Bodies thicken. After that come the diminution of stamina, the minor aches, and so forth. These things are hardly unique to community, and I believe that they are easier to bear at Twin Oaks than in the world at large. This is because we are determined as a culture not to let arbitrary distinctions like age interfere with our enjoyment of life.

Recently Piper, our oldest member (age sixty-eight) fell and broke her ankle. At her age it takes a long time for a bone to heal, and we do not yet know how much function that ankle will recover. What worries her is not so much the difficulty of walking with a cane but the possibility of having to stop dancing! Twin Oaks dances are one of her major pleasures in life.

The physical problems of aging hit each individual differently and are usually met with surprise and indignation, then varying degrees of accommodation and acceptance. Recently we had a forum about aging at Twin Oaks, featuring four members over sixty, each telling his or her experiences of living here while being older than most members. All four of them emphasized the unwelcome onset of physical weaknesses as their major age-related problem. The Community got high marks for its attitudes, both official and personal.

Aside from physical problems, there is an aspect of pioneering in being old at Twin Oaks that isn't much fun. We can remember perfectly well what it was like to be younger, but the younger people have no reciprocal memories, and the simple fact is that they frequently don't believe our complaints. We older people may ask for something special because of a special need—a larger than average room, because we can no longer climb a ladder to a loft bed, an electric cart to save our feet or hip joints, an air-conditioned space, because we feel ill in hot weather. Eventually we generally get what we ask for, partly because we are careful to be reasonable and mostly because the average Twin Oaker is a compassionate person. Before we get it, however, we must endure the unsympathetic criticism of some who have not yet experienced bodily weakness and don't believe they ever will. The general line they take is this: If people eat right and exercise, they won't be weak in their old age. They generally know several old people who still work in the garden (or do yoga, or dance the polka) at age seventy. They imply, without actually saying so in public, that the Community should not indulge people who did not take proper care of their bodies and are now reaping the consequences. They even imply that the older people are exaggerating their ills because they are self-indulgent people who like luxuries.

This is very hard to contradict, because, indeed, who can deny that there are self-indulgent and luxury-loving people among the old? The point, of course, is that we want the same comfort and mobility that the self-indulgent, comfort-loving young person gets.

Underneath all these grumbles I think I can hear something else. I think what the young are trying to do is avoid believing that the weaknesses of aging will happen to them. If they can believe that we older people are exaggerating and pretending, then they don't have to fear their own futures.

Until very recently a look at our demographics showed that the Twin Oaks population was aging. I mean more than the obvious biological fact about individuals. The average age of the group as a whole had been rising fairly rapidly. Here are some contributing factors:

Some members have decided to spend their lives here, and of course they keep getting older. These career communitarians could be any age, but the ones I am sure of are all over forty.

The Sixties generation, which continues to dominate our culture, is now about forty to forty-five years old. Those people are likely to feel comfortable with Twin Oaks values and assumptions and therefore be more likely to join us than any other age group. In ten years the Sixties people will be in their fifties. Will they still be joining? Quite possibly.

People who have been attracted to the Twin Oaks idea for years but had children to raise are now sending those children off to college and are free to follow their own paths. Some of those paths lead here.

This trend could be alarming. If we got to the point that the average member became prone to back problems or heart conditions, we could have a hard time getting the work done. Much of our activity is big-muscle work: sawmill, construction, lifting heavy pots or milk cans, or hay bales, or cases of rope, or trays of dishes, repairing cars, loading and unloading, forestry. Getting into and out of our vans requires secure knee joints. Even hammock-making takes a toll on backs, shoulders, and wrists. As long as our average age is in the thirties, we don't have to think much about this, but if the average age got to be forty-five, perhaps a quarter of us would be asking for useful work not involving much heavy lifting, bending, climbing, or straining any particular set of muscles.

We're not just going to sit around and wait for this to happen. We'll be thinking and working toward finding income-making areas and other useful work for older people to major in. We may also find we need to get machines to help with tasks now done by human muscles. Our architectural planning already reflects a felt need to keep public rooms on one level, accessible to all.

While it is sensible to plan for older people, our worries about failing to attract the young have proved needless. The young are once again interested in Twin Oaks, and our age groups seem to be balancing out once again.

Here are some actual figures for the ages of our population as of the end of 1992:

Age

20 - 25	12
26 - 35	29
36 - 45	24
46 - 55	13
56 and older	7

It is important for the Community to keep the flow of young people coming in to the Community. We have only fifteen children with an adult population of eighty-five, so are not a natural village. Those children we do raise are typically unwilling to spend their teen years here and unlikely to settle down in the place where they grew up. This means that our member replacements come entirely from the outside, and so our ultimate survival depends on attracting people in their twenties.

What are these young people looking for, and to what extent can they find it here? Many of the ones we meet are strongly idealistic. They feel that the preceding generations have made a mess of things, and they want a chance to help put the world on a healthy track. Who can argue with them? Twin Oakers who came of age in the Sixties are particularly sympathetic. As a Community we are engaged simultaneously in several different idealistic efforts to help out with global problems. Nevertheless, frequently new young members are unsatisfied with what Twin Oaks did before they came. They have an understandable desire to use their energy in newer, more dramatic ways, to make a deeper impact, and to feel that they have personally made a difference. Pitching in with ongoing efforts doesn't always provide a big enough kick.

A young people's commune, in which a group of age peers take on radical change as a group, providing both the leadership and the follow-through, would be a satisfying experience for these young people, but it is not realistically available for most of them. Starting a new community takes either a big hunk of money or a great deal of luck, and probably both.

The next best thing, then, is to join an existing group that comes as close as possible to their ideals, and work within that group to change it into the community of their dreams. The infrastructure is already here, having been provided by previous generations of communitarians.

So here we are at Twin Oaks, with years of experience behind us and a fairly stable economy, idealistic in our own ways and already putting as much energy as we can spare into our own interests. Are we eager to see new young members come in and provide leadership for us, tell us what is wrong with our little world, what a mess our preceding generations have made, and how we can turn from our evil ways (wasteful, compromising, politically incorrect, whatever) and take our places in the avant-garde of the latest correct thinking? Well, not exactly. What we really want is for new people to come in and help us out for a few years with what we're already doing, and save their fresh ideas until they know enough about the Community to be effective without rocking our little boat too much.

This, too, is unrealistic. Consider: these young people are freshly adult. They have left their parents and their colleges. They are at the height of their mental powers, and they get very testy at the suggestion that some of their ideas will change as they mature. They are ready to make a mark on the world, and they don't see why they can't do it here.

In many ways our Community is a wonderful environment for this age group. Most Twin Oakers have been rebels at one time or another and either still are or can remember it. Even though a certain amount of social conformity is necessary in any group, we keep it at a minimum. Age is no barrier to political participation, and young people can step into management jobs at will. Nobody treats them like kids, and since we're trying to be egalitarian in general, we all tend to forget people's ages. This all works well for the young person who is interested in being part of what Twin Oaks is.

The difficulty comes when the young person sees Twin Oaks as a stepping stone to the community he or she really wants, and sets about to struggle for Community changes, long before getting the experience to make judicious choices. The chances are high that their efforts will upset older or longer-term members, and the resultant backlash may send the younger member off in search of a more compatible environment.

Wendell and Joan

I remember a couple I'll call Wendell and Joan. They were in their twenties and gave out an aura of definitely knowing how the world should be run. Their ideas were "radical," in the sense of the political Left, and it was clear that radical meant correct, without much examination. Wendell posted O&I papers intended to alert communitarians that we were in danger of committing some conservative act, such as voting at the polls or subscribing to a magazine put out by hunting and fishing devotees. His general manner to all except his co-radicals ranged from the briefly caustic to the barely condescending. For her part, Joan busily shoved mild-mannered communitarians aside in order to take on managerial jobs. Her idea of being House Manager (a job created primarily to oversee housecleaning) was to ignore the gathering cobwebs and dust-bunnies and spend her energy boycotting Colgate-Palmolive and researching how to spend the budget on politically correct cleaning products.

The vote on Wendell and Joan when their provisional period expired was "Extend," by which the voters probably meant to shake them up a little and subject them to a Feedback meeting (mandatory for any provisional member who gets an "extend" vote). I don't think anyone meant to reject them, ultimately. The time had in any case come for politically correct house products; Joan wasn't the first pushy person we have moved aside for; and as to Wendell's opinions about voting or hunting, there are several members who agree with him. This pair's behavior was almost within the acceptable range. All that was lacking was a stronger sense of humor and a little dash of humility.

They didn't stay for the Feedback. They left, and it's really too bad. I admit that for me it's a relief not having them around stirring up trouble, but this is short-sighted. In spite of their irritating ways they didn't deserve to be rejected for their excesses of enthusiasm.

I keep remembering the community's beginning years, when I was the only "older" member around (thirty-five years old at the time), and kept out of the way when the rest were having serious fun. What bothers me about the memory is recognizing that we built this Community on the efforts and energies of those young people. I took them seriously as peers, because I didn't have any choice, and they came through, in between their parties and their clumsy love affairs and erratic comings and goings, and in spite of their three-month average length of stay. They believed in Twin Oaks, briefly, and while the belief endured, they invested themselves. Of course they overrated their own knowledge and wisdom, but so what? At that time there weren't many "conservatives" here for them to rebel against. They were 1968's version of "radical," but they were in the majority. By default they were the backbone of the Community.

Today's young Twin Oakers missed that experience, and some of them chafe at the loss. I recall Wendell's goodbye paper in which he gave as one of his reasons for leaving "the presence of people at Twin Oaks who may have been considered radical in the Sixties, but at this point can be called nothing but conservative." I had the feeling he meant to wound us with the remark or perhaps to stir us out of our lethargy. Personally I didn't feel either insulted or inspired, just amused and nostalgic. I remember when "radical" meant living on a commune and being rigidly egalitarian about money and about nonpossessiveness in love. Radical used to mean Red. Now it means Green. My own opinions these days tend to pastels.

Chapter 31

Twin Oaks Plants an Acorn

I can't stand waiting lists. I am appalled at the spectacle of dozens of people knocking on our door for admittance and being told, "We're full." I can not see any reason why the people who happened to get here first should have the benefits of this lifestyle while those who came later should be denied it.

It is not as if the current members of Twin Oaks had been the pioneers, now perhaps entitled to the fruits of their earlier efforts. On the contrary, the current members are all inheritors of the comfort and security provided by people long gone.

As I recounted at the end of the chapter on turnover, the renewed national interest in community took Twin Oaks by surprise. We accepted as many members as we had private bedrooms for, and then we closed the door. There are now over thirty people on our waiting list, and we can't count on taking in more than ten of them in the coming year.

The issue is more complicated than just the number of applicants. Some of the people on that waiting list are relatives, lovers, or close friends of current members, who are waiting impatiently for them to be admitted.

In some ways it feels like 1972 all over again. The big difference is that this time I am not alone in feeling the urgency of the problem. This time the waiting list tugs at the consciences of a large number of communitarians.

The first and most obvious proposed solution to this problem is to increase our numbers by adding housing. We now have a large residence on the drawing boards, and we will probably start building it this summer.

The building will take a long time, and we could do more than that. There have been at least six proposals for creating additional housing quickly. All have been rejected or shelved, based on a variety of objections, many of which boil down to a reluctance to taking any big step in a hurry.

There are members who do not feel any obligation to the people on the waiting list. Some of them feel that Twin Oaks is big enough already, or perhaps too big. Some feel crowded in the dining hall. Others fear the derailment of their hopes for other projects if the Community pours its resources into growth. For whatever reason, between six and twenty communitarians can be counted on to oppose—probably block—any proposal for increasing the numbers of Twin Oaks members at this time.

This political situation feels so familiar to me from previous experience that at a very early stage I predicted a negative outcome to growth efforts, and therefore turned my energies in a different direction. My instincts told me that we growth-oriented people were not going to be politically successful soon enough to catch the people on the waiting list. The Community would be likely to prioritize peaceful process and try to avoid disrupting the flow of normal communal living. Though many people wanted to see applicants taken care of somehow, they would not want to make their fellow communitarians unhappy, and therefore they would not insist on growth.

I had a theory, based on history, that the opportunity to build community with those eager potential members would not last forever. I gave it three or four years maximum. If anything was to be done about it, we needed to do it soon.

I tried out the notions of forming another branch of Twin Oaks or proceeding with the "grow-split" theory like the Hutterites. It was obvious that a branch proposal would meet heavy opposition from McCune and others who had lived through the first branch experiment and thought the idea bad in principle.

As to grow-split, I did propose it and got a lot of verbal support, but the differences between us and the Hutterites soon became apparent. The Hutterites are accustomed to obedience, and as individuals they do not prioritize personal preferences or happiness. When their leaders recognize the time for splitting one of their communities in two, their people go or stay mostly according to what is deemed best by their elders.

Twin Oakers are of course not like this at all. I soon realized that there would be few volunteers to be part of a splinter. So much for that idea.

The only politically practical solution I could see was to start another community, the same conclusion that had, years ago, resulted in the founding of East Wind. However, I didn't see anybody ready to take on the leadership responsibilities for such an effort, and I couldn't envision myself having the stamina to do it again.

While the Community was pondering the old grow-split idea, rumor went out via one of our newsletters, and it reached a woman named Deborah, who had been an early and influential member of East Wind. One day I received a letter from Deborah saying "I hear you're starting a new community. That's great! Can I do it with you?" At first I laughed at the way rumor can twist information, but that night I found myself taking the idea seriously. Deborah, that dynamo of energy, opinion, and sense, might be just the person who could do what I could not do. Maybe we could form a new community nearby, and I could be a sort of consultant.

My memories of the earliest years of both Twin Oaks and East Wind provided me with a guide to what I thought the new community needed in order to succeed. It would need land, but the price of land had risen out of proportion to ordinary wages and savings, and the kind of people who were applying to Twin Oaks probably did not have much capital. Could Twin Oaks be persuaded to buy the land?

A new community needed an ongoing source of income. Outside jobs had been an extremely bad way to make money in the past. Present conditions were if anything worse. Meanwhile Twin Oaks had sales opportunities it wasn't using and jobs going undone. Perhaps Twin Oaks could offer enough jobs to the new community to keep it going for a while.

The people I was trying to serve were interested in joining Twin Oaks. It made sense, then, to use the same general form of organization that we had tested. We could quite openly say, "This community will be independent but similar to Twin Oaks."

A new community needs a founding population of at least ten people, and should rise to fifteen within the year. Those fifteen have to be housed. No land that we could afford would provide enough housing. Could Twin Oaks lend money for a big residence, along with water, sewage, and initial utilities?

I thought Twin Oaks might respond positively to a request for a large amount of money, because its savings were at this point quite substantial. On the other hand, I didn't think a new community should get a handout. It should stand on its own feet. The help I envisioned from Twin Oaks was a loan, to be eventually repaid in full, with interest.

What was needed, then, was a suitable piece of land, a guarantee of some Twin Oaks employment, an adequate building loan, and a group of people willing to be pioneers.

It took eight months to accomplish this. Two other communitarians, Gordon and Ira, joined me in an informal committee to get the new group off the ground. We split the work. Ira handled the Communities Conference where we did the initial recruitment. Gordon did the land search. I took on writing the papers that we hoped would convince Twin Oaks. I also wrote the resulting inter-communal contracts and kept up a correspondence with the people who wanted to be part of the founding group.

I saw the whole process as a balancing act. In order to persuade waiting list people and other potential communitarians that the project was viable enough for them to invest themselves in, we needed a piece of land and a source of income. In order to get the land and income, we had to persuade Twin Oaks to back us. In order to get Twin Oaks' backing, we had to produce a group of people willing and eager to create a new community. The Acorn Committee, as we three called ourselves, provided the faith that it could and should be done.

The political process, seen in retrospect, went smoothly and quickly by Twin Oaks standards, though it didn't feel quick while it was happening. It seemed to me that our offer to get Twin Oaks off the hook in the matter of growth ought to be accepted with thanks and not quibbled with. To be fair, a lot of people reacted just that way, which probably accounts for our ultimate success. But there were a number of Twin Oaks members who tried to change the project in one way or another that the Committee felt sure would not work.

Some wanted Acorn to form itself far enough away so that its members would seldom set foot on Twin Oaks soil. Others wanted Acorn to start out entirely with its own industries and not expect to get employment at Twin Oaks. For some, the amount of money we were asking for seemed too much. They imagined that Acorn could get by on half that amount. The fact that the Committee would not (could not) budge on these issues caused some people to call us stubborn and uncompromising. We didn't want to be stubborn, but we also didn't want to fail. The three of us had all in the past been founding members and leaders of egalitarian communities. We felt strongly that we knew what we were talking about when we set our minimum conditions.

I wouldn't be writing this chapter if it hadn't all worked out. Gordon's untiring research eventually netted us a rundown but potentially beautiful farm about seven miles from Twin Oaks. Thanks to Ira's efforts, Twin Oaks consented to let the potential Acorn people have two gatherings here, so they could settle among themselves some of the big questions about what kind of community they were committing themselves to. The Board of Planners gave us friendly encouragement and did their process work promptly on the various agreements. Friends of the new community gave the Acorn Committee the encouragement and appreciation we needed to keep going.

Acorn Community was founded April 1, 1993 and as of this writing is one month old. Twin Oaks shows a fascination with it that reminds me of the way people feel about new babies. The former naysayers have accepted it without apparent rancor. A few of them have openly admitted they are glad about the way things turned out. Most Twin Oakers have visited Acorn at least once. You can get there by bicycle or even by canoe, since both communities are on the South Anna River. Income-area managers are eager to get Acorners involved in their shops. Acorn invited Twin Oakers to a party, thinking only a few would come, and half the Community showed up. Other than running out of food, it was a great success.

Acorn's attitude toward Twin Oaks is equally positive. For one thing, nearly half its membership is made up of people on the waiting list. But quite apart from that, Acorn's very first decision, agreed to unanimously and unilaterally, was that it would not bad-mouth Twin Oaks or Twin Oakers publicly, regardless of provocation, and so far everybody has kept to that resolution, except maybe me, once in a while.

People on the Twin Oaks waiting list are welcome to be part of Acorn for the interim. When their names eventually come to the top of the list, they'll have their choice between the two communities, and Acorn will try not to make them feel guilty if they decide in favor of the older community.

The social benefits of the overall increase in our population have already been felt, even in this first month. One Acorner comes to Twin Oaks for choir. A Twin Oaks beer brewing project is being expanded to include some Acorners. The first inter-community love affair started up after a mere two weeks on the land. It is probably not the last.

If my window theory has any validity, the crush at the front door of both communities should ease off about 1995. Acorn should by that time be a medium-sized, sturdy community quite able to recruit on its own merits.

Some people don't believe in the window theory. Taylor visited Twin Oaks recently and took issue with that part of my planning. "This country is never going back to the way things used to be," she said, referring to the national affluence of previous decades. "The job market is permanently changed. Community ought to be a viable and attractive option for the forseeable future." If that should turn out to be true, then Acorn won't be enough, either.

Did I mention that East Wind is also full to bursting and has just reluctantly started its own waiting list? My cup runneth over.

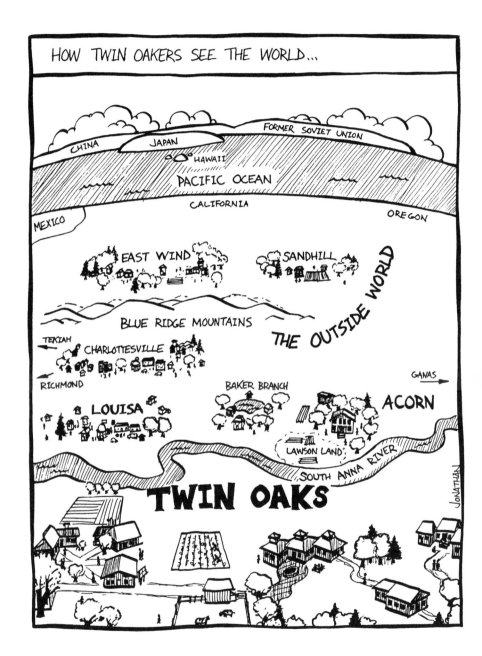

Chapter 32

And in Conclusion...

I'm trying to bring this book to a close, and I'm having a hard time. How am I supposed to end a story that hasn't ended?

Maybe I'm supposed to sum up the meaning of it all. I remember one time a television producer was here at Twin Oaks trying to do a show about us. Her photographer had filmed interviews with dozens of members, and she had abundant footage on every conceivable topic, but she wanted someone to help her summarize the whole thing. "Tell me," she said, "how all this relates to the ordinary person watching the show."

That one stumped me. "I don't think it does," I said.

It isn't the "ordinary people watching the show" who are likely to be affected by this story of the struggles of a Utopian community. It is the people who have at one time or another imagined themselves joining one. That's who this book is for, and I'm guessing that's mostly who will read it.

The impact of reading about the communal experience will vary with the reader, just as the meaning of living here varies with the member. If this book stirs you to want to visit and maybe add your name to the waiting list, write to us at the address at the front of the book. If the Acorn project turns you on, write to me at the same address, and I'll pass on the message. If you can't join but want to give some financial help, Acorn and I would be grateful. If you're seeking a community somewhat different from the one I've described, get hold of a *Directory*. We sell them.

Or maybe your interest is less direct. You're settled in your life and not discontented with it, but somewhere in the back of your mind you've wondered what your life would have been like if you'd ever followed up on that interest you once had in Utopian communities.

I suppose every writer has an fantasy reader in mind—the reader who will pore over each paragraph with intense interest, smile with delight at each happy phrase, and not miss a nuance. I know who my fantasy reader is. It's me. It's the person I would have been if I had done something else instead of doing community. I figure she's out there somewhere, the Kat Kinkade in a parallel universe. I really wrote this book for her.

So here's your answer, my counterpart in Outside World clothing. Yes, you would have been reasonably happy. You'd have a comfortable sense of having spent your life doing something rewarding and interesting and possibly even significant. Maybe it would have been better than what you have chosen. Maybe not.

I've been frank enough about the problems of communal living. Obviously Twin Oaks isn't Paradise. For one thing, I'm no angel, and if you were here, you wouldn't be one, either. Ordinary mortals can't create Paradise. We can, however, strive for Utopia. Never mind that we haven't quite got there yet. We're working on it.

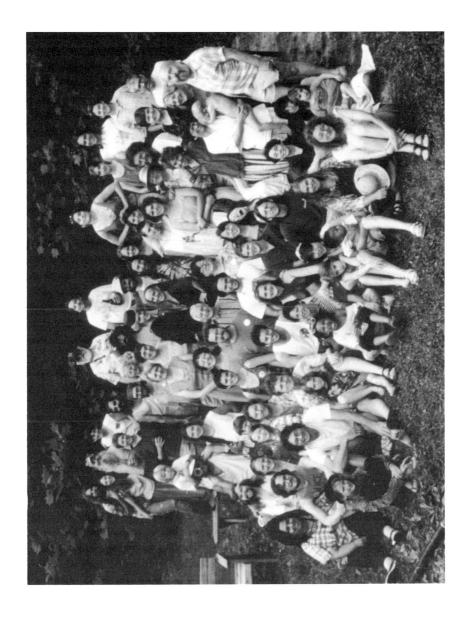

INDEX

Aaron, 81-82
Acorn, 300-305, 307
Address of Twin Oaks, ii
Affinity groups, 97, 100-101
Age and Aging, 29, 226
   physical problems of, 293-94
   in relationships, 182, 185
   and youth culture, 292
Ageism, 213, 293, 299 (cartoon)
Aggression
   physical, 195-96
   verbal, 194, 196, 218-19
Agriculture, 65, 115, 140, 155, 257.
   see also Dairy program;
   Farming; Garden
Air-conditioning, 199 (cartoon), 226,
   234, 293
Alexis, 133, 134, 136
Allowances, 43, 44, 51 (cartoon), 64,
   67, 99, 118, 167, 217
Amateurism, 135
Amri, 147
Anarchist, 205
Animal rights, 40 (cartoon), 122
   (cartoon), 200, 209
Appeals, 21, 157, 246
Apprentices, 129, 149, 236, 249, 250,
   253
Architecture, 79, 81, 96, 131, 261, 262
Arts, 268
Autonomy, 98
   of branches, 252
   and small living groups, 253

Bank accounts, 42, 43, 46, 48, 49
Baseline expenses, 64, 68
Battery-driven carts, 8 (cartoon), 226,
   293
Behavior
   of children, 148, 150-51, 167
   macho, 228, 247
   middle class, 194
   standards for, 209
Behaviorism, iii, 141, 201
Bellamy, Edward, i, 31
Better world, 89, 124, 223, 266, 295

Bill, 55-57
Blacks, 193, 214, 215
Blues, 218
Boys, the, 53, 244-45, 246
Branch experiment, 301
   end of, 101-2
   Merion, 97-99
   and social planning, 252
   Tupelo, 99-100
Buildings, 20, 49, 162
   contracting out, 82
   design of, 79, 137 (cartoon)
   New Age culture, 200
   opposition to, 127, 136
   see also Construction; Design;
   Housing; Residences
Bull seals, as metaphor, 261
Bylaws, 21, 23, 26, 49, 282
   and verbal aggression, 219

"Candy store" phenomenon, 183
Career, 43, 168
   Twin Oaks as, 250, 294
Carl, 259-60
Caroline, recommendations of, 149-50
Carrol, 105, 208
Cash box, 213, 246
Celibacy, 176, 177, 182
Child Board, 149
Childcare, 11, 22, 91, 97, 111, 143-44
   complaints about, 147
   father's role in, 152
   original concept of, 146-48, 151
Children, 68, 91, 92, 287
   behavior of, 148, 150-51, 167
   communal authority over, 147
   education of, 145-46
   funds for, 43, 46
   at Merion, 98
   and opinions on food, 116-17
   and parents' relationship, 180
   in residences, 169
   and theft, 217
   in Walden Two and Twin Oaks
      compared, 140, 141
Children's building, 79, 82, 98. see

also Degania
Choir, 66, 269
Christopher, 169-70
City job rotation, 53, 111
Classism, 194-95, 197
Cleanliness, 104, 112, 125, 126, 160
Closed door policy, 87, 171
Clothing, 3, 44, 193-94
    New age culture, 199 (cartoon),
        200, 211 (cartoon)
    see also Commie clothes
Commanding the sun to rise, 138, 141,
    273
Commercial farming, 91, 93-94, 155
Commie Clothes, 76-77 (cartoon),
    193-94
Communal movement, 29, 36
Communal treasury, 42-43, 281, 282
Commune, Twin Oaks as, 4, 77
    (cartoon)
Communistic idealism, i, 88, 186
Community, sense of, 288-89
Competition, 186, 258
Compost Cafe, 281
Computers, 30, 66, 105, 106, 112, 257
Conferences, 251, 303
Conformity, 5, 195, 202, 295
    to behavior standards, 196, 209
Consensus, 22-23, 85, 148, 238
Construction, 32, 78-82, 87, 123
    finishing details, 136
    low-commitment workers in, 129,
        135, 136
    managers of, 129
    of new dairy barn, 156-59
    post-KDC push, 133
    women in, 135
    of Zhankoye, 124-31
    see also Buildings
Consumption, 45, 63-70
Controversies, 90, 119
    Acorn, 301, 303, 304
    KDC, 123-35
    microwave, 203-9
    new dairy barn, 156-62
    planner appointments, 236
    population growth, 68-69, 86-87,
        97-98, 238, 301
    swimming options, 67, 126, 224

Cooks, 31, 121 (cartoon), 258
Cooperation, 206, 256, 273
Cooperative and communal economy
    compared, 5
Cooperative leadership, 136, 260-61
Councils, 18, 21, 243
Counseling, 35, 93
Courtesy, as community norm, 195
Courtyard, 2-3, 7 (photos), 25, 125
Cows, 11, 98, 139, 155, 157-58, 164
    (cartoon)
Craft Fairs, 55
Crime, 212
    bribery, 218, 220
    rule-breaking, 245
    see also Theft
Criticism, 26, 85, 136, 169
    mutual, 92
    of old by young, 294
    from visitors, 11-12
    of visitors, 195
Crowding, 69, 86, 100, 171
Cuddling, 182
Culture, 268-74
    musical comedies, 270-73
Cynicism, 45, 48, 90

Dairy barn, 133, 156-62, 163 (cartoon)
Dairy program, 68, 155-60. see also
    Milking crew
Daniel, 285-86
Death, 91, 94, 259, 287
Deborah, 302
Decision-making, 23, 26, 35, 63, 98,
    257
    of Child Board, 149
    and new members, 161
    by Planners, 237, 243
    process of, 168
    role of parents in child program,
        147
    time cutoff for, 162
    tradeoff game, 65
Deck, Zhankoye, 130, 131
Degania, 81, 91, 92, 129, 144, 147,
    148
Delancey, 286-87
Democracy, 21, 22-23
Demographics, 292, 294

Dependents, 33
Design, 96, 97
    for KDC, 128
    for new dairy barn, 156, 158-59
    residential, 79-81
    of visitor cottage, 133
Desserts, 116, 119
Dexter, 107
Dianne, 135-36
Dining hall, 3, 125, 140, 144, 152. see
    also Kitchen-Dining
Complex; Llano; Zhankoye
Directory of Intentional Communities, 1,
    172, 173, 308
Dishwashing, 32-33, 105-6, 218
Disillusionment, 89, 90, 94, 104, 169
Diversity, 4, 10, 141
    and classism, 194-95, 196-97
    ideological, 25, 68
    ideology of, 192-93
    racial, 193-94, 198 (cartoon)
Donations
    to causes, 46, 64, 67, 68, 123, 224-25
    to Twin Oaks, 49, 106
Donna, 135, 136
"D" (pseudonym), 214-15
Dress, style of, 140, 179-80
Drinking glasses, 105-7
Dwight, 11, 68, 85

Early years, 9-13, 111
    housing in, 78-82
East Wind, 90, 91, 98, 99, 249
    cleanliness at, 104
    Gerri as pioneer, 243
    history of, 87, 88-89, 302
    tax exemption of, 280-81
Ecology, 226-27
Economic planning, 20, 43-44
Economy,
    communal and cooperative compared,
      5
    defined, 42-43
    effects of, 49-50
    and equality, 46-49
    problems of, 43-44
    vacation earnings, 44-45, 46
    weeds and knots, 45-46
Egalitarianism, 13, 45, 89, 168. see also

Equality
Ego, 135
    bruising of, 26, 258
    lack of, 243
Election, 19
Emerald City, 272
Energy saving, 67, 131, 226-27
Equality, ii, 12-13, 112, 170
    and communal economy, 46-49
    political, 24, 25
Ethics of community members, 203
Example, Twin Oaks as, 223-24
Exploitation, 88
Expulsion, 220, 245, 246

Facilitators, 24-25, 149
    and sexual relationships, 181
Families
    outside, 147
    privacy needs of, 97
    see also Children; Housing
Fanatic, 84
Farm, The, 92
Farming, 11, 155
    commercial, 91, 93-94, 155
    see also Dairy program
Federation Desk, 279
Feedback, 195, 285
Feedbacks, 10, 85, 92, 215, 219
    mandatory, 216, 219, 296
Feminism, 92, 145, 196, 209, 228, 231
    (cartoon)
    and dairy barn, 158
    and relationships, 183
    in theater, 270
Financial crisis, 53, 157, 249, 263
Financial rules, 49
Financial statements, 280, 281
Flies, 156, 158, 161, 200
Flying Tomatoes, 270, 275 (photo)
Food, 115-16
    children's opinions on, 116-17,
      121 (cartoon)
    and New age culture, 138-39, 200
    processing, 287-88
    wars, 117-19
Freedom, 35, 36, 58, 89, 169
    personal, 265
    sexual, 175, 183, 185

Free enterprise system, 89, 170
Friendships, 184, 258
Fulano, 34
Funky atmosphere, 127
Furniture, 104, 105, 227

Garden, 2, 66, 98, 138-40, 155, 236
    manager of, 17, 115
Gaskin, Steven, 92
Gender ratio, 185
General manager. See Products
        manager
General Managerial Team (GMT), 18
Generation gap, 69, 203
George (choir director), 269, 275
        (photo)
George (planner), 246
Gerri, 25, 128, 134, 265
    and government, 254
    and Mel, 246
    as Planner, 243-47
    as Products Manager, 247-48, 249-
        50
    and social planning, 252-53
    and Will, 248, 249
Getting straight, 92, 93
Gift money, 44, 45, 46, 48
GMT. See General Managerial Team
"Good Communitarian" (song), 271-
        72
Gordon, 206, 237, 303, 304
Government, 17-26, 254, 255
    excellence in, 24
Graffiti, 225
Grow-split theory, 85, 172, 301-2
Growth, 97, 112
    process for, 301, 303
    see also Controversies, population
        growth

Halcyon, 157
Hammocks, 3, 32, 60, 61 (cartoon),
        62, 98, 263
    and the Boys, 245, 246
    and growth of the business, 53-54,
        58, 263
    pushes, 248
Hammock shop, 105, 134
Happiness, 10, 12, 70, 186

and relationships, 183
Hard line, 47, 85
Harmony, 78, 111, 285
Health practices, 200
Health team, 18, 252
Henry, 79, 81, 128, 129, 136, 267
    and government, 254
    and social planning, 252
Hierarchy, 17-18, 23, 264
High South, 94, 287
Hildegard, 157, 159
Hippies, 12, 201
Holidays, 41 (cartoon), 113, 267
        (cartoon), 270
Home schooling, 145
Homosexuality, 177
Honchos, 124, 135, 136
House, management of, 18, 277, 296
Housing, 86, 136, 144, 166, 301, 302
    current, 2-3, 112
    design and construction of, 32, 78-
        82, 96, 156
    early, 9-10, 11-12, 103, 111, 242-
        43
    Morningstar, 106, 107, 135, 152
    women only, 228, 231 (cartoon)
    see also Residences; Tupelo
Hutterites, 301

Idealism, 47, 48, 88, 89, 104, 170
Ideological diversity, 25
Ideology, 57, 67, 169
    communal, 256
In-box, 112, 113
Incentives, 12, 46, 48, 89
Income, 44, 45, 52-59, 98, 111, 112
    loss, 263
Income-sharing, 4, 170
Indexing, 55-57
"I need the eggs," 266
Insulation, 227
Intellectual freedom, 5
Intentional community, defined, 1
Intermediate membership, 282
Internal Revenue Service, 279-83
"In Your Face" phenomenon, 184
Ione, 106-7
Ira, 193, 194-95, 258, 303, 304
IRS Code 501(d), 279, 280, 282

Jake, 236
Jealousy, 175, 180, 184
Jewelry-making business, 213
Joanie, 169
Joint Hammock Agreement, 247
Joshua, 33, 245, 246
Josie, 11, 84, 101, 204
    dropping membership, 168-69
    KDC and, 126, 127
    spiritual movement and, 92
    Tuesday Group and, 108-9
    Tupelo founding and, 99-100
Joyce, 169
Juniee, 237
Justice, 10, 48

Kat
    early years, 10-13
    and power, 25-26, 32-38, 85, 265
    on strict financial rules, 46-49
    and Tradeoff Game, 65-66
    Degania construction, 80-81
    leaves Twin Oaks, 84-90
    returns to Twin Oaks, 104-9
    not fitting in, 138-41, 201-9
    social class, 197
    as planner, 234-37
    writing by, 285
KDC. See Kitchen-Dining Complex
Keenan, 133, 134, 135, 136, 166, 238
Ken, 53
Kibbutz, 43, 50
Kitchen-Dining Complex (KDC)
        (Zhankoye), 3, 132 (photo)
    cost overrun of, 130-31
    need for, 124-26
    political process for, 126-28
    Will as honcho for, 128-31, 248,
        261
Knicely, Mr., 281, 283
Kodiak, 225
Komar, Ingrid, ii, 91, 143-44, 252

Labor
    assigning of, 30
    desirability of, 31-32
    outside, 53
    physical, 294

variety of, 10, 29
Labor credit mentality, 36
Labor credits, 55, 56, 95 (cartoon),
        235
    for childcare, 143, 147, 151-52
Labor credit system, 5, 29, 36, 83
        (cartoon)
    flexibility of, 5, 30, 35
    manipulation of, 31, 39 (cartoon)
    and non-workers, 33-35, 37
        (cartoon), 38 (cartoon)
    variable credit experiment, 30-32
Labor hole, 34-35, 299 (cartoon)
Labor quota, 29, 44, 166
Land purchases, 97, 112
Land use, as objection to building, 124
Leaders, 4, 26, 89, 254, 255
Leadership, 24, 205, 253, 265-67, 295,
        302
    cooperative, 136, 260-61
    See also Gerri; Taylor; Velma
Leaves of absence, 34
Leaves of Twin Oaks, The, 10, 91, 93
Leaving
    papers, 166, 169
    Taylor's reasons for, 254-55
    See also Turnover
Leftists, iv (cartoon), 226, 296
Leisure, 30, 35, 123, 170
Leslie, 134, 207, 259-60
    and theater, 270-71, 273
Less-Involved, The, 150-52
Library, 12, 43, 46
Living the Dream (Komar), ii, 91,
        143-44, 252
Llano, 79, 86, 125, 127, 132 (photo)
    remodel of, 133, 261
Logan, 235-36
Looking Backward (Bellamy), i, 30
Louisa, town of, 49, 168, 214, 245,
        246
Love affairs. See Relationships;
        Sexual norms and practices
Luxuries, 59, 224, 294

Macho behavior, 228, 247
Managers, 43, 63, 252
    accounting, 215
    building maintenance, 63-64

computer services, 261
construction projects, 129
dairy, 156
garden, 17, 115
house, 227, 296
labor, 218
new industries, 56
products, 247-50, 263-64
qualities of, 272
turnover of, 18-19
and variable labor credits, 32
vehicle use, 245
Velma as, 257-59
see also Products manager
Mandatory kitchen shift, 32-33
Margaret, 94
Marriage, 97, 177, 183, 184
Mating environment, 96, 177-79
McCune, 127, 168, 301
    as dairy barn honcho, 158-59
    and energy conservation, 226
    as KDC opponent, 135, 136
    vs. Will, 130-31
Meat, 68, 107, 116, 117, 118, 155
Media, 88
    television, 212, 307
    TIME magazine, 1
Meetings, 22, 30, 131, 245
    childcare workers', 147, 148
    Planner, 20, 236
    and process, 289
Megas, 144
Mel, 213, 246
Members
    average age of, 167
    intermediate, 282
    leaving, 88, 254-55
    provisional, 34, 296
    selection of, 89, 201, 213, 215, 251
Members, long-term, 86, 167
    moving beyond group control,
        205-6
    resistance to new members, 94,
        128, 170-71, 296
Members, new, 69-70, 214
    compromises made by, 170-71
    presence of, 97
    "reinventing the wheel," 161, 169
    Tuesday Group and, 65, 107

Membership team, 18, 251
    and sexual relationships, 185-86
Memory, selective, 161
Merion, 97-99, 252
Metas, 144
Microwave controversy, 199 (car-
    toon), 203-9
Middle class, 127, 170, 194
Midis, 144, 148
Milk, 99, 117
Milking crew, 22, 31, 157-60, 257. see
    also Dairy program
Milking parlor, 157-60
Milk-processing, 66
Money, 265
    personal, 44-45, 46, 153 (cartoon)
    See also Allowances; Consump-
        tion; Economy, communal;
    Income
Monogamy, 175-76, 177
Morningstar, 81, 106, 107, 135
    as family housing, 152
Multiple relationships, 177, 180, 184
Music, 269-70
Musical comedies, 270-73
Mutations, as metaphor, 170
Mutual criticism, 92

Name changes, 9, 92, 187 (cartoon),
    191 (cartoon)
Needs
    of aging population, 293
    communal, 42-46
    of long-term members, 86
    sexual, 185
New Age culture, 200-202, 209-10,
    216, 284 (cartoon)
New communities, 173, 295
    requirements for, 302
Non-violence, 195-96
Non-workers, 33-35, 37, 38 (cartoon)
Novagene, 235-36
Nudity, 10, 20, 193, 194, 200

O&I Board, 27-28 (cartoons), 106,
    109, 141, 166, 296
    about sexual relationships, 185
    dealing with theft, 216
    and microwave controversy, 204,

208
on new dairy barn, 158
as tool for discussion, 21, 22, 139, 149
Older people and sex, 178
Oneida, 78, 133
Open door, 5, 86, 87, 89, 171
OPP (Overquota Products for Projects), 46
Organic, 57, 67, 115, 139
OTRAs (One Time Resource Allocations), 64-65, 66-67
Outside work, 53, 82, 111, 302
Outside world, 73 (cartoon), 81, 91, 172, 178, 306 (cartoon)
and classism, 194-95
compared to community, 90, 167, 168, 181, 223, 308
and dress styles, 74-75 (cartoons), 180
and leadership, 265
and waiting list, 172, 250
Over-quota, 30, 48

Pam, 286, 287-88
Paper napkins, 107
Parents, 92, 141, 143, 152
less-involved threat to, 150
vs. childcare workers, 147-48
Parties, 68, 113, 214, 292, 293
Partnership, 279, 280
Patent, 54
Paul, 208, 249-50, 263
Paula, 236, 275 (photo)
Permanent home, Twin Oaks as, 44, 168-69
Personal money, 45-46, 167, 170, 245. see also Allowances
Personal property, 23
Personal service credits, 273
Pier One, 248, 249
dependence on, 53-54, 264
Pine, 106, 126, 127
Pioneers, 87, 300, 303
Piper, 293
Planners, 66, 108, 134, 149, 208
and Acorn process, 304
current methods of, 237-38
dealing with theft, 216, 217, 220
and decision-making power, 232-33
decisions of, 20, 21, 29, 94, 97
functions of, 17, 19-23
Gerri as, 243-46
Kat's experience as, 234-37
and new dairy barn, 157, 159-62
and power, 23-24, 233-34, 238-39
selection of, 19-20
and sexual relationships, 185-86
term of office, 19, 20, 26, 228
and turnover survey, 166-67
and Will, 133, 134
Political action, 225
Political correctness, 154 (cartoon), 229-30 (cartoons), 296
Political debate, 109
Political equality, 24, 25
Political incorrectness, 24, 295
Pond, 224
Pool, 67, 126, 224
Population, 54, 68, 97
growth of, 69, 86, 98, 123
see also Controversies, population growth
Poverty, 59, 89, 104, 194
vow of, 281, 282
Power, 21, 24, 108, 232-33
and Gerri, 248
and Kat, 25-26, 32-38, 85, 265
of less-involved, 150
of managers, 19
and Planners, 23-24, 233-34, 238-39
Velma's, 258
Primary time, 59, 180
Private rooms, 88
Privilege, 45, 46, 168
Process, 16 (cartoon), 105, 149, 289-90
of bookwriting, 285, 286
and growth, 173, 301, 303
and KDC cost overruns, 130, 131
and microwave controversy, 204, 206, 208
of play production, 272-73
social planning as, 252-54
and Velma, 257
Process Team, 216, 286

Products manager
  Gerri as, 247-48
  Paul as, 249-50, 263
  Velma as, 263-64
Professionalism, 134, 135, 235
Profit, 58, 93-94, 139
Progress, 124, 167
Proposals, 20, 21, 53
  to build KDC, 126
  for SLGs, 100
Prosperity, 69, 170, 171
Provisional members, 34, 94
Public schools, 145, 225
Punishment, 34, 246. see also
  Behaviorism

Quality of life vs. expansion, 69

Rammed earth, 11, 78
Recruitment, 88, 139, 140, 174
  (cartoon), 303. see also Visitors
Recycling, 11, 227-28
Relationships, 188-89 (cartoons), 228
  breaking up, 182, 184, 190
    (cartoon)
  celibacy, 176, 177, 182, 190
    (cartoon)
  as community problem, 185-86
  and monogamy, 183-84
  multiple, vi (cartoon), 177, 180,
    184, 190 (cartoon)
  negative aspects of communal
    living for, 181
  partners, availability of, 177-78
  positive aspects of communal
    living for, 178-81
Religious beliefs, 4, 93, 199 (cartoon)
Replacement, choosing, 249-50, 260
Residences, 86, 106, 136, 144, 166
  Acorn, 301
  design and construction of, 32, 78-
    82, 96, 156
  women only, 228, 231 (cartoon)
  see also Harmony; Housing;
    Morningstar; Oneida; Tupelo
Retreat cabin, 15 (cartoon)
Rico, 108, 170
Rituals, 200, 209
Rollie, 63-64

Room size, 112, 123, 169, 293
Roth, Jonathan, iii
Rudy, 227

Salvadoran refugees, 195-96
Sandhill Farm, 68
Sandy, 275 (photo)
Scott, 206
Screamies, 91, 93
Self-discipline, 36, 151, 215
Selling, 53, 58
Sense of community, 288-89
Seth, 94
Sewage, 79, 86, 112
Sexual freedom, 175
Sexual norms and practices, 175-77.
  see also Relationships
Shakers, 280, 281
Shal, 237
Shana, 159-60
Sharon, 292
Sheltered workshop, 249, 263, 264
Shops, 136
Sick leave, 29, 30, 42, 43
Simon, 68, 213
Simple life, 54, 68, 98, 99, 166, 171
Sixties, The, 88, 173, 294
Size of community, 5, 85, 301
Skinner, B. F., i, 31, 146, 182
Skirts, on men, 140
Small businesses, 52, 55-57
Small living groups (SLGs), 100-101,
  107, 166, 252, 253, 292
Smokers' retreat, 281
Social planning, 100, 252-54
Social security, 42, 43, 279
Solar water-heating, 226
Species survival, as metaphor, 170
Spiritual movement, 92
Standard of living, 86, 171, 224
  vs. expansion, 68-69
State Department, 57
Statistics, Twin Oaks, 2
Stereotypes, racial, resistance to, 215
Steven, 53, 81
Stretcher-making, 58, 136
Support groups, 228
Surveys, 63, 208, 253
  by Planners, 22, 48, 54, 115, 238
317

on turnover, 166-67
Survival, reasons for, 5-6, 25, 53, 54, 84, 192-93, 201
Symbols, 106, 124, 209
Systems and Structures Packet, 279

Taxes, 46, 171, 279-83
Taylor, 56, 259, 260, 265, 266
  difficulties in joining, 250-51
  as Planner, 235-36, 237
  reasons for leaving, 254-55
  and social planning, 252-54
Teen-agers, 292
Theater, 270-73
Theft, 213-14, 220
  by the Boys, 245
  by children, 217
  dealing with, 215-16
  petty, 216-17, 222 (cartoon)
Tobacco, 10, 52
Todd, 65, 204, 205, 259-60
Tofu, 57, 116, 117, 136, 200, 201
Tomatoes, 66, 139
  processing of, 32, 287-88
Tours, visitor, 4, 10, 14 (cartoon)
Town trips, 71-77 (cartoon), 214, 215, 245, 246
Tradeoff Game, 63-68, 107, 128, 133, 140
  and children's education, 146
  and donations to causes, 224-25
  and solar devices, 226
  Song, 66-67
Travel, 55, 170, 226
  costs of, 45, 46, 67, 167
  and love relationships, 177, 178
Tripper, 245, 246
Trisha, 145
Tuesday Group, 107-9, 118
Tupelo, 81, 101, 106, 107, 252
  beginnings of, 99-100, 251
  as family housing, 152
Turnover, 11, 112, 113, 133, 283
  and children's program, 146-48, 152
  and new dairy barn, 160-61
  reasons for, 44, 165-68, 254
  and sexual relationships, 177, 184, 186

and waiting list, 250
Twentieth Anniversary, 259

Unemployment, 33, 172
Utopia, 1, 43, 139, 186, 239, 256-57, 307, 308
Utopia (play), 271

Vacation, 34, 58, 136, 152
  average length of, 22
  earning of, 30, 55
Vacation Earnings (VE), 44-45, 46
Variable credit experiment, 30-32
Vegans, 118, 119, 120 (cartoon)
Vegetarians, 116, 117-19, 155
Vehicles, 2, 11, 67, 99
  car-pooling, 226
  personal use of, 43, 168
Velma, 107, 205, 248
  and community ideology, 256-57
  dealing with Carl's death, 259-60
  leadership role of, 265, 266-67
  and managerships, 257-59
  as Products manager, 249, 262-64
  service orientation of, 255-56
  and Will, 261-62
Vertical integration, 58
Veto, 19-20, 26, 235
Visitor cottage, 133-34, 166
Visitors, 2, 97, 125, 166, 209, 218
  barred from hammock shop, 245
  and behavior norms, 195
  and sexual relationships, 178
  tours, 4, 10, 14 (cartoon)
Voting, 19, 22, 34, 94, 296
Vow of poverty, 281, 282

Wages, 46, 53, 58, 279
Waiting list, 87-88, 171, 172, 173
  and Acorn, 300, 301, 303, 304
  at East Wind, 305
  and Taylor, 250-51
Walden Two, 13, 34, 182
  abandonment of, 25, 141, 201, 202
Walden Two Experiment, A (Kinkade), ii, 52, 84, 85-86, 176
Walden Two (Skinner), i, 9, 17, 23, 24, 30, 68, 140, 141, 253, 269
Washing dishes, 32-33, 105-6, 218

"Washing machine" conversation, 285-86
Weeds and Knots, 45-46, 48, 273
"Why you?" argument, 46-48, 69
Will, 236, 254, 265
    and Gerri, 248
    and KDC, 126, 127, 128-31, 136
    and Velma, 261-62
"Window" theory, 173, 301, 305
Wood heat, 200, 226
Work. See Labor
Working it out, 181, 182, 273
Wrenn, 245, 246

Youth culture, 292, 295

Zhankoye, 3, 132 (photo)
    see also Kitchen-Dining Complex